Travel Easy

Travel Easy
The Practical Guide for People over 50

FIRST EDITION

Rosalind Massow

An AARP Book
published by
American Association of Retired Persons
Washington, D.C.
Scott, Foresman and Company
Lifelong Learning Division
Glenview, Illinois

Cover illustrator: Iosif Teodorescu

Copyright © 1985
Scott, Foresman and Company, Glenview, Illinois
American Association of Retired Persons, Washington, D.C.
All Rights Reserved. Printed in the United States of America
12345678-KPF-8988878685

Library of Congress Cataloging in Publication Data

Massow, Rosalind.
    Travel easy.

    Includes index.
    1. Travel.   2. Aged—Travel.   I. Title.
G151.M37 1985   910′.2′020880565   84-27626

ISBN 0-673-24817-8

To my mother, Ida Massow,
who understands my wanderlust,
and to my husband, Toolie,
who shares it.

AARP Books is an educational and public service project of the American Association of Retired Persons which, with a membership of more than seventeen million, is the largest association of middle-aged and older persons in the world today. Founded in 1958, AARP provides older Americans with a wide range of membership programs and services, including legislative representation at both federal and state levels. For further information about additional association activities, write to AARP, 1909 K Street N.W., Washington, DC 20049.

Contents

Preface

Older people have never been younger!
They fly planes at 68, ride bikes at 70, compete in marathons at 54, play a hard game of tennis at 65, travel to the Arctic at 80, go on African safaris, assist in archaeological digs in Israel, and even manage the awesome climb up the Great Wall of China.

In short, people past 50 get around.

Forget the stereotypes of the rocking chair crowd. That's antediluvian. The current young-old generation is the first off the tourist bus, willing to try new things, and gung ho for new adventures to the best of their physical ability.

This book will provide the information you need to facilitate your journeys. It will tell you how to plan your trips, both here and abroad, and how to get the most for your money and time. It will let you in on hundreds of good travel tips. Potential troubles are identified and solutions suggested.

If you are planning your first trip ever, a hearty welcome to a thrilling world of new sights, sounds, and experiences.

If you've been around some, but not recently, you'll find travel styles and opportunities have changed. It's the same old world, but you can fly around it faster, and now you can have company—escorts and other enthusiastic travelers like yourself. The array of tours available at home and abroad is truly remarkable for variety and scope.

Experienced travelers, too, will find something of value in the up-to-date information within these pages. I know I learned a lot doing the research. Many more options and opportunities are now available. You no longer have to do everything yourself. Travel agents with computers can work out the details of a trip for you in six minutes to your six hours of checking costs, arrivals and departures, and other details.

Perhaps you might want to steer the family car around little-known places in the United States, or maybe drive through the peaceful Maritime Provinces of Canada, or even wander down Mexico way. Maps and detailed routings are readily available from tourist offices and auto clubs.

Possibly the time has come to activate your lifelong dream of taking a long train trip. A scenic transcontinental ride across the United States or Canada would be a rewarding adventure. There are other rail trips to choose from, too. You might want to splurge and take the exotic Orient Express in Europe, or have a thrilling experience riding a narrow gauge railroad in the Peruvian Andes and seeing llamas in their natural habitat.

Travel by bus has been elevated to a new class of luxury. Gone are the days when employees at posh hotels looked down their noses at people who arrived by bus. Motorcoach tours have never been more luxurious, and first class hotels now offer a hearty welcome to travelers who choose this form of group travel.

Cruises have been touted as the nearest thing to living like a millionaire without actually being one. Comfort and luxury are truly outstanding on cruise ships, whether they veer out to sea or ply the rivers and big lakes. If you choose the water route, there are even opportunities to travel on deluxe barges. No, not like Huck Finn, but a lot fancier.

Years ago, while studying geography in grade school, I made a secret pledge to myself to dip my toes in every major ocean and river in the world. It was a childish dream, but through the years I managed to fulfill a good deal of that fantasy.

The waters of the South China Sea, the Ganges, the Zambesi, the Caribbean, the Aegean, and even the muddy Mississippi all washed over my big toes. I admit I stopped short of my mission several times, as when I learned about piranha in the Amazon River and schistosomiasis in the Nile, but that naive girlhood dream served me well. Subconsciously, it was the motivation for a lifetime of travel.

All of us harbor great dreams of adventure. Our education, childhood memories, the people around us, and our exposure to other cultures all contribute to building and shaping the direction of our romantic flights of fancy.

That comfortable armchair of yours may have served as a magic carpet many times through the years. The time has now come to put wings and wheels under your dreams and take off, while you are still reasonably healthy, curious, and interested.

Your travel goals today may have undergone a slight revision since your younger days. Then, you may have yearned to scale the Alps; today, you might be content just to see them. It doesn't much matter which path you choose to an Alpine adventure, as long as you get there.

This book was custom written for you, whether you've just hit 50 or are enjoying advanced youth at 85. Its goal is to share my enthusiasm for travel with you, not put any impediments in your way. Travel is the most exciting, enjoyable, and stimulating way to stay young, whether you travel for a week, a month, or even a year. So let's get started.

Acknowledgments

Ten years ago I came to the conclusion that most leisure travelers had passed life's equator. For the past decade, I have been researching and writing for the traveler over 50. Despite my labors, this book owes much to the enthusiastic assistance of many travel professionals as well as to friends and acquaintances. Their valuable input is reflected throughout this book. Of the people listed below, I want to especially thank Dr. Norton M. Luger, Dr. Lyonel S. Hildes, Dayton Lehman, and Steve Pisni for their extraordinary cooperation and help.

Thanks go to Juergen Arnold, German Federal Railroad; Susan Baumgartner, Carlson, Rocky and Associates; Luceille Candeletti, Travelers III, Fort Lee, N.J.; Patricia Duricka, Travel Industry Association of America; Phyllis Epstein, Stevens Travel Management, New York City; Ewen Gillies; Evelyn Heyward, Heyward Associates, Inc.; William E. Jackman, Air Transport Association; Roslyn Kaiser, U.S. Department of Transportation; Garry LaBella, Recreational Vehicle Association; Dayton Lehman, Consumer Affairs of the C.A.B.; Norton M. Luger, M.D., consultant on medical affairs to the Society of American Travel Writers; Samuel J. McKelvey, Canadian Consulate General, Tourism; Steve Pisni, Air Canada; Robin Prestage, British Tourist Authority; Ron

Rubinow, Spencer & Rubinow, Inc.; Adele Reingold, TV
Travel, Dayton, Ohio; Dag Scher, French National Railroads; Peter Tauck, Tauck Tours; and Pat Wilson, American Bed and Breakfast Association.

I appreciate, too, the suggestions and help of Alice
Dyson, Teresa Pialek Ely, Barbara Gillam, Phyllis Gitlin,
Lyonel S. Hildes, D.D.S., attorney Malcolm A. Hoffmann,
Mimi Miller, Frances Needles, Kay Pomrinse, Vidya
Chandra Rasmussen, Lena Reid, food and travel writer
Myra Waldo, and Dr. George Silver, Professor of Public
Health, Yale University. Thanks also to Joan McDermott,
and Robin LaBollita.

The constructive comments of people who reviewed
the whole or sections of the manuscript were especially
appreciated. These people include Ethel Blum, travel writ-
er and broadcaster; Connie Coning, *Chicago Tribune*; Thom-
as A. Dickerson, Esq.; Robert Forbes and his staff special-
ists Hal Norvell and Barbara Alderman of the AARP
Travel Service; Cathy George, Space Travel, Inc.; Ray
Greenly, American Society of Travel Agents; Eve Kronen,
Hyatt Hotels Corporation; John McLeod, Amtrak; Diana
Orban, Cruise Lines International Association; Charles
Shapiro, M.D.; John Snyder, American Bus Association;
Allan Wilbur, American Automobile Association; Donald
Williams, Olson-Travelworld, Ltd., and Herbert B. Zak,
D.D.S.

CHAPTER 1

Choosing a Destination

How do you select a destination?

Most of the time, people have inside of them a secret trip deeply rooted in romance, adventure, or religion. Chances are, those special places have been with you for a long time, maybe ever since your grade school days, when that travel poster in your classroom or pictures in the *National Geographic* kept nudging you in the direction of Capri, Yosemite, Carcassonne, or fairy tale castles on the Rhine.

Anything can trigger your choice of destinations. Countries, cities, and regions glamorized by television, movies, and books may play a major role in your travel decisions.

Napa Valley, for instance, the major center of the wine-making industry in California, has always been a popular tourist attraction, but ever since "Falcon Crest" became a top television show, Napa Valley has been flooded with travelers who want to see where the lifelike principals "live."

Successful plays and movies may evoke an interest in seeing an area. While jazz and food have made New Orleans a tourist mecca on the Mississippi, visitors are still looking for Blanche from *A Streetcar Named Desire.*

Literature, too, impacts on travel. The recent revival of interest in the works of Marcel Proust has tour operators mapping out new itineraries in France's Normandy country. And what literary buff could travel to Czechoslovakia and walk the streets of Prague without thinking of Franz Kafka?

And how about the good old days? They probably weren't any better than life today, but symbols of history and nostalgia are especially cherished as the world of high tech envelops us all. Preserved historic areas and restoration villages have become attractive destinations to a widening segment of the traveling public. If you don't nose your own car in the direction of eighteenth and nineteenth century U.S. shrines, you can be sure there's a wide array of motorcoach package tours that target into those areas. The exquisitely restored eighteenth century village of Colonial Williamsburg, Virginia, is the centerpiece of America's restorations, but within an easy drive are other Virginia landmarks for those who would look back in time.

Travelers who would like to unearth the real roots of America will find Massachusetts is the state for beginnings. Plymouth Rock on Cape Cod is where the Pilgrims made their first step for freedom in 1620. The fires of revolution were stoked all over the Boston area. Today you can follow the well-marked Freedom Trail and trace the movements of those early revolutionaries.

Touring with a theme is a wonderful approach. It puts all your special interests to work for you. The knowledge you've accumulated in art, music, architecture, antiques, Indian lore, quilting, or any other subject, will come to life for you and those around you in a tour zeroing in on those special interests.

World War II veterans might find a trip to the battle sites in Europe a bittersweet nostalgic experience. Every year, one tour operator or another runs such a trip. And on the other side of the world, maybe your evenings weren't so enchanted in the war-torn South Pacific, but traveling there now in normal times would certainly be an exotic and interesting experience.

Spa Vacations

Health and the pursuit of it provide a dual purpose in selecting a travel destination. It's a perfect vacation combo for those who want a new place to visit while courting health. You don't need physical discomforts to visit these watering spots; there's more going for them besides thermal springs and sulphur waters. Spa resorts are found everywhere in the world, from the hot springs in Japan to the Hot Springs of Arkansas.

In the U.S., spa resorts have literally bubbled up into islands of culture, entertainment, and sports activity while remaining havens for health, beauty, and diet. In New York State, for instance, Saratoga Springs used to be a pleasant little resort town where the horsey set met and came to drink from the salubrious mineral springs. Old pleasures still remain, but Saratoga Springs now caters to a wider spectrum of people. The more cultured, especially, flock to the area now that it's become a center for the performing arts. Every summer, the New York City Ballet Company and other ballet groups captivate audiences with their excellence. The Philadelphia Orchestra fills the "sulphured air" with classical music, and theatre groups bring Broadway hit productions to upper New York State.

Out near the Ozarks, curative mineral springs come with a different entertainment package, more akin to the culture of the area. Hot Springs, Arkansas, offers country music, thoroughbred racing, beauty pageants, outdoor theater, and a host of festivals practically all year around. There's also fishing, golf, and tennis. Part of the National Park System, the area boasts more than 40 thermal springs. Doctors and others working in the hydrotherapy institutions are qualified by the federal government to administer the treatments. You may even get your vacation partially paid by Medicare; there are hospitals in the area where such treatments are reimbursed.

For a more exotic spa experience, Europe has wonderful old spas that have been attracting Europeans for centuries. Anyone from the New World exposed to grand spas of old can really see how important these mineral oases were to generations of Europeans. Hotels are located in wooded dells of picture book beauty. Treatments are about the same as anywhere else—mud baths, wet and dry massages—but at the more famous spas, concerts and casinos offer other attractions.

Eastern European countries like Poland, Romania, Hungary, and Czechoslovakia are dedicated to the concept of spa vacations, and many Americans have found their way over on packaged tours. Romania, the home of the Dr. Ana Aslan Geriatric Institute, has been very active in organizing such tour programs for olds who would be younger.

You might not think of going to Mexico for "the waters," but people do—for spa waters. Our neighbor just south of our border has very attractive spa resorts. What makes Mexican spas so desirable is that they are affordable, nearby, and beautiful. Hollywood scouts looking for a locale for a Humphrey Bogart movie thought so highly of the spa resort of San Jose de Purua in Morelia that they filmed the movie *Treasure of the Sierra Madre* there. Another spa popular with Americans is Ixtapan de la Sol, about 89 miles from Mexico City.

Fair and Warmer Climes

People select destinations for a host of other reasons as well. Some use a travel experience as a means of scouting out retirement sites or looking for a second home. Arizona, southern California, Florida, and Hawaii are visited again and again by middle-aged people with that thought in mind. Others look for a destination that will provide an inexpensive vacation.

While many people past their 50s and 60s are not enamored with tent camping, they do use recreational vehicles to "camp out." RVs are allowed to overnight in 145 National Park Service areas. In addition, there are pleasant lodges in or around the parks that are reasonable and right in the heart of the great scenery. One of the nation's most spectacular beachfront parks is in the Virgin Islands. Cinnamon Bay has campsites, but there are other places to stay, mid-priced between Cinnamon Bay and its very wealthy sister, Caneel Bay Resort, host to celebrity vacationers.

Another unique national park destination is Hawaii Volcanoes National Park, located right on the rim of a crater, but a good distance away from the lava and fiery eruptions of Hawaii's two active volcanoes. The volcanoes, the biggest attraction for tourists on the Big Island, can be seen from an interesting and inexpensive hotel, the Volcano House. For about $40 a night, double, you can sit out and wait for nature's biggest fireworks display.

Some people travel to play golf. Golf and tennis packages, cross-country ski weeks, and other all-inclusive sports vacations are offered by many resorts in cooperation with airlines, car rental agencies, and even trains and buses. It's not necessary to carry cumbersome equipment, since rentals are available on the spot.

Learning Vacations

Going back to school in later years has been gaining in popularity. It's an excellent way to keep your mind young and active. Learning and travel are a natural twosome. The combination provides a purpose, a destination, and a stimulating path to new ideas and new experiences.

If there's any doubt of the popularity of this exciting approach to travel, look at the statistics of Elderhostel, Inc., the foremost proponent of study and travel for 60-plusers. This past year, more than 110,000 older persons attended Elderhostel classes in more than 700 universities and schools in the United States and abroad. When the program started in 1975, only 200 students took classes at five schools in New Hampshire.

There are now many educational offerings geared to older travelers sponsored by travel agents, language schools, cruise lines, and historic communities. Elderhostel gets seniors and institutions together for quick courses on hundreds of different subjects. In addition, students explore the area in which the college or learning institution is located. They can take advantage of art and cultural activities both on and off campus.

Currently participating institutions are located in 50 states, Washington, D.C., all the provinces of Canada, Bermuda, Great Britain, Italy, Denmark, Finland, France, Holland, Norway, Sweden, West Germany, and Israel.

The fact that one-week or longer classes are held at such prestigious schools as Cambridge University, Williams College, and Brigham Young University doesn't mean that students must have a Ph.D. or some equally impressive degree. There are no educational requirements, not even a high school diploma. All that is required is interest and a desire to learn something new or relearn something old.

A wide variety of subjects are offered. A small sample includes medieval music, Greek and Latin roots of American words, a study of stress, the mystery novel, geology in Britain, cowboy art, music appreciation, folk life, plant life, and what computers can do for you.

Apart from its educational programs, Elderhostel is a sought-after experience because of its low cost. Students are put up inexpensively in school dorms or simple accommodations near the campus. Not at all spartan, accommodations are comfortable. Some have shared baths, but don't expect bellboys or coeds to carry your luggage. Room, board, and classes cost under $200 a week. You eat in school cafeterias, just like the other students.

Though by no means as inexpensive as Elderhostel, there are other travel-related educational programs available for mature students. Language studies are popular, especially Spanish. Programs are keyed to total immersion in the language. There are at least 11 language schools in Cuernavaca, Mexico. Rates for tuition can run about $135 a week; room and board with a local family about $10 a day. More information may be obtained by writing the Oficina Federal de Turismo, Avenida Morelos, 105, Cuernavaca, Morelos, Mexico. One school, the Center for Bilingual Multicultural Studies, offers minicourses in Spanish plus studies in pre-Colombian civilizations and other Mexican subjects and field trips.

AARP Travel Service has also caught the learning bug. Eight new learning vacations are being introduced this year which span a number of subjects from arts to antiques to chateaux and more.

There are many other educational travel outlets available. The American Institute for Foreign Study has been serving as registrar and land and air packager for several European universities in Great Britain, France, and Spain. The student age ranges from 20 to 80, and in recent years the Institute has noted an increase in the number of mature scholars taking part in its programs.

The National Registration Center for Study Abroad is another coordinating operation for educational programs overseas. Its listings include schools and institutions of learning in Latin America, Europe, Britain, and Ireland. Some programs are more suited for the 50 to 80 year group.

Schools aren't the only locale for learning experiences. Sometimes destinations themselves have educational offerings packaged in with recreational travel. Historic Colonial Williamsburg in Virginia sponsors winter Learning Weekends every February. Each of these weekends is keyed to an aspect of Americana.

Resources for Learning Vacations

Elderhostel, Inc., 100 Boylston St., Suite 200, Boston, MA 02116

AARP Travel Service, 5855 Green Valley Circle, Culver City, CA 90230 (1-800-227-7885)

American Institute for Foreign Study, 102 Greenwich Ave., Greenwich, CT 06830 (1-800-243-4567)

Institute for International Education, 809 United Nations Plaza, New York, NY 10017 (1-212-883-8200)

National Registration Center for Study Abroad, 823 North 2nd St., Milwaukee, WI 53202 (1-800-558-9988)

Looking Up Roots

Nostalgia isn't limited to the United States. Many millions of Americans look back nostalgically on life in "the old country," even though they may have been born here. Stories told them by parents and grandparents who emigrated from foreign lands have fanned a lifelong interest in those nations.

With so many of us one or two generations away from those countries, seeing where and how our forebearers lived makes a compelling reason to travel there.

Many have relatives still living in foreign countries and want to connect with old ties. Others may just want to tour through towns and villages where parents and grandparents lived. It might come as a surprise to find your name on street signs in those far-off communities.

Tracing roots provides a very personal reason to travel, and many countries are now helping Americans look up their ancestors. For years, Ireland has maintained a special genealogical office in Dublin to help people of Irish extraction find their relatives, living or dead. Now Germany is providing information for North American tourists. In Hamburg, for instance, the Historic Emigration Office in the Museum for Hamburg History will provide information about relatives who emigrated from Europe if you give them the name of your forebearers with the year they left for North America. Hamburg was a principal port for European emigration between 1850 and 1914, and when people from Eastern European countries, Germany, and Italy sailed from Hamburg, their names, ages, occupations, family members, and home towns were recorded by city officials. The information is still there, and for a fee you can find out more about your relatives and where they came from. France, too, will help you look for roots.

I've given you a few ideas and told you a few stories. Now it's up to you to put your own dreams into action. You will have to deal with your own practicalities: how much time to spend, the kind of weather you enjoy, how much comfort you require, the amount of activity you want, and many other factors.

Now read on to learn the art of travel.

CHAPTER 2

Alone or With Someone

Traveling Alone

Women who have worked and lived alone for a number of years have few problems in traveling alone. Whether they want to is another story, but they can deal with money, handle hotel bills, get to airports and train stations on their own, and are not troubled too much by sitting at a table for one in a restaurant. They have made a life for themselves as a single in a world of doubles.

As widowed or divorced men and women get older, on the other hand, they find it more difficult to adjust to a single state, especially on a vacation trip. They are used to traveling as a couple and are unsure of their ability to cope as a single. Loneliness is the biggest fear, but worrying about making arrangements and luggage handling are equally troublesome.

A 55-year-old friend, widowed two years after a 30-year marriage, decided the time had come to try her wings again. She had always traveled with her husband, but never on her own. Italy was her goal, but none of her friends had the time nor the money to go with her. Taking a trip alone was her objective; she wanted to avoid taking a tour.

She didn't know anyone in Italy, and wasn't sure she could manage her luggage or the detailed arrangements of getting there herself. While competent and capable, she was scared.

Her approach, however, was sound. She planned the trip meticulously. She read about Italy, got names of stores and restaurants, talked to people who had been there, and when she felt she was properly prepared, she took off.

Worried friends were relieved when she returned home filled with enthusiasm, confidence, and satisfaction. She also had three new Italian dresses.

How did she do it? She had the right personality and approach. She found that being alone paved the way for a few adventures she would never have had otherwise. It started when the plane was delayed. She struck up a conversation with a pleasant woman traveling alone who was also going to Rome. They made plans to meet for dinner one night. That date gave her a prop—one night was accounted for. Next, she went to a restaurant alone. There were three Italian men who spoke English at the next table. She smiled, they included her in their conversation, and they ended up as friends.

Being upbeat, energetic, charming, and interesting are traits that certainly help a lone traveler, but being able to manage under unfavorable conditions is also an asset. The plane delay proved that she could turn a bad situation into a positive one.

If you, as a single, can be positive and a little aggressive, traveling alone can be a very pleasant experience. You don't have to worry about a companion's feelings. You can sleep late, spend hours shopping or sightseeing, and you have no one but yourself to account to. You are not subject to group movements or restrictions.

Adventures, too, come your way. Couples often find a solitary traveler interesting. You may get an invitation to join them for a meal. If that happens, keep the friendship alive by paying your own check.

Traveling alone becomes a little more difficult the older you get. It's tied up with the inconveniences of travel arrangements, hauling luggage, and dining alone.

Both men and women find solo travel not as adventurous as when they were youths.

Some personalities definitely should not undertake a trip alone. People who are overly sensitive, who are easily taken advantage of, and who have a tendency to feel sorry for themselves should be the first to sign up for a group tour. Those who have led a sheltered life and have had limited worldly experience could also benefit from group interaction. If you wonder about your own ability to go it alone, see how you make out answering the following questions.

A Mini-Quiz for Would-Be Loners

1. Are you gregarious? Can you talk to strangers easily?
2. When you encounter problems, can you assert your rights?
3. Are you a self-starter? Can you plan your days?
4. Do you have a good sense of humor?
5. Can you read a city map? Do you have a sense of direction?
6. Can you afford to stay at a first-class hotel? (Very important because they usually have their own dining room, should you choose to stay in for dinner.)
7. Can you go into a hotel bar alone, sit down, and order a drink without pain and suffering?
8. Are you flexible?
9. Do you enjoy your own company?
10. Can you get to the train or plane on time?
11. Can you limit your luggage to what you yourself can carry?
12. Are you in good physical health?
13. Can you handle solitude?

Be honest with yourself. If you score more noes than yeses, do yourself a big favor and investigate a group tour. It will be a wise investment and you'll have a better time. If you score a high percentage of yes answers and are determined to travel by yourself, there are some more points you might pay attention to.

If your plans are to travel in a foreign country, do you know at least one foreign language or at least enough phrases to get by? Do you have one or two people you could look up? Are you upbeat enough to turn delays or other inconveniences into positive experiences? Being in the same boat as others offers an opportunity to start conversations and maybe even make friends with a pleasant single going your way.

Tips for Independents

☐ When you make hotel reservations, guarantee your room by sending a deposit. It will help hold the room for your arrival.

☐ Inform the hotel when to expect you. Especially after traveling on a night flight over the Atlantic, you'll want a room available when you arrive in the morning so you can rest. You may not get it, but it doesn't hurt to ask.

☐ Single accommodations are the least pleasant rooms in a hotel, often no bigger than utility closets. If you request a large single you will probably get a better room. Larger singles are often used as doubles when hotels get crowded. Another alternative, of course, is to pay for a double room.

☐ Reconfirm your plane reservations. In doing so, you may find that your flight was canceled. If that's the case, have the airline telex your hotel and change your reservation. In some countries air reservations are canceled unless confirmed. Check rail and bus departures, too.

☐ Before you leave on your trip, read about the destination and plan a sample itinerary. When you get to where you are going you will know what to do with your time. Without plans, you would have too much time on your hands, and you could get lonely.

☐ When you first get to your destination, a city tour will help acclimate you to your surroundings and give you an opportunity to meet people like yourself who may be looking for company.

☐ Leave for airports, trains, and buses with time to spare in case you get lost.

Dining Alone

Probably the hardest experience for an individual traveling alone is dining in a restaurant at a candlelight table for two when you are all by yourself. Both sexes find it difficult, but women especially suffer embarrassment, fear of rejection, and the uncomfortable feeling that everyone must be staring. While it's certainly more agreeable to have company at meal times, it shouldn't be such an ordeal that you end up eating alone in your room, or sitting at a counter in a coffee shop.

At issue is how you feel about yourself. If you have a good self-image there's no need to view the experience as unsettling. Being alone can actually be a relief. You don't have to listen to dull conversations. You can enjoy your drink and food in your own distinguished company at whichever restaurant you choose.

If the headwaiter hides you at a small table near the kitchen, you can complain or you can use your hideaway position as a good vantage point to observe the clientele. People-watching in an unfamiliar city or country can be educational. It might give you a clearer insight into the local scene.

Rejection is a problem women, more than men, encounter in dining alone. Not being seated can be a crushing blow. One woman had her heart set on eating at one of the great restaurants of Paris. The concierge of her hotel made the reservation at the height of the dinner hour. When she got to the restaurant, it was very crowded. The headwaiter denied she had a reservation. If you want to dine alone at a very popular special restaurant, don't make the reservation at peak hours. Make it before or after, when the restaurant is less busy.

Tips for Single Women

☐ Book a hotel room in the center of town where you can walk to shops, restaurants, and maybe even to a nearby museum or a famous church. (Don't do this if the center of town is rundown and host to the criminal element. A good travel agent would inform you of this.)
☐ Make sure the hotel you stay in has a dining room. If you get cold feet about going out at night alone, you can at least eat in your hotel.
☐ A luggage cart or light luggage with wheels is a good investment. You might have to carry your own suit-

case. It usually gets heavier every day with the things you buy.

- ☐ It's difficult maneuvering a luggage cart or luggage with wheels down stairs. Look for ramps or elevators at terminals.
- ☐ When you go to a good restaurant alone, be well dressed. You will be taken care of better if you look as if you know how to tip.
- ☐ Try not to travel at night. Daylight hours are more friendly, and there's less chance of getting lost or mugged.
- ☐ A smile goes a long way.
- ☐ If you need help getting off a train, don't hesitate to ask those around you for a hand. People are usually helpful to women.
- ☐ Take along plenty of coins or small bills for tips. If you're traveling overseas, a slim wallet-sized calculator will help you convert foreign currencies to U.S. dollar equivalents quickly. (It's done wonders for me.)
- ☐ Choose a country friendly to women. People always seem to take care of younger and older women. Try an English-speaking country, or one with a warm climate—cordiality seems to thrive along the Mediterranean and in the Caribbean.

When You Need a Friend

There are times when even the most self-confident person needs a little company. When that happens just go back to basics.

- ☐ Take a city tour, either by day or night, and be friendly with fellow passengers.
- ☐ Have a drink of club soda or whatever at the bar in your hotel and be approachable.
- ☐ Ask the local tourist office if there's a Meet the People program at your destination. You might find the experience one of the most memorable of your trip.
- ☐ Don't forget about senior citizen groups. Even if you're not so senior, you just might have a good time and meet some interesting people. Contact AARP's Field Service Dept., 1909 K St., N.W., Washington, DC 20048 to

find a local chapter. Other organizations are listed in the Yellow Pages of the phone book under Clubs.
□ Look up professional or business counterparts. If you were or are a teacher, lawyer, or chef, for example, visit schools, lawyers' clubs, or restaurants.
□ If you're a classical musician, you might find a string quartet group to play with. A bridge fan might try to locate a bridge club.
□ Stay in bed-and-breakfast accommodations where you will meet people.
□ Look for cultural exchange organizations whose goals are to foster friendship between people of diverse nationalities.

Traveling in a Group

A whole other set of circumstances confront the person traveling alone in a group. The villain in this situation is not loneliness but the penalty for being alone—the dread single supplement. Hotels and cruise ships require that you pay extra for occupying a double room by yourself. The supplement can amount to several hundred dollars extra for a tour, a very high price for privacy.

The solution is to find a friend to share your room. When that isn't possible, tour operators often try to pair off single travelers to share a room. Some operators might absorb the cost of the double room if they can't find you a roommate.

Strangers in the Night

Incompatibility in a roommate could spoil a trip if you let it. Petty annoyances become magnified in small, shared quarters. If it's true with a husband and wife or best friends, then it's certainly true with a stranger, though many of us can exhibit more control with strangers than with our loved ones.

Single or doubles, everyone wants some privacy. It's difficult and repressive for one adult to adjust lifelong habits to please another adult, but it can be done.

If you must share a room with someone you don't particularly like, ask the tour leader if the arrangement can be changed. When another roommate cannot be found and economic reasons dictate double occupancy, clear the air and discuss the problem.

Work out an agenda where each of you will have the time you need alone. When it's a question of two really clashing personalities, pay the extra money or give each other a lot of space during the day. Take different tours and sit with other people at meal times and on motor-coaches. The idea is to minimize exposure to each other. You can't do anything about the nights, but you certainly can handle the days.

A Little Matchmating

Finding a suitable roommate is not easy, but it's not impossible either. If travel agents or tour operators can't help, there are agencies, like widow's travel clubs, travel adventure clubs, divorced persons clubs, and other groups dedicated to introducing travel-minded people to each other. The newest one to achieve national celebrity is the Travel Companion Exchange, a membership organization of single travelers in search of partners in travel. For information write Travel Companion Exchange, Box 833, Amityville, NY 11701, or phone 1-516-454-0880. Membership is $4 a month with a minimum six month membership.

Another alternative for finding roommates is to place an ad in leisure publications. Some large tourist operators and wholesalers with newsletters also allow clients to run a few lines in their own publications to help single travelers get together.

CHAPTER 3

Doing Your Homework

You know how it is with presidents. Every time they go abroad a retinue of experts is ready to cram the chief executive full of facts. It's a good way to assure a successful trip. The presidential staff does all the homework.

You, too, have a staff. A whole industry is at your command, ready to help you with your travel homework. The more you learn, the greater your pleasure, because planning a journey can be almost as exciting as taking the trip.

The travel industry has billions of dollars riding on your itinerant nature and spends millions to educate and inform you about destinations and all the services involved in getting you there and hosting and catering to your touristic needs.

Literally tons of reading matter pour off the presses annually from every city, state, country, and resort. The thrust of that information may be a little self-serving, but there's solid information on attractions, costs, how to get there, and how to get the most from your trip.

Backing up that mountain of matter is more reading produced by tour operators, cruise lines, motorcoach companies, book publishers, travel agents, magazines, newspapers, and even newsletters.

And don't forget the auto clubs. They, too, can fill you with information about destinations, adding practical advice on the best ways to get there. If you don't belong to an auto club, don't fret; fuel companies, too, maintain touring and informational services with the same kinds of data.

The free material available from all sources is staggering. The British Tourist Authority, for instance, estimates that they prepare more than 1,000 individual pieces of free tourist information. In the U.S., states and localities send free booklets in addition to everything else—dining and visitors' guides, pocket-size handbooks, and newsletters chock full of well-organized and inviting information.

You can write for maps and lists of special festivals and sports events. From the material offered, you can learn when craft exhibitions are held, when the racing season starts, where to camp, when to camp, when to whale watch, where to rent a houseboat, how to get tickets for concerts, when, where, and what to fish for and how to get a license, and hundreds of other facts to make your trip more enjoyable.

In Appendix A you will find the addresses and phone numbers of state tourist offices and selected foreign tourist offices. When you request information, be specific. If you want to know about bed and breakfast accommodations, ask for that especially. For information about accommodations, ask for lists and rates of hotels plus information about cottages, condos, inns, and tourist homes. Get a good selection of what's available; you may want to go deluxe in one place and economy somewhere else.

Timetables and schedules for transportation services—buses, trains, ferries, boats, etc.—are also available, as are the names and addresses of companies that operate tours through various areas.

Prepared brochures come on just about every subject.

Research on the Home Front

While you're waiting for this information to arrive, visit your library and look for books and articles about places you are thinking about visiting. The *Readers' Guide to Peri-*

odical Literature will direct you to magazine articles about destinations under consideration. Browse through book shelves for travel books or related books that explore the area's history, customs, and social life. Read the card catalog for what else is available. And don't forget the bookstores! Get a notebook and write ideas down.

Talk with friends who have traveled. Get their ideas on what they considered interesting. Read the travel sections of newspapers and look at the ads. You might even clip stories and ads or take notes from those that seem pertinent. If ads indicate there is literature available, call or write for it. Attend some travel lectures and search out movies shot in the locale that interests you.

While collecting material, give some thought to your own expectations and the kind of things you would like to see and do. When there are two of you, discuss each other's interests, and make accommodations to satisfy each other's needs.

If health is central to your travel plans, where and how far you go may be determined by your physical condition and your energy level. If taking a tour is on your mind, do you have enough endurance to keep up with a regular group, or should you choose one that's slower paced and stays longer in each place? Walking problems, too, need consideration. If you have a trick knee or troubles with your hip, heel, or ankles, try to eliminate places with uphill and uneven terrain. Ask people who have been there. Think about the climate for the time of the year you want to travel.

Be Flexible About Time

For those who are no longer at the mercy of school vacations, it's helpful not to have to take trips at Christmas, Easter, or during the summer months. Transportation facilities are less crowded off-season. You can see places when they are normal, not overcrowded with tourists.

There are certain places, however, where off-season months are definitely not the time to go. In the early fall months, for instance, Caribbean islands and the southern U.S. may be subject to heavy rains and hurricanes.

Choose off-season months when the weather is pleasant.

Climatic conditions are topsy-turvy in this world. When it's freezing cold in most of North America, it's nice and warm in South America. When Australians are sitting on their beaches acquiring a tan, many Americans are digging themselves out of snowbanks.

Be aware, too, that winter and summer are not always "on" seasons. Sometimes spring and fall are the height of the season. Take Hong Kong, for instance. There, winters are cold and summers rainy. Tourists who want the best weather conditions visit in October and November or April and May. New York City, too, is beautiful and exciting in the fall and spring.

If you do go off-season, find things to do that will compensate for lack of sun. Winter is a good time to enjoy the cultural life of a region or country. That's when everything is in full swing.

When not to go is also a consideration. Being somewhere during a national or religious holiday can be disappointing. In England, for instance, practically all tourist activity and public transportation stops on Christmas and the day after (Boxing Day). Most restaurants, too, close up on Christmas Day.

Consider Your Comfort

Timing is certainly important in planning a trip, but safety, cleanliness, crowds, ease of getting around, and your ability to weather discomforts are equally significant.

A woman on a photographic safari to Africa had a choice of taking a tour with comfortable lodgings in a game park or being billeted in tent camps out in the bush. Wishing to really get the "feel" of Africa and dazzle friends with all her courage and derring-do, she chose the tent safari.

The nights she spent out in the bush in "tent city" were sleepless ones. She interpreted every click, beep, grunt, and croak heard in the darkness of night as harbingers of evil and danger.

To make matters worse, she developed a bladder infection. Tents don't yet come equipped with modern plumbing, and getting up in the blackness of the African night to go to the outhouse was a frightening experience.

There was no need for her to have had such a bad experience. Lodges in the African bush are comfortable and deluxe, some even have swimming pools. A little realistic self-analysis would have made her trip much easier.

When to Go

Travelers should pay attention to inner fears, dislikes, and pet peeves when they plan their trips. People who hate crowds, for instance, should not choose to go to Rio de Janeiro during Mardi Gras. Cariocas push and shove to get close to the music and dance. Instead, plan to visit Rio after Carnival, when you can hear the winning songs, enjoy the city in a less hectic atmosphere, get into good restaurants, and receive personal attention in hotels, no longer pressed by the crowds.

If your plans are to visit an area with unique events and features, like California's movie and television studios, Paris fashion openings, or the opera and ballet in New York, getting tickets in advance is recommended.

Part of doing your homework involves learning about regional and national customs. The Middle East, for instance, is culturally unprepared for women in shorts. Thais find it offensive if you show the sole of your shoe. And if a Portuguese family invites you to dinner it's customary to send flowers ahead of time. These little tidbits of information do come in handy. What's more, they are nice to know.

What Can You Afford?

You can't travel without money. Before you figure how much a trip will cost, consider how much you can afford.

It's not necessary to go deluxe all the way. If you can't afford to indulge yourself and book the Princess Suite, moderate accommodations are just as acceptable. You don't spend too much time in your room anyway. Small hotels, bed and breakfast places, and tourist homes keep costs down. People who want to make their own arrangements should know that independent travel often comes with a higher price tag, especially if you fly to a destination. Take advantage of independent tour programs with hotel packages, or visit countries or places that are less expensive.

Motorcoach travel will have to be substituted for air, or charters might be considered instead of regularly scheduled air flights for overseas travel. In Europe, a Eurail pass for train travel will cut costs.

How about group tours?

When you want full value for your money, prepackaged tours are the answer. See Chapter 7 for more information on tours.

Perhaps you are thinking about taking a cruise. Some people love the idea of a floating resort. Staying put for a week or more on a ship and getting off at romantic ports is just the kind of relaxing vacation some people dream about. For others, a ship's environment is too constraining. The constant ebb and flow of food, the same people and the often frenetic programming of activities on a ship may be too rich for some vacationers.

All elements of your own personality and taste must be considered when planning a vacation. After you've analyzed your goals and digested the material you collected, you can get some sense of how and where to spend your travel money.

All this preparation takes time. Six months is about right for letting the ideas percolate in your head.

How Do You Begin?

When you're set for serious planning, start with a list of destinations you might like to visit. Write down what you want to do and see in each place. Talk about it with friends. Add or subtract places from the list. The more you think about it, the more your ideas will gel.

The Tools You Need

Methods for planning a trip may vary, but the tools are the same. The following can be obtained from government tourist offices, airlines, libraries, travel agents, and bookstores.

☐ Several up-to-date guide books
☐ Lists of lodgings with prices
☐ New maps of the region, and specific maps of the cities or towns you plan on visiting
☐ Itineraries from already prepared package tours, available from travel agents, airline, bus or rail offices
☐ Timetables, airline schedules, train, ferry, cruise, hydrofoil, and bus schedules, whichever are appropriate to your journey
☐ Lists of events to see, with dates and available times— The Taj Mahal in moonlight, a Van Gogh exhibit in a museum, an azalea festival, championship tennis matches, a regatta, etc.
☐ Weather charts
☐ Critiques of places to visit. You can cull these from your readings of newspaper and magazine articles and from opinions of travelers. Some tourist attractions are "must sees," others are expendable.
☐ If going abroad, get phrase books and start learning some words in foreign languages. Your reception over there will be much warmer.

Rely on guide books for pre-digested material, but not for exact prices. Information about costs should come directly from the facilities involved or from listings provided by municipalities.

Now That You've Made Your Decision

When you are sure of your destination, start blocking out a proposed itinerary. Some of your research on expenses can be incorporated into your travel budget later.

☐ Determine when you want to go and for how long. Some people plan their trips with time at the beginning to rest. That free time gives them a chance to catch their breath after the hectic days of preparing for a trip, but it also provides time to absorb the atmosphere of a new locale and to get the feel of the region. Other travelers plan time in the middle of a trip to reflect on

what they've seen and done and to relax without packing and unpacking. Others program rest time at the
conclusion of a trip, before coming home.

☐ How do you want to get to your destination? Make
some determination on your method of travel, which
may be a combination of buses, rail, rented cars, and
planes.

☐ Crib a little from all those package tour itineraries in
your possession. What kind of trips do tour operators
offer to the same destination? Study the brochures of
all of them—AARP Travel Service, American Express,
Thomas Cook, TWA, Olson-Travelworld, Tauck Tours,
Grand Circle Tours, Maupintour, Cosmos, Cartan,
Saga, or others. What do the tours highlight? How
much time do they spend in each place? What hotels do
they use? How much do the trips cost?

☐ With those package plans as your guide, construct your
own rough itinerary. Take it day by day, and fill in the
attractions you want to see.

Constructing an Itinerary

Take a sheet of paper and draw large squares on it for
each day of your trip. In the squares, write where you
want to be and what you want to do each day. The following tips will help you make your plans.

☐ Don't plan to do too much. You can't see everything. Be
selective. When you see things in depth, you'll remember them better. Cram too much into an itinerary and
your impressions will be blurred.

☐ Do not rely on old maps or old information. Travel is a
dynamic industry, constantly changing. Neighbor-
hoods once slums have been rebuilt and restored to
former glory. You can witness such restorations in
New York, Baltimore, Philadelphia, and elsewhere.

☐ Avoid one-night stands. A relaxed schedule will allow
you to savor a place and give you opportunities to talk
to people, try culinary specialities, and enjoy cultural
spectacles. A day here, the next there, is unrewarding
and exhausting.

☐ If you can, avoid night flights. Plane seats are too narrow for a restful sleep. A day flight, especially across

time zones, is the best assurance of maintaining your body clock. If you can, break your journey and get a good night's sleep; then continue your trip the next day. You will be rested and raring to go.

☐ If you can't arrange your schedule for day flights, do not make any plans for the first day after a long flight. Get some rest before you start your hectic life as a tourist.

☐ If you want to dine in a famous restaurant and you're only going to be in the area for one or two days, write or call ahead for a reservation so you won't be disappointed. It's as necessary for some of New Orleans' restaurants as it is for the five star dining establishments in France.

☐ Everyone has his or her own strategy for planning a trip. You might visualize your itinerary better if you have maps of the region or city in front of you. With a magic marker, pinpoint the places you want to visit on the map and ring the attractions. Draw a dotted line to the margin of the map, indicating opening and closing hours in the margin if that applies. When you arrive at your destination you will have the map showing all the pertinent information you need.

☐ If you are committed to doing all the planning and reservations yourself, make your travels easier by using one city or town as your headquarters. Take day tours from that center point. It is probably the most relaxing plan you can make, since you are assured of a comfortable and familiar place to return to at the end of each day. You eliminate daily packing and unpacking, and you can pace the trip to your energy level.

Before you finalize your itinerary, ask your travel agent (or yourself, if appropriate) the following important questions.

☐ Have you explored all excursion and promotional rates open to you—hotel packages, specials on car rentals, air fares?

☐ Are the hotels located near the sights and services you require? Do they have impediments (steep stairs, no elevators) that might pose problems for you?

☐ Will transportation to and from the airport be provided by the hotel?

☐ Are the dates you selected close to or on a national holiday? If so, is that likely to create special problems for you?

☐ Is weather generally good at the time of your trip? What is the mean temperature? How much rain might there be?

☐ Can you buy tickets in advance for special events?

☐ Will the famous museum or other public building you want to see be open, or is it closed for repairs?

☐ If you're planning on playing golf or tennis at a championship course, will there be a tournament on during your visit that will preempt the course or court for the likes of you? And while you are inquiring, ask about the charges for greens fees or for the use of the tennis courts.

☐ If traveling by car, did you get a routing from your auto club? Did they mark the interesting things to see en route between destinations? Do you have the mileages available, so you can determine when to stop for the night?

☐ If traveling by plane, are you allowing enough time between flights to go through customs (if necessary), or to get your luggage transferred to another carrier?

☐ If you buy your cruise, plane, rail, or bus tickets in advance, are there any penalties if you have to cancel?

☐ If going abroad, have you applied for your passport or checked the validity of the one you have?

☐ Have you checked your list of priority attractions with someone who's been there recently?

☐ Have you considered staying put in one place and making daily trips within a radius of 75 to 100 miles?

☐ Have you found out who to contact for sightseeing tours when you get there?

Budgets, Money, and Related Matters

With your years of experience in handling money, you probably have a built-in budget mechanism. You know how much you have, how much you can spend, and are probably able to keep your expenses within that frame-work.

Your heaviest travel expenses will be air fare, hotels, meals, and, if traveling by car, the expenses of running your auto.

Life-styles, too, determine how much money you'll require for a trip. If you like going deluxe all the way and would be miserable in budget accommodations, I hope you have the means to keep yourself gloriously happy.

Some destinations are more costly than others. If you go to Tokyo, you'll have to allot more funds for travel than if you were just driving through the bayou areas of Louisiana.

Most people splurge in one place and economize in another. Whatever your private strategy is, be realistic about travel funds. Set that sum down front and center. If you've done your homework, you have a lot of figures in front of you—a range of hotel prices, the least expensive air fares, an approximate idea of how much your meals will cost.

How much would you have to spend for three meals a day in restaurants at home? If you live in a place with a moderate cost of living standard, add about 25 percent to get the daily cost of meals while traveling.

Figuring Costs

To determine approximate costs for your trip, make three columns on a sheet of paper—one for escorted tours, another for group charters, and a third for independent travel.

The escorted tour column is easy. You have the overall prepaid cost. Add the extras and items not included. How many meals are you being offered? Does the tour skip meals in big cities? If it does, remember that food costs are higher in big cities. Is the air fare included? If not, what special fare do they offer? How about tips, porterage fees, optional attractions? Will you have to pay to go on sightseeing tours? Are taxes included? If you're going overseas, does the tour price include departure taxes from foreign airports? What other expenses could you incur? Do you like a full breakfast in the morning?

You will have to pay extra if the tour only offers a continental breakfast (coffee, roll, and marmalade or jam).

Do the same thing for group or charter travel. Take it step by step. What are you going to have to add to the prepaid cost—transfers between airport and hotels, cost of meals, sightseeing trips, car rentals, cabs, porter fees?

Independent travel has its rewards, but it does require more work and checking. How much will your transportation cost? What is the lowest air fare you can get, the best excursion rates by rail, any promotional fare from the bus company? If traveling by car, how many miles can you get on a gallon? Figure other costs of running your car—tolls, garages, emergency repairs, etc.

Evaluating Other Expenses

Do the same thing for hotels as you did for tours. Make three separate columns for different hotel categories: deluxe, first class, and economy. Write down the daily cost of rooms for each. Remember that some hotels list double room rates, which include two persons; others may charge per person (double occupancy). With the various options spelled out in front of you, it will be easier for you to determine where to indulge yourself and where to economize.

Your next consideration is food. These estimates and tips, trips, and cabs all go on a special cost sheet. These items can be controlled somewhat. Estimate the cost of meals, snacks, and drinks per day. Multiply by the number of days you will be traveling. In the next column, figure transfers to and from the airport, bus, or train terminal. Multiply that by the number of arrivals and departures. Your next column will be automobile expenses, if you drive. Figure daily parking fees and multiply by the number of days you will have parking fees. Also figure expenses for running your car. Sightseeing costs, tips, and sundries each get a column. When you add each column on each worksheet, you'll have a pretty good idea of how much it's going to cost you.

Charter packages are less expensive at the outset because of lower air fares and inclusion of hotel costs. But there may be more extras than you thought possible—

sightseeing and optional trips. Remember that charter flights can be very tiring. Delays are more the rule than the exception.

Do-it-yourselfers will have to dovetail schedules, make reservations, get porters and cabs, and take care of all the details. Weigh all the advantages and disadvantages for the three modes of travel. Don't let cost alone sway your decision. Pick the plan that will bring you the most enjoyment. If you've never traveled before, taking a group tour will be a good learning experience should you want to travel alone the next time.

As you will see, budget-making is easier when you buy an all-inclusive prepaid tour or cruise. You know in advance what you will spend on the major portion of your trip, and you can even cost out the per diem rate by dividing the price by the number of days on tour. Tour operators often include the days you travel to and from your destination as tour days.

As a quick guide to help you figure the cost of your trip, check off items on the following list. If expenses listed are absorbed by your tour, delete them from your computations.

- ☐ Fees for baggage handling
- ☐ Transfers from hotels to airports and back
- ☐ Local transportation—cab fares, subways, buses
- ☐ Car rentals plus extra insurance
- ☐ Wines and other spirits
- ☐ Train, plane, and bus fares
- ☐ Sightseeing tours (You may be offered some free; others are "optional"—translated, that means you have to pay extra for them.)
- ☐ Tips
- ☐ Admissions to attractions
- ☐ Evening entertainment—theatrical, musical, etc.
- ☐ Night clubs
- ☐ Gifts for grandchildren, children, neighbors
- ☐ Buying souvenirs for yourself
- ☐ Calling home
- ☐ Laundry costs
- ☐ Snacks

☐ Port taxes if on a cruise (Airport taxes in foreign coun-
tries are discussed elsewhere. On a cruise ship with a
lot of stops, port taxes can amount to $50 or more.)
☐ Costs of passports and visas
☐ Preventive shots and pre-trip visit to your doctor
☐ Hosting others
☐ Cost of buying traveler's checks
☐ Trip cancellation insurance, medical insurance, luggage
insurance
☐ Additional charges for taking extra luggage
☐ Spending money strictly for enjoyment (Perhaps you
want to rent a car for the day.)
☐ Emergency money

The Cost of Last Minute Changes

While spontaneity can be exciting, it usually is an
expensive luxury when it comes to travel. Usually you
can't pick up and go at the last minute without paying a
premium for accommodations on air fares, cruises, and
hotel rooms. With rare exceptions, there are no last minute supersavers. All the inexpensive staterooms have
already been sold on cruise ships, and if you show up at a
hotel, you're going to be charged the rack rate.

Travel Agents—How They Can Help

Travel agents have become the indispensible middlemen
of the tourist industry. They can save travelers time,
money, and frustration. Being well connected helps, and
the computer has given them an edge over an ordinary
traveler without those "connections." More than 90 percent of the 24,000 travel agents in the United States today
have access to computers. Information on package tours,
low-cost fares, and special places are available to travel
agents in a matter of minutes.

The services of travel agents are free to the public.
Agents are paid commissions by carriers, hotels, tour
operators, and motorcoach companies when they sell a
trip.

There are times when an agent may charge you for his or her time or extra expenses—long distance phone calls, telexes, cables, and other special services. It's a small fee for the service you get.

Agencies handle commercial and vacation travel. Within those classifications there are sub-specialties— cruise travel, freighter travel, ethnic travel, charters, groups, European travel, Pacific destinations. In large cities there are those who handle specific destinations.

Agencies specializing in commercial accounts will take on vacation travelers, but they often don't have the patience or time to hold the hands of and reassure neophyte travelers.

There are large agencies, small agencies, and middle-sized agencies. Whether you consult one over the other is purely subjective, but the bottom line is your personal agent. How good, interested, and knowledgeable is that person? Will that agent fight for your rights, try to get you the best for the least cost, and make your trip the joyous experience you want it to be?

Agents working for a smaller agency, might have more time to find you a trip that best fits your life-style, stamina, personality, and taste.

If you have hotel or car rental discounts coming to you through memberships in clubs, the agent may get them for you as a courtesy even though that discount represents their commission.

On the minus side, small agencies may sometimes take on inexperienced help who don't know enough about the field, and generally the small agency may not have access to information that larger agencies have. The complexities of new rules and regulations take a long time to learn, and you, the client, may be missing out.

Cash flow problems may impede a quick refund when you are cancelling a trip. In addition, small agencies with limited business may have trouble standing up to wholesalers who don't deliver what they promise. If you have only one small travel agency in your area, ask for the most traveled agent in the office.

The best reason for dealing with larger agencies is that they have more clout and more connections. Hard-to-get airplane and hotel reservations may be easier to obtain from an agency that does volume business with carriers and hotels. Because they do business on a larger scale, they are probably more financially sound. If you had trouble with your tour, a hotel, or other services along the way, a large agency might fight harder for your rights. All agencies will try to help, but some take out more insurance to cover errors. There's also a greater range of experience in a large or medium-sized agency. If your individual agent doesn't know about a destination, usually someone in that office can provide up-to-date information.

How They Operate

Travel agents function as middlemen between you and your journey. They may pull all the components of your tour together or find you a tour operator who has the kind of package you want.

For instance, there's a two-week tour to Vienna. The tour operator will provide your agent with all the documents you need for your trip. The agent will make sure you have your air tickets, vouchers for hotels (if it's not escorted), and a detailed itinerary. Your trip will probably include transfers at the airport, porterage help, hotel accommodations, a city sightseeing tour, maybe tickets to the opera, an evening tour of the Grinzing, with stops at four Heurigens (wine bars) for food, wine, and music, and the choice of taking coffee and cake at Demel's, the famous pastry shop, or having a Sachertorte and coffee at the equally famous Hotel Sacher.

If you want a custom designed tour, the agent will do that for you, too. He or she will contact the people the agency works with in specific destinations to provide you with a car and guide, sightseeing services, hotels, air flights, and anything else you require. This foreign independent tour (FIT) is more expensive, since it requires personal attention from the beginning of your trip to its happy ending.

Just remember, it is your trip, your choice of destination, and the agent should be counted on to tell you about availability—not tell you where you should go.

Here are some tips that will help you find the travel agent who is right for you.

☐ Recommendations from friends who have used the agent and were satisfied with the way trips were handled is a big plus.

☐ Experience is important. These days many professional travel agents have taken advanced training to polish up their skills. The CTC written after their names stands for Certified Travel Counselor, which means that they have at least five years of agency experience and two years of courses. Agents without the CTC after their names downplay this training as unimportant, but anyone who pursues additional knowledge is likely to be more professional about his or her business.

☐ Membership in the American Society of Travel Agents tells you that the agency has some standing in the travel industry and is regulated by its code of ethics.

☐ If the agency has approval from the Air Traffic Conference, it can issue domestic airline tickets; if it has approval from the International Air Transport Association (IATA), it can write tickets on international airlines. This is important, because it indicates that the agency meets the strict financial criteria of those important organizations.

☐ Does the agency have a computer hookup?

☐ If the office has up-to-date issues of *Travel Weekly* and *Travel Agent* magazines, it is some indication that the agency keeps up with news and trends.

☐ If you like the agent, but aren't sure of the agency's credentials, check them out with the Better Business Bureau in your area and find out if any complaints have been lodged against it.

Before you decide on a travel agent, interview several of them. Determine which one may serve you best. Everything you can do to protect yourself and your own interests should be done. After all, it's your vacation, your hard-earned money, and your expectations on the line.

Great Expectations

Here's a list of what you can expect from a travel agent.

☐ To be your personal advocate in putting together a vacation that is long on quality and short on price. That includes the best packages and the lowest air fares from one point to another.

☐ To offer a package by a reliable tour operator, one with whom the agency has had no problems.

☐ To be able to sell you all types of travel/health insurance to cover you for unexpected eventualities.

☐ To provide you with advice on money-saving opportunities like charter flights and tell you all the pros and cons of such an arrangement.

☐ To be well informed about the industry and changes that may affect the services you get. The agent should keep pace with new places and good buys.

☐ To have a sense of your style and to deal ethically with you.

☐ To pay attention to your needs and not try to sell you a tour because it will bring in a heavy commission.

☐ To go to bat for you if you've been wronged and return your money as quickly as possible if you have to cancel your trip.

☐ To give you advice about clothes to take, weather you may encounter, and health tips, and to get you all the documents you need for your trip.

☐ To be honest about the fact when he or she does not personally know the hotel booked for you.

☐ To make all your reservations, order tickets, find out all available services for you, take care of requests for special diets, make arrangements for certain celebrations, and compute your costs for you.

Your Obligations to Them

What's fair is fair. If you expect all those things from a travel agent, you owe the agent some candor, too. Here's your checklist.

☐ Be honest with your agent. Are you really serious about taking a trip or are you just picking his or her brain.

☐ Level with the agent about how much money you have for your trip. Don't fudge about price. If the trip is too expensive, say so.

☐ If you have personal piques about people, places, and politics, tell the agent about your feelings. Also tell the agent what you like to do and relate your previous travel experiences.

☐ Be prepared when you go to an agent. Have some concrete ideas of where you would like to go. Listen to suggestions and keep an open mind. You have your own research to back you up.

☐ Make an appointment with a travel agent so you know he or she will have time to sit down with you and discuss your vacation expectations.

☐ Don't expect a travel agent to get you a pension in Greece or a small hotel in Paris without charging you for the long-distance call or telegrams. That hotel and that pension will probably not pay your agent a commission.

☐ If you are a total stranger to the agent and you are asked for a deposit before work is done on your itinerary, it is fair. It's the agency's only way to know if you really mean to take that trip. For your part, get specific points in writing—cancellation refund policy, agent's policies, and supplier's policies.

Despite all the care you take in finding the right agent, nobody's perfect and things can go wrong. Keep notes on where, when, and what happened, plus receipts and names of people with whom you had problems. It will help the agent serve you and others better in the future.

CHAPTER 4

A Home Away from Home

Where to stay and where to eat are questions frequently asked when travelers get together.

And why not? Food and shelter are an essential part of our daily lives. They become especially important when we travel. A great meal and a good night's sleep in pleasant surroundings can only enhance a tourist's experiences.

Where to Stay

We're in luck in the U.S. There are more than 55,000 hotels, motels, and resorts willing and eager to put travelers up for the night. There are almost as many hotels in this country as there are in the rest of the world.

That number provides plenty of variety. You can stay at luxurious modern hotels, historic antebellum guest houses, glass-sheathed commercial hotels, motels on the interstates, resorts with country club–like services, small privately-owned hotels, and old-fashioned rambling caravansaries. If your goals are less grand and more homey, bed and breakfast establishments, boarding houses, tourist houses, and less formal guest houses will answer your needs for overnight stays.

The Star System in Hotels, Motels, and Resorts

Unlike most foreign countries, the United States does not have an official rating system for hotels and motels. Instead, self-styled hotel critics, guide book authors, auto clubs, and hotel associations dole out diamonds, stars, gold keys, and other rating symbols designating fair to excellent accommodations.

Each group has its own set of determinants as to what represents the best. Mobil Guides and the American Automobile Association actually send out crews of critics to judge accommodations. Other hotel raters send out questionnaires, while travel writers are more subjective. The higher the rating a lodging has, the more costly the rooms. That's fair, since establishments work harder to earn those meritorious awards.

What most people want in overnight accommodations is cleanliness, safety, proximity to attractions, a pleasant host, and perhaps television. Most of the time you are out of your room anyway. Extras like ice machines, a handsome lobby, and a swimming pool are nice, but not essential.

Resort accommodations are another story. When you're spending a week or more in one spot, amenities become more important. Resorts are supposed to provide that total vacation environment.

Hotels—What Can You Expect?

In the U.S. you can count on an inexpensive hotel room to have a private bath or shower, a radio or television (or maybe both), a phone, a reading lamp with a bulb that's probably not bright enough (there's never enough light) to read by, the usual towels and soap, and fresh linen on the bed. There may or may not be someone to carry your bag, but there will be someone at the front desk to field your requests and answer questions.

More expensive hotels may have amenities like dining rooms and/or coffee shops, swimming pools, gyms, boutiques, nicely furnished rooms, well-trained personnel, and perhaps even 24-hour room service. They often place expensive soaps and shampoos in the bathroom, provide a plastic shower cap, and maybe even a terry bathrobe. A newspaper may be dropped at your door in the morning and chocolates placed on your pillow when the maid comes in to turn down your bed at night.

Your room may have a mini bar—a small refrigerator stocked with a variety of sodas, mini-sized liquor bottles, beer, cheese and crackers, and bars of chocolate. Warning: the contents are not free. Every day the housekeeper checks the fridge and charges missing items to your bill.

Hotels may be individually owned or a franchise or part of a chain. Chain hotels and motels are usually linked together by a central reservation system with a toll-free (800) number to reserve a room for your next stop.

Travelers who want full services and all conveniences choose hotels over less costly types of overnight accommodations.

Motels

Motels have traditionally been roadside lodgings appealing to motorists because of free parking, inexpensive rooms, and convenience to the road. The very low cost motels limit amenities.

In recent years some have upgraded their services and raised their prices. They now list themselves as "motor inns" and "motor resorts." Swimming pools, restaurants, bars, fireplaces, video game rooms, and even putting greens are now featured, and some even have bellmen to carry your luggage. They've come a long way from those roadside cabins and are rated and priced accordingly. Rooms in motor resorts can cost almost as much as resort hotels of equal quality.

Strictly an American invention, motels have been copied in other parts of the world. Canada, Mexico, the Caribbean, Europe, New Zealand, and Australia now have them.

Resort Hotels

The U.S. is rich in resort hotels. Some are noted for their food and entertainment, others for their grand style. Most are built close to woodlands, beaches, lakes, scenic wonders, and historic areas. Many feature tennis, golf, dancing, fine restaurants, and health spa facilities.

Palm Springs, Las Vegas, Miami Beach and many other Florida locations, Scottsdale, Arizona, and Saratoga Springs, N.Y. are noted for resort hotels. But to be fair, every state in the union has very special vacation hotels offering meal plans and often free use of all sports facilities.

Usually, a minimum stay is required for this type of resort. When a resort offers an all-inclusive package plan, it's a good vacation investment. All or most of your meals are included, and you probably have full use of all the facilities. Many offer golf and tennis packages. Sometimes, too, the resort, acting in concert with airlines, can offer lower air fares than you can get yourself.

Books written about resorts abound in your libraries. Consult the reading list in Appendix B.

Checklist for Planning Hotel Stays

Specify your needs. In writing for a reservation, detail your needs. If you want a quiet room, ask for one on a high floor or specify one not facing a busy thoroughfare. If you want a double bed, request it. People with walking problems should ask for a room near the elevator.

Request rates. Always ask for special rates; you never know when you may uncover a real bargain. Seniors should ask about special discounts. Avoid the "rack rate," the highest price for any room. It's the price listed on the hotel's rate sheet.

Ask for confirmation. Get a written confirmation of your reservation and room cost, especially if at the height of a tourist season. Take the confirmation with you.

Prepay. Ask your hotel's guarantee policy, then prepay for the first night. Use a credit card. Hotels are unlikely to book someone else into a prepaid room. If you don't like the hotel after one night's lodging, you can leave without worrying about getting money back.

Call if delayed. When you'll be late arriving, call to tell the hotel when to expect you. Late arrivals who don't call and don't guarantee may be disappointed.

Try smaller hotels. If you're destined for a big city, try a smaller, less expensive hotel. Large commercial hotels

attract convention groups, which tax facilities. Smaller
hostelries may be more responsive to your needs.

Choose convenient locations. Consider the location. If activities
are centered downtown, that's where you want to be.
Cab fares mount up. If a hotel is a distance from the
hub, is there free transportation?

Check phone charges. Hotels impose a surcharge on the phone
calls from your room. Charges can be 70 cents to a
dollar per call. Ask about the hotel's policy on phone
surcharges.

Follow safety rules. When you arrive in your hotel room,
check emergency exits, and double lock your door
when inside.

Check bills. Always check your hotel bill. You don't want to
pay for someone else's champagne when all you had
was a beer.

And a Few Tips About Resorts

☐ When planning to stay at a resort hotel, make your
reservation at least six months in advance. Resort hotels are popular, especially around holiday periods.

☐ Resorts usually ask for a deposit and full payment
before you arrive. Ask about their policy on cancellations. They usually return your money if they can fill
the space. They may have disclaimers about this over
major holidays.

☐ If you're an angler or a hunter planning on fishing or
hunting, get required licenses ahead of time.

☐ Resorts sometimes include a 15 percent service fee in
the total price of your room. You still tip about 15
percent for special personal services. Inquire about tipping policies.

☐ Hotels or resorts sometimes offer free transportation
from and to the airport. If not, find out how much they
charge.

Hotel Tipping

How often have you been a party to this question,
"How much do we tip?"

No matter how rich, famous, or sophisticated people
are, something happens to them when it comes to tipping.

Hidden insecurities emerge. Are you giving too much or too little? Do you look cheap or foolish?

Many people seem to think that tipping is a dead giveaway as to their character. It isn't, of course, but many try to avoid the confrontation at any cost. Do Not Disturb signs go on doorknobs so the chambermaid won't know they are packed and ready to leave. A bellman delivering luggage won't find them in the room; they are waiting in the lobby until the coast is clear! "I don't have any change," is also a common out.

It would be easier if we lived in a tipless society like Tahiti. Maybe that's why they call that island a paradise. Since we live in a real world where a smile just isn't good enough, learn a few guidelines to ease the anguish of tipping.

The Doorman. If he opens the door to your cab and nothing else, forget it. If he takes your baggage to the registration desk, tip a dollar per bag. If he just brings your bags to the door, 50 cents will do. If he gets you a cab, 25 to 50 cents.

The Bellman. He's got your room key and bags and shows you to your room. When he's ready to leave, tip him a dollar. If he also opens the drapes, checks for towels and hangers, and puts your bags on a luggage rack, he deserves a little more. If you're on a tour and tipping is included, a smile and thank you is fine. Generosity, however, is appreciated.

Room Service. If you ask for ice and a couple of glasses, 50 cents is fine. If you're having a few friends in and you need glasses, ice, beer, and soda, $2 is acceptable. If meals are served in your room, tip 20 percent of the bill.

At the Bar. If you're at a table in the bar, tip 15 to 20 percent of the check. If you're at the bar itself, 50 cents a drink.

Laundry, Dry Cleaning, or Pressing Service. Hotel laundries are expensive enough; a tip of 50 cents is sufficient for the person who brings back your clothes.

Chambermaid. If you're staying at a deluxe hotel, there may be two maids, one who makes up your room in the morning and one who turns down your bed at night. The chambermaid or man gets a dollar a day for two of you, plus an extra dollar or two if you stay a week; 50

cents a night for the evening shift. If the chambermaid is helpful, tip more, if sloppy, tip less.

Dining Room Service (Resort). If you're on the American plan (all your meals) or a modified American plan (breakfast and dinner) and have the same waiter for all meals, tip about $2.50 a day per person if service is not included.

Taxi Drivers. Some cities don't have this custom, but in large cities in the United States, Canada, and more affluent nations, tip about 15 to 20 percent of the fare.

Finally. Have the courage not to tip. When a waiter, cab driver, or other service person is rude or couldn't care less, show your displeasure by not leaving a tip. Maybe he or she will be more pleasant next time.

Some Other Housing Options

New "Cottage" Industry—Bed & Breakfast

Years ago, they were known as tourist houses with "Rooms to Rent" signs out in front where motorists could see them. Today, with the addition of breakfast and the involvement of more private home owners, many have been renamed and redecorated to become bed and breakfast accommodations, and they are all the rage.

And why not? It's more interesting for a traveler to sleep over in a real home than to stay in an impersonal hotel or motel. You get a homey environment and can touch base with local residents. You can learn first hand about the things to do and see in the area, get directions, find the special restaurants, and maybe even make new friends.

Bed and breakfast accommodations can be as simple as a room and shared bath in a contemporary house in the suburbs to a lavishly decorated room with a fireplace, a canopied four-poster bed, and period wallpaper in a restored Victorian mansion.

You'll find B & Bs in A-frame homes in ski areas, rustic cottages in the mountains, Cape Cods at beach fronts, farmhouses, and townhouses.

What B & Bs have in common is that they are run by mostly friendly folk with a sense of adventure. Many are retirees, others "empty nesters," whose children have left home. Spare rooms are rented to defray costs of electricity or even home improvement expenses.

The cost of an overnight in a B & B can be less than in a hotel or motel, but not always. The fancier the home, the more expensive the rate. B & Bs can rent for $120 a night, but the average is about $35 per couple.

Finding a B & B

A number of local and national reservation systems have been organized in the U.S. representing individual bed and breakfast hosts. No one organization yet represents all B & Bs in the U.S., but one organization is the American Bed and Breakfast Association, P.O. Box 23294, Washington, DC, 20026 which represents at least 137 reservation systems and over 5,000 homes. The Association publishes two books of listings (see reading list in Appendix B).

A library catalog file too, will show a rash of new books specifically listing individual bed and breakfast homes as well as the reservation systems representing them. Because this type of lodging has become so popular, the reservation system may have instituted a toll free number instead of the long distance numbers listed in many books. Check first with 800 information—1-800-555-1212—to determine if there is a toll free number and save yourself some money on that long distance call.

Travel agents are another resource for finding a B & B. Many agents use computerized reservation systems which serve individual hosts. One of these is P.T. International, 1318 Southwest Troy St., Portland, OR 97219 (phone 1-800-547-1463). P.T. has listings for 25,000 rooms in 49 states plus Australia, New Zealand, the Canadian west, and the Caribbean. Another resource with more than 3,500 B & Bs listed in the U.S. and overseas is Bed and Breakfast Reservations, 16801 Iliff Ave., Aurora, CO 80013 (phone 1-800-824-7008 or, in Colorado, 1-303-695-0544).

A new bed and breakfast plan has been organized by the Evergreen Club for people 50 and over. Members can stay in each other's homes for $10 per night per person, or

$15 for a couple. You must be willing to host fellow members, and your home must be available for use for three months consecutively. Membership, which costs $20 a year, includes a directory, updated four times a year, and a newsletter. If you're unable to host other members, there's an associate membership for $35 a year, which includes the directory. For more information write Evergreen Club, P.O. Box 44094, Washington, DC 20026.

Finding a B & B without advance information or a directory may be a little problem. Because of zoning regulations and attitudes of neighbors, B & Bs usually don't have signs announcing their side business. Check the Yellow Page phone directories in the place you want to visit because some now are listing this classification.

Chambers of commerce or tourist offices in various localities may be able to direct you to B & B accommodations. They know about the privately published booklets that describe and list homes in the locality.

If a Bed and Breakfast experience appeals to you, when contacting the host or reservation service you should ask the following questions.

☐ Is there air conditioning?
☐ Is there a private bath with tub or shower, or both?
☐ What kinds of breakfasts are served and at what time? Do you have to make your own?
☐ Does the room have double or single beds?
☐ Is there a television set?
☐ What are the rates? Is the rate less expensive for two or more days? Can you pay by check or credit card?
☐ What is the house like in size and location?
☐ Is parking available?
☐ How accessible is the house? Some particularly old houses have dozens of steep steps leading to the entrance hall. If climbing steps is a consideration, don't forget to ask about them.
☐ If the hosts work outside their home during the day, what time can you check in?
☐ Are there outdoor activities available? Some B & Bs have swimming pools, tennis courts, and other sports facilities.

Inns and Small Hotels

Country inns and small historic hotels can be very delightful places to stay, especially those built before World War I. When weather is nippy, there's sure to be a working fireplace and maybe even a large wooden bowl of apples at the desk.

Antique furniture, made by master craftsmen, is usually an outstanding feature of such places, and while floorboards may creak, modern plumbing is in place. Many inns are friendly gathering places for the local gentry on Saturday nights. Food is usually good.

Inns with only six or seven rooms are not usually available through travel agents, but larger ones are. Local chambers of commerce and a number of books can be of help in finding them. Some inns are included in B & B listings (see reading list).

Lodges in the Parks

Camping out under the stars in our national parks might be a nice adventure and certainly is priced right— about $6 for a camping fee. However, if cold-water showers and chemically treated toilets no longer appeal to you, you can still enjoy our parks. Hotel rooms with hot and cold running water and private baths can be found in the heart of many of the older parks. Yellowstone, Grand Canyon, Yosemite, Mount Rainier, Glacier National Park, Crater Lake National Park, Shenandoah National Park, Big Bend National Park, and others have rustic, stately, old-fashioned hotels with big fireplaces. While these hostelries are run by concessionaires, prices are reasonable, from about $40 to $52 a night, double.

Make reservations far in advance for these accommodations. A special brochure is available from the National Parks Visitor Facilities and Services, Conference of National Park Concessionaires, c/o G. B. Hanson, Mammoth Cave, KY 42259. Cost is $3 plus $1.05 for postage. Kentucky residents add 5 percent sales tax.

State parks, too, have lodge accommodations for travelers, if not within the parks, just outside. Information about these overnight facilities and their current rates are available from state tourist offices (see Appendix A).

Back-to-School Housing

College and university housing between semesters is another method of keeping high hotel rates out of your travel budget. You probably will have to share a bath, but the prices of the rooms are incredibly low, about $50 a week, and you can dine in the school cafeteria at student prices. The Elderhostel organization has been using this type of accommodation for over-60 students taking its courses. Reservations are usually required. For more information contact colleges directly to determine if they have this kind of program.

And while in a youth mode, don't be put off by the name, American Youth Hostels. This vintage organization has 5,000 or more members who are over 50. The organization has supplemental accommodations providing hotel-like privacy for two in a room with a bath. Special facilities are listed in the *AYH Handbook,* which comes free with membership. For further information contact the American Youth Hostels, 1332 "I" St., N.W., Washington, DC 20005.

Houses and Apartments

The high cost of hotel living has made economy-minded tourists more innovative in finding alternative accommodations when traveling.

People now offer to house sit, house swap, or trade time-share accommodations. Others rent homes or lease apartments and condominiums.

House Swapping

When your travel plans are to stay and play, house swapping is a good solution. You can save money on accommodations and food and keep tabs on diets more easily. Sometimes the house comes with a car, a boat, or even a set of built-in acquaintances. An exchange of residences is also good insurance against burglaries. While you're enjoying someone else's house, there's activity in yours. Mail and newspapers are collected daily, lights go on and off at night, and a daily presence warns house thieves to stay away.

Apart from money saved, swapping reaps other rewards. By living in someone's home in a distant destination, there's an opportunity for a more authentic, in depth cross-cultural foreign experience, which hotel stays could never match.

Crucial to the success of a house swap is finding someone who wants to exchange homes with you at the same time. Probably the best candidates for this type of arrangement are retirees.

Finding the perfect house to swap requires effort, research, and fortuitous timing.

A number of directories are available for do-it-yourself house swappers. (See end of this section.) They carry names and addresses of home swappers, abbreviated descriptions, personal information about the owners, and lists of the attractions in the area. Some carry photos of the homes.

If you fail to find a match in the directories, they also list agencies that arrange swaps. These charge both a search and a closing fee. Chambers of commerce, state tourist boards, and especially tourist associations in foreign countries have records and information about swapping arrangements.

Ads in the area's newspapers may produce some prospects too. Travel-related magazines and "personals" in general magazines run ads that can hasten an exchange.

House swapping is not a U.S. invention. In 1953, a group of teachers in Great Britain, the Netherlands, and Germany started sending out names of teachers who were willing to exchange homes during vacation time. From that casual beginning an American affiliate was established. David Ostroff, a school principal now retired, started the Vacation Exchange Club in 1960. Now there are many others.

Ostroff points out that if you're planning a swap, you should leave plenty of time to explore the suitability of your candidate.

Six months is a reasonable period in which to get to know that other family via an exchange of letters, photographs of the house or apartment, and phone calls. Ostroff also advises that you find out about the family's life-style, neighbors, and neighborhood. References, too, would broaden the picture.

House swapping is a great idea if you are not uptight about your possessions. If you are going to worry how your swapping partner looks after your home, the money you save may not be worth your anxiety. Last-minute cancellation of the swap can also create problems, especially if you bought non-refundable charter air tickets or air tickets like APEX, which carry cash penalties if canceled.

Since there is no real supervision of your house or apartment, just the friendly interest of a neighbor or friend, you have no real protection against severe damage to your property except, perhaps, your home owner's insurance. A written agreement between you and your "guest" about how to pay for damages is essential. Check with your lawyer and insurance broker.

Guidelines on Swapping or Renting Houses or Villas

List the things you must have in a house to assure your comfort and well-being. Tell the broker or agency how many rooms you want and how much you can afford to spend if you are renting a house or villa. The more specific you are at this point, the happier you will be later on. Consider the following.

☐ Do you want people around? Is the house secluded, or in a developed area?

☐ Is the house all on one level, or will you have to climb stairs?

☐ Is the house on a steep hill, with a long stairway to its entrance?

☐ Does it have your kind of kitchen, one compatible with what you are used to?

☐ Is a car included? If it is, discuss insurance and liability. Get your own insurance broker in on the details. If no car is available, what alternative transportation is available?

☐ Are there stores nearby where you can shop for food?

□ Do you have any fixed ideas about the appearance of the house or its furnishings?

□ Does the bathroom have a tub, a shower, or both?

□ Is the local water safe for drinking?

□ What medical facilities are nearby, and how good are they?

□ If the house is in a foreign country, are there English-speaking people in the area?

□ How much will utilities cost? In a swap, who pays for what? Decide ahead of time.

□ Will there be an available phone in the house?

□ Will you have access to maid service if you want it?

□ How many people can the house accommodate?

□ If overseas, what kind of electrical current is used, and what converters or outlet plugs will you require to use your own small appliances?

□ If you are using a broker, will he or she evaluate the house for you?

□ What does the home owner's property insurance cover?

□ What are the emergency numbers of plumbers, electricians, doctors, or friends who can be called upon for help if needed? Leave such numbers in your own home, too, in a swap arrangement.

□ Are there mechanical features in the house that require explanations?

□ Are the property and fire insurance premiums paid up?

□ Have valuables been locked up?

□ Have some drawers and closets been cleared out for the visitors' use, with plenty of hangers left in the closets?

Renting Time Shares and Condos

Much less complicated than swapping homes is renting a time-share or condominium apartment, or swapping your own time-share apartment. Time share is the vacation plan in which an apartment is purchased in a resort community for several weeks out of a year for a number of years, even up to 60 years! The owner has the exclusive use of the apartment every year at the same time. He or she can also swap an apartment with another time-share owner for a more varied vacation.

Sometimes, however, time-share owners can't use

their property or anyone else's in a given year. So, many choose to rent out their apartment instead. It provides an inexpensive vacation.

Another alternative is renting a condominium. Quite a few resort condominiums provide full maid service and linen. A resident manager oversees the property in the absence of the owner. Condominium apartments are only as good as the management looking after them. Other condominiums have no such services, and you deal directly with the owner.

Rental agents, individual owners, and computerized services advertise time-share and condominium apartment rentals in the classified sections of newspapers. Lists of these rental facilities and their agents also are kept by travel agents and local, state, and foreign tourist offices.

Apartments on the Package Plan

Recognizing that some travelers like to do their own thing, tour operators now offer travel programs that cater to independent travelers who want some housing arrangements made for them. Apartment and rental programs, for long or short stays, are offered by the American Association of Retired Persons Travel Service, Grand Circle Tours, SAGA, and others. Apartments and condominiums are located in some of the world's most favored vacation spots—the Hawaiian Islands, Spain and Portugal, Vienna, London, Paris, Florence, and other special places.

Resources for Housing

For further information on house swapping, time sharing, and other alternative housing possibilities, contact agencies specializing in various vacation housing arrangements. The following lists are just a small example of such organizations. Some directories may be available in your public library.

HOUSE SWAPPING

Vacation Exchange Club, 12006 111th Ave., Youngtown, AZ 85363 (phone 1-602-972-2186). A directory, published semiannually, includes about 6,000 listings in 40 countries. One issue costs $15; $22.70 for two issues.

International Home Exchange Service, P.O. Box 3975, San Francisco, CA 94119 (phone 1-415-383-7368). Directory lists about 500 homes and costs $45, including your listing. Published in spring with updates.

Interservice Home Exchange, Box 87, Glen Echo, MD 20812 (phone 1-301-229-7567). Publishes directories in February and April, with 1,000 listings. Costs $24 with your listing.

AGENCIES

Home Exchange International, 22713 Ventura Blvd., Suite F, Woodland Hills, CA 91364 (phone 1-213-992-8990). Has overseas offices.

Villas International, 213 E. 38th St., New York, NY 10016 (phone 1-212-685-4340 in New York or toll-free 1-800-221-2260 elsewhere). Lists 30,000 homes, apartments, chateaux, castles, and live-in windmills.

At Home Abroad, Sutton Town House, 405 E. 56th St., New York, NY 10022 (phone 1-212-421-9165).

Caribbean Home Rentals, Box 710, Palm Beach, FL 33480 (phone 1-305-833-4454). Houses and villas in the Bahamas and Caribbean.

COMPUTERIZED SERVICES FOR TIME SHARE, CONDOS, RESORTS

Creative Leisure, 951 Transportway, Petaluma, CA 94952 (phone 1-707-778-1800 in CA., 1-800-426-6367 elsewhere). Condos in Palm Springs, Mexico, Hawaii.

Holiday Condominiums, 7701 Pacific, Suite 300, Omaha, NE 68114 (phone 1-800-228-0002). Over 110,000 listings of time share and condos in U.S., Caribbean, Europe.

M. D. R. Telecom, 13464 Washington Blvd., Marina del Rey, CA 90292 (phone 1-213-823-1200 or toll free 1-800-423-6377). Time-share rentals in U.S., Caribbean, Hawaii.

Vacation Time Condo, P.O. Box 12379, Birmingham, MI 48012 (phone 1-800-882-6636, or 1-313-540-3020 in Mich.). Condo rentals in Florida, Colorado, Hawaii, Caribbean and other places.

APARTMENT RENTAL PLANS

AARP (American Association of Retired Persons) Travel Service, 5855 Green Valley Circle, Culver City, CA 90230 (phone 1-800-227-7885)

Grand Circle Travel Inc., 555 Madison Ave., New York, NY 10022 (phone 1-800-221-2601; in New York City 688-5900).

SAGA (Saga International Holidays), 120 Boylston St., Boston, MA 02116 (phone 1-800-343-0273; 1-800-462-3322 in Mass.). Apartments in southern Spain and condominiums in Florida.

Overseas Accommodations

Travelers willing to forgo traditional American-like hotels can be rewarded with unique housing experiences overseas. Ancient castles, monasteries, princely hunting lodges, country homes, royal mansions, and great houses converted into tourist accommodations not only provide interesting places to stay but offer travelers insights into a life-style that existed hundreds of years ago.

You can stay in castles in Spain, Portugal, Germany, Austria, Great Britain, and France. For those who would like less lordly shelter but closer contact to the peoples of Europe, bed and breakfast accommodations, small hotels, farms, pensions, and guest houses are all low-cost alternatives that are mostly accessible by car but also by rail, boat, air, bus, and sometimes motorcoach.

Castles in Spain and Elsewhere

For many years now, Spain has taken its most precious castles and monasteries and turned them into exquisite housing for travelers. These castle hotels, ancient convents, and elegant country homes, operated by the Spanish government, are part of its system of *paradors*, some as old as the thirteenth century. Accommodations for a couple can be had for as low as $50 a night, including breakfast.

In addition to paradors, Spain has museum hotels that are partly run by the Spanish government, partly by private business. These Entursa hotels are a little more expensive; rates start at about $75 a night for two, with breakfast. Some buildings served as hospices for pilgrims in the fourteenth century. Information about both types of accommodations can be secured from the Spanish Government Tourist Office (see Appendix A) or from the government's official representatives for this housing, Marketing Ahead, 515 Madison Ave., New York City, NY 10022 (1-212-759-5170). Outside of New York, phone 1-800-223-1356.

Neighboring Portugal also has a network of historic castles, monasteries, and convents, which have been converted into *pousadas*. These beautiful and elegant hostelries offer a combination of medieval charm and modern plumbing. Prices are very low, about $37, including breakfast, for two. Portuguese palaces all offer home-style meals with house wines. Information is available from the Portuguese Tourist Office (see Appendix A).

French chateaux are the country's deluxe contribution to specialty hotels. Chateaux are all luxury class, with overnight accommodations at about $100 to $140 or more per night. Information is available from the French National Tourist Office (see Appendix A).

Germany, too, has its share of castle hotels, and even boasts an association of 55 of these, scattered throughout the wooded scenic areas of the country. These romantic hotels, called *schlosse* (castles), cost as little as $45 a night with breakfast.

Listings of these castle accommodations are included in the booklet, "Gast Im Schloss," free from the German National Tourist Office (see Appendix A).

Austria has 30 castle hotels—some pleasure palaces, others simple hunting lodges. Prices for overnight stays range from $40 to about $95 for a couple, including a typical hearty Austrian breakfast.

While Great Britain is better known for its manor homes, there are a few castles in Great Britain where visitors may stay. One has a special history. Culzean Castle, of eighteenth-century vintage, located in Maybole, in West Scotland, was given to the National Trust of Scotland. An eight bedroom flat in it is available to tourists. The apartment was given to General Eisenhower in 1945 for his lifetime use as a gesture for his services in the war. Now anyone who can afford the rates—about $110 to about $148.50—can stay there.

Britain's country homes are no castles, but delightful, peaceful places to stay, many with fine restaurants. The average cost for doubles is about $60. A free booklet that lists and describes these country hotels and other guest properties is called "BTA Commended Country Hotels, Guest Houses and Restaurants," available from the British Tourist Authority (see Appendix A).

Bed and Breakfast and Other Low-Cost Lodging

While B & Bs have become Americanized and are now a part of the U.S. lodging system, this bargain housing started in Britain and swept through 21 countries in Western Europe. Prices are low, and the atmosphere friendly. In Britain you could be getting the best room in someone's house. B & B reservation services are available, but local tourist offices in each town can book rooms for you as you travel. They'll even phone ahead for a small fee. B & B accommodations run from about $10 a night per person to a high of $20. If you stay four days to a week, it's even cheaper.

Travelers to other European countries will find B & Bs all over the map. If you stay in non-English-speaking homes in Germany, Italy, France, or anywhere else, you'll find that a few words of the language will help in communicating with your hosts. Computerized reservation services are available. One such service is European Tourist Information, 1300 Dove, Newport Beach, CA 92660 (in California phone 1-714-851-1787/8; elsewhere phone 1-800-621-1934). It features 35,000 listings for pensions, hotels, and guesthouses.

Farm Stays or City Apartments

For more bucolic experiences, there are farm holiday programs in Denmark, Great Britain, and other countries, where you can actually do farm chores. Renting apartments in Europe has been discussed elsewhere. For these and other non-hotel lodgings, contact the countries' tourist offices.

Special Safety Tip

Bathtubs in many European hostelries and castle hotels are much higher than you are used to. Getting in and out of tubs may be a problem for some people. Request a room with a shower and ask for a suction-type bathmat.

CHAPTER 5

Wings or Wheels— Your Choice

When it comes to vacation travel, the means may be as important as the ends.

Take a plane and you're buying speed. When the flight is over you've seen the country from on high, but nothing much—clouds, maybe a crazy quilt of farmlands, ribbons of highways, mountain peaks, tiny blue-green swimming pools, and clusters of buildings. You do get to your destination quickly and efficiently, though.

With cars, trains, cruise ships, buses, or even recreational vehicles, the mode of travel is an important part of the vacation package.

From the window of a bus or car, you get a closer view of homes, people, farms, and mountains. Traveling by car and recreational vehicle, you have the flexibility of stopping anywhere you choose. In a motorcoach tour, interesting sights will be pointed out from your window, and getting on and off the bus will put you in closer touch with what there is to experience.

You are a relaxed spectator when traveling by train. Peek in on the backyards of America to see how people work and live. From the inevitable lines of drying laundry or from the outdoor play equipment for children, you may even guess life-styles. You are at ease while sweeping views of America rush past. You can take a three-car walk and stretch your legs. And you can exult in seeing speeding cars on adjacent highways and know that you're going faster than they are without the effort or pressure of driving yourself.

Before you choose your mode of travel, read, talk to other travelers, and study all your options.

Taking the Car

The car is the backbone of travel in America. For touring, it is the most popular way to go. Eighty percent of all vacationers travel by car. With you at the wheel, you do as you please, stop when you like, eat when you're hungry, see what interests you, and shop when you feel like it. You are the master of your vacation, with no one to orchestrate your schedule, except perhaps your fellow passengers.

Costs are not as low as they used to be, but are within reason. According to the American Automobile Association, this past year the average cost of an auto trip for two, including gas, oil, moderate accommodations, and modest meals, was about $112 a day ($52 for meals, $53 for lodging, and $7 per 100 miles for gas). Admissions to special attractions and "happy hours" are extra, as are bridge tolls and tunnel charges. Increase that figure by about 75 percent more for stays in larger cities and deduct 25 percent for smaller ones.

The car has no equal for people who love being behind the wheel, with time, energy, and the inclination to zip along the interstates, meander the back roads, and enjoy the challenges of driving through unfamiliar territory. Others, however, may find the constant vigilance of driving not particularly relaxing, and maybe even stressful. Different driving styles in different regions could be a cause for concern. A 70-year-old couple from Nantucket found that out when they motored through California.

Coming from a gentle community with polite drivers, they were unprepared for West Coast motorists on California freeways. They were not able to drive as defensively as they should have and were unnerved by the freeway traffic. For safety's sake, they compromised their time schedule and ended up on the much slower side roads. Because of that, they didn't have time to see some of the places they had set out to visit.

If you don't think you can or want to endure long-distance drives but still want a car on your vacation, don't give up; there are alternatives.

Consider sharing the driving; it's the easiest and most pleasant solution. Not only will it ease stress, but it will give you a chance to enjoy the scenery, too.

A second possibility is to send your car to your destination. Auto delivery companies ship your car on trailer trucks of the same type used by car manufacturers in delivering new vehicles. It's expensive, but if you are planning an extended stay in an area far from home, it might be worth the cost. Prices vary, but as an example, the cost of sending a car from New York to Florida in season is about $450.

Automobile driveaway services, too (companies that assign drivers to chauffeur your car to your destination) are helpful in delivering your car to vacation areas. Even though these companies provide certified drivers to drive your car while you travel by other means, be cautious about this alternative. The Interstate Commerce Commission regulates driveaway services because they are in the business of driving cars across state lines. Officials urge consumers using these services to read their contracts very carefully, because they are very specific as to liability.

Many people who spend winters in warmer climates use these services annually. Driveaway services may be found in the Yellow Pages under Automobile Transporter and Driveaway Companies.

Advertising in a newspaper for a driver is another means of getting your car to where you want it. Usually students or peripatetic young people will sign on for driving chores. They will drive you and your car or just your car. Some charge, others accept the use of your car as a trade for getting to their destinations. Check their references and driver's licenses carefully and your own insurance coverage for non-family drivers. It is not always the best alternative.

On the East Coast, the Auto Train transports you and your car from Lorton, Virginia, just outside of Washington, DC, to Sanford, Florida, about 20 miles from Orlando. Operated by Amtrak, this special train takes about 500 passengers and a little more than half that number of cars. Shipping your car one way costs about $200, plus one-way rail fare in coach, about $150, meals included. Sleeping car accommodations are also available on the 17-hour trip. Write Amtrak Distribution Center, P.O. Box 7717, Itasca, IL 60143 for more information.

Renting a Car

Renting a car at your destination is another solution. Check around before you leave home to find which car rental agency gives you the best price. Inquire about discounts for monthly and longer-term rentals. Club members in such organizations as the Automobile Club of New York, American Association of Retired Persons, and others, can arrange discounts on car rental costs. You should be aware that some car rental franchises don't always honor discounts offered by parent companies.

People who seldom rent cars may find the following information of value.

Ask about drop-off charges. These are extra charges if you return the car to another city or state. Some agencies impose drop-off charges if the car is not returned to the exact place from which it was rented. If you return the car to a dealer in another state, be prepared for extra charges.

Add taxes and gas. When computing rental costs, don't forget to figure sales taxes and the cost of refueling. Unlimited mileage does not mean unlimited fuel. Fill the fuel tank up at a service station before returning the car. It's cheaper that way.

Check insurance. Most auto rentals are insured against collision, fire, theft, and bodily injuries. However, there is usually a deductible on the coverage. The deductible might be the first $200, or over $1,500, or even the cost of the car.

You are probably responsible for the deductible, but additional insurance is available at about $7 a day. If the deductible is very high it may be worthwhile. Perhaps your own auto and liability insurance will cover a rental situation. If you are traveling south of the border, Mexico requires that auto insurance be purchased on their side of the border. Canada will recognize your U.S. insurance if you get a Yellow Card from your own insurance broker and show it to the rental agency.

Use a credit card. Rental companies do not usually handle cash payments. Credit cards are preferred. A credit card establishes your credit and gives the agency a method of checking on you.

Shop around. Competition among car rental agencies could yield handsome savings. Compare rates even among franchises of the same company. An airport rental might be less expensive than a city rental.

Auto Clubs

Anyone contemplating a trip by car should think about becoming a member of an automobile club. These clubs provide assistance in planning your journey, but, more importantly, they help when you're in trouble on the road.

Call a toll-free number and an emergency tow truck is dispatched to you when you've had a breakdown on the road. The mechanic on duty will try to restart your car, but if he can't, you'll be towed to a service station. The towing fee may be picked up by your auto club directly or reimbursed to you later. Each club sets its own maximum amount they will pay for towing, from $15 to $75. Save your receipts for that refund.

Emergency help is only the beginning of a catalogue of services available from auto clubs. Some sell insurance, issue free credit cards, rate the quality of hotels and motels, publish tour books, provide maps, plot your itinerary, act as travel agents, get you discounts at hotels, motels, restaurants, and car rental agencies, and even make it easy for you to get emergency cash.

The American Automobile Association, with its 168 regional member auto clubs and 1,012 local clubs, has over 24 million members. There are other million-member clubs, too, including Amoco, Montgomery Ward, Allstate, and Gulf. Essentially, they all provide the same services with some significant differences. Eligibility for membership may require that you have a credit card with the gasoline company or that you buy insurance first. Because rules and regulations are constantly in flux, use the toll-free numbers of several motor clubs to find one that will suit your needs.

Finding a Motor Club

American Automobile Association. Look for a local AAA club in your telephone directory or write: 8111 Gatehouse Rd., Falls Church, VA 22047 (1-703-222-6334).

Amoco Motor Club (through American Association of Retired Persons, Diners Club, American Express), P.O. Box 9048, Des Moines, IA 50369 (1-800-334-3300).

United States Auto Club Motoring Division, P.O. Box 660460, Dallas, TX 75266-0460 (1-800-348-2761).

Allstate Motor Club, 30 Allstate Plaza, Northbrook, IL 60066 (1-800-323-6282).

Montgomery Ward Motor Club, 2020 Dempster St., Evanston, IL 60202 (1-800-621-5151).

Exxon Travel Club, 4550 Dacoma, Houston, TX 77092 (does not have toll-free number: 1-713-680-5723).

Shell Motor Club, 6001 North Clark St., Chicago, IL 60660 (in Illinois: 1-312-338-7028; elsewhere in the U.S.: 1-800-621-8663).

Readying You and Your Car

It's elementary that unless you have a new car or just had a tune up, your car requires a pre-trip examination before exposing it to a long drive. Get a mechanic to check the brakes, lights, battery, transmission, directional signals, tires, wheel alignment, oil, fan belt, and heating and cooling systems.

Give your auto club plenty of time to work out your routing—at least a month. You will want time to study the route and make reservations for at least your first overnight stay.

When you're ready to leave, make sure there's a magnifying lens in the glove compartment to make it easier to read maps. Take along a flashlight, too. Take your car registration, your driver's license, your physician's phone numbers, and your health insurance documents, pre-moistened towelettes, paper tissues, a first aid kit, and sunglasses. And don't forget the medicines and vitamins you take.

Safety First

A long distance motor vacation requires a lot of thought and planning. To make your trip more pleasurable as well as safe, take note of the following suggestions.

Set a reasonable goal. Drive no more than 300 miles a day on good roads, or 250 on poorer ones. Take plenty of rest stops to relieve the monotony, to stretch and unkink your joints, to "use the facilities," and to keep your blood flowing normally.

Keep air circulating. If you or your passengers are smokers, keep the windows open. You need all the oxygen you can get.

Choose safe roads. Although driving on highways does not afford the best views of the countryside, highways are usually more predictable and safer than subsidiary roads with unexpected or hard-to-see traffic lights, hidden driveways, and other dangers. If you are uncomfortable on freeways with fast-moving traffic, take other routes.

Drive in daylight. Dusk is probably the most dangerous time to drive because the light is so poor. Night driving isn't so easy either. Glare is your enemy. Flashes of bright lights from oncoming headlights can cause temporary loss of sight in older eyes.

Avoid rush-hour traffic. When driving in or near cities, plan on arriving or leaving before hordes of work- or home-bound motorists clog the roads.

Eat lightly. Too much food can make you sluggish and sleepy. Save your big meal for evening hours, after you've stopped driving.

Note medication effects. Some medications slow down reflexes and cause drowsiness. Keep that in mind on a long trip if you take such drugs.

Reserve rooms ahead. Reserve hotel and motel accommodations ahead so you won't have to search for a place to stay after a hard day at the wheel. Motel and hotel chains can call ahead.

Avoid one-night stands. If you can afford the time, try to stay at a place for a day or so and absorb the atmosphere while giving yourself a reprieve from driving.

Protect temperature-sensitive items. Keep most cosmetics and medications with you in a small carry-on bag or plastic carrier. Do not leave them in the trunk, where extremes in temperature can affect their potency or usefulness.

Keep extra car keys. Have a set in your pants pocket or purse at all times.

Pack lightly. Even though you have that big trunk in which to pile all sorts of luggage, hold the amount of clothing you take down to a minimum. The more you take, the more you have to look after and carry.

Be prepared for emergencies. Most highways and major roads are marked with a standard white *H,* for hospital, on a blue background. Note it as you pass. A citizens band radio (CB) could come in handy to summon aid, especially when driving through a desert or other unpopulated areas. Keep flares or reflectors in your trunk in case of road emergencies.

Thwart thieves. Don't leave clothing and luggage visible through the windows of your car when you park it. A skilled thief can empty your car in three minutes. Lock luggage in your trunk.

Busing, an Easy Way to Travel

When you want someone else to do the driving, the logical solution is to go by bus or motorcoach. These vehicles can and do go everywhere. For the sake of clarity, and to distinguish between their services, the use of the word *bus* here will mean point-to-point scheduled service, while the word *motorcoach* will be used to signify charter or tour buses.

Big carriers in the scheduled bus service field—Trailways and Greyhound Lines, Inc.—have stations all over the country and can take you to almost as many points on the map as your car. With deregulation, new bus companies have entered the business, offering point-to-point as well as charter and tour service, heating up the competition. Look in your Yellow Pages under Bus Lines for listings of all types of bus service.

If you've never traveled by bus, prepare yourself for a great time. Tourists who travel on these comfortable vehicles from city to city are friendly, down-to-earth people from all walks of life who want to see America's sights while keeping transportation costs down. You'll find many foreign visitors on board, too. They've discovered that buses are an excellent and inexpensive way to see the country.

Point-to-point buses never run more than five hours without a rest stop. Drivers too, have to get out and stretch their legs. Bus vehicles these days have adjustable seats, tinted windows to cut down the glare and heat of the sun, and on-board toilet facilities. Drivers usually offer a hand with luggage.

Travelers who plot their own trips should start by asking bus companies about special promotional fares. Frequently there will be discounted rates to a variety of destinations. Some are good for mid-week excursions, others for limited time periods. If you tour during discount-rate days, you can trim your costs even more. Folks 65 and over are almost always the recipients of discounted fares. Usually it's 10 percent off the regular price. Take along proof of your age, such as a driver's license. Remember to be persistent in asking for discounts. Membership cards, too, make a difference.

National bus companies have 7, 15, and 30-day trip tickets priced competitively. Trailways calls its ticket *USA Pass*, Greyhound names its plan *Ameripass*.

Seven-day trips this past year were about $190, 15-day journeys about $254, and 30-day trips about $350. Call the companies for the exact current amount for these trips.

The fixed-price passes permit passengers to get on and off buses whenever and wherever they choose. For $10 or so extra per day, you can extend your trip beyond the pass expiration date.

When contemplating this kind of journey, seek help from the bus company's tour office. They can advise you about better hotel accommodations and interesting stops. Try not to schedule more than six hours a day on a bus. More bus hours could be exhausting.

Charter Buses

There are now about 2,500 companies licensed by the Interstate Commerce Commission to operate charter motorcoach services. Clubs or organizations can book one of these for one-day trips or arrange holiday packages lasting a week or more. Packages usually include hotels, meals, sightseeing, and, of course, motorcoach transportation. Charter divisions of Trailways, Greyhound, and individual charter operators work up a number of sample itineraries. Organizations wishing to arrange tours can study these itineraries and modify them for their own group. Charter trips have no escorts. The person promoting the organization's tour is the one in charge. That is usually worth a free trip for the promoter.

Complete planning assistance is offered by the charter company. This includes selecting suitable hotels and restaurants, getting tickets for special events, and arranging for other amenities. The real beauty of this type of trip is that you can travel with your own friends and design your own itinerary.

Tips for Bus Travel

Arrive early. There are no reserved seats on scheduled buses. It's first come, first served, and anyone with a ticket is guaranteed a seat. Not all buses are alike. They vary in size, and some are likely to be more crammed with passengers than others. The number of passengers a bus carries will determine the best and worst seats. Some people prefer a front seat because it affords an unobstructed view. But in some buses with a tight configuration, that front seat is not adjustable, and there's little leg room. The mid-bus seat, between the rear and the driver, will give you the smoothest ride. The least desirable seats on all buses are the very last row, because they do not recline.

Note the smoking rules. There is no smoking in the front two thirds of a bus. The Interstate Commerce Commission dictates the rules. Seats for smokers are in the rear. That's usually where the lavatory is located.

Learn the luggage regulations. With each ticket you are permitted to check two bags bags free of charge. These go into the belly of the bus and should not exceed 100 pounds. You can also take a carry-on bag. Luggage can be sent to the furthest point on your ticket to await your arrival. Major companies will store luggage without charge for three days. After that, it's 50 cents per bag per day, not to exceed $10 a month. (Some exclude weekends.)

Take essentials with you. Take your medication with you in your carry-on bag. You might also want to take a thermos of tea, coffee, or whatever snacks you like to stem hunger. Some companies may not permit food on buses. Ask ahead.

Take advantage of relief stops. When given an opportunity to "use the facilities," never pass that opportunity up. It's more comfortable at a stop than on a moving vehicle.

Prepare for cool air. Take along a sweater or some warm covering in case the air conditioning is too strong.

Wear comfortable clothes. Women who choose to wear pants to travel should wear slacks with an elasticized waistband; it's less restrictive.

Take notes. A notebook can be very helpful to jot down impressions and names and addresses of people you meet if you want to keep in touch.

Check on credit. Credit cards can be used for payment of most bus fares, but take along travelers checks, too. Since policies do change, check with the company before buying your ticket.

Take insurance information. Don't forget your health insurance cards, just in case you need a doctor or hospital.

Bring citizenship information. If you are traveling across the border into Canada or Mexico, you will need some proof of citizenship. For Canada, a U.S. voter's registration card or a passport will be helpful. If you're going into Mexico, you'll need a tourist card, which you can get at the border.

For more information on bus travel, consult the Greyhound and Trailway offices in your community or use the Yellow Pages to contact smaller local companies.

Recreational Vehicles—A Home on the Road

If you love driving and think you might enjoy life on the open road, consider a home on wheels. Buying one can cost $25,000; renting one is better for beginners. Share one with another couple to cut costs; they are expensive even to rent.

In a recreational vehicle (RV) you're always at home, even away from home. There's no need to pack or unpack; your hotel room is just above the transmission. And as for food, your kitchen is open 24 hours a day.

Today's recreational vehicles are built like elaborate second homes with wheels. They have wall-to-wall carpeting, fiberglass bathrooms with showers and/or tubs, and stainless steel sinks. The galleys, where meals are prepared, come with a refrigerator and a range, some with eye-level or microwave ovens. Air conditioning and heating keep you comfortable.

While presumably you can live in these self-contained motor homes independent of support systems for water and electricity for a period of time, few would want to use up all their own water reserves or power. Camp sites are the answer. There are literally thousands of them outside big cities, in resort areas, and in a network of trailer parks all over the United States, Canada, and Mexico.

Some campgrounds are very luxurious, with swimming pools, sports facilities, recreation halls, health clubs, cable TV, phone hookups, and other deluxe amenities. Others are simple places where, for a small fee, you can hook up to the electrical current, the water supply and drainage, take a shower, and use the toilet facilities. There's usually a general store on the premises to restock your larder.

The six million Americans who own recreational vehicles and those who rent them usually target in on the national parks when they vacation. Each park has its own rules and regulations about camping and motor homes. Facilities are described in the booklet, *Camping in the National Park System.* Write the Superintendent of Documents, U.S. Government Printing Office, Washington, DC 20402. The booklet costs $1.50.

You can reserve campsites in some national parks through Ticketron outlets. There is a small reservation fee, plus nightly campsite fees (under $10). For more information, contact a Ticketron office in your city or write Ticketron, P.O. Box 26430, San Francisco, CA 94126. No telephone reservations are accepted.

Renting an RV

Simple self-contained motor homes, with kitchen and bath, are recommended for inexperienced RV renters because they are easy to drive. A 19- to 21-foot home is ideal for four adults. Some agencies charge a daily rate of about $69 plus 18 cents a mile for this size home, while others have unlimited mileage packages that run about $763. Prices depend on size of vehicle, season, and number of miles you plan on traveling. Always ask, too, about special senior rates and promotional bonuses.

Small travel trailers, which can be hooked up to the family car, rent for about $150 to $200 a week. They offer the most flexibility. They can be unhitched and parked at a campsite while you take off in the family car. They sleep four, but are not self-contained. You need hookups for water and toilet facilities. There is a modified kitchen in the unit.

RV Resources

RENTAL AGENCIES

Agencies that rent recreational vehicles are located all over the United States. They include the following.

American Safari National RV Rental System, with 88 locations around the country, is one of the larger agencies. National headquarters is at 420 Lincoln Rd., Suite 316, Miami Beach, FL 33139 (1-800-327-9668; in Florida, call 1-305-531-4202).

Altman's Recreational Vehicle Center, 1155 Baldwin Park Blvd., Baldwin Park, CA 91706 (in California, call 1-800-258-6261;

elsewhere, 1-800-258-6267). Altman has franchises in 28 locations.

American Land Cruisers, 7740 N.W. 34th St., Miami, FL 33122 (1-800-327-7778). Fees for drop-offs at seven locations: Los Angeles, San Francisco, Denver, Miami, Tampa, Orlando, and Nutley, N.J.

You can get more information, too, from the *RV Rental Directory*, which lists 100 dealers and gives costs and availabilities of RV rentals. It costs about $4.00 postpaid. Write to the Recreational Vehicle Dealers Association of North America, Suite 500, 3251 Old Lee Highway, Fairfax, VA 22030. Call 1-800-336-0355; in Virginia, 1-703-591-7130.

LARGER CAMPSITE CHAINS

Kampgrounds of America, P.O. Box 30558, Billings, MT 59114. Has 700 sites.

Outdoor Resorts of America, 2400 Crestmoor Rd., Nashville, TN 37215 (1-800-251-3006). Has 10 locations, 5 in Florida.

CAMPSITE DIRECTORIES

Woodall's Campground Directory of North America, 500 Hyacinth Pl., Highland Park, IL 60035 (1-800-323-9076). Directory costs about $12.30. Updated annually.

Trailer Life Campground Directory, 29901 Agoura Rd., Agoura, CA 91301 (1-800-423-5061). Costs $6.95, plus $2 handling, from publisher; in book stores, $13.95. Updated annually.

Wheeler's Campground Guide, 1310 Jarvis Ave., Elk Grove Village, IL 60007 (1-800-323-8899). Costs $9.95, plus $1.50 handling. Updated annually.

GENERAL INFORMATION ON MOTOR HOME TRAVEL

Write for information and send self-addressed stamped #10 envelope to Recreational Vehicle Association, P.O. Box 204, Dept. R., Chantilly, VA 22021.

Helpful Information on Recreational Vehicles

The Tryout. Before you rent an RV for a long trip, take one out for a weekend close to your home. If you're comfortable driving and living in one, then you are ready to roll for a longer period of time.

Credit References. Rental agencies will require credit references, a security deposit for cleanup work after use, and often advance payment.

Extra Insurance. While companies provide minimum insurance coverage, an RV is costly, so check with your own insurance agent for other protection.

Combination Packages. Amtrak has a tour combination with motor home rental agencies to provide both rail transportation and RV rentals. Some companies may also pick you up at airports. Inquire when making your rental arrangements.

Golden Passport. If you are visiting National Parks and are 62 or over, bring proof of age and apply for a Golden Age Passport when entering the park. It gives you free access to parks and a 50 percent discount on campgrounds and other user fees. Those under 62 who plan on using many parks can buy the Golden Eagle Passport for $10. Park entrance fees run about $3 per car. Write National Park Service, U.S. Dept. of Interior, Washington, DC 20240 for further information.

Steam Engines Were a Hoot

Train travel generates its own head of steam for millions of Americans. It brings back youthful memories of the old toy set of Lionels, Casey Jones, and dreams of being a train engineer.

You may remember politicians riding in the back open cars on whistle stop campaign tours before election time. Movie stars, too, glamorized train travel by posing in front of the Super Chief en route to Hollywood. And veterans of World War II will never forget their train experiences 40 or more years ago when they traveled from coast to coast and post to post. The more nostalgic will remember the open windows but forget the soot and flying embers from the locomotive's engines.

Rail travel is much different today.

Amtrak, the National Railroad Passenger Corporation, which now runs the passenger railroads, has installed new and better equipment. Some trains now clip along at 120 mph, and faster ones are on their way.

Deluxe superliners with wrap-around, glass-enclosed double decker observation cars are now used in the West. Spectacular vistas elsewhere can be enjoyed in Vista Dome cars. As for service, long distance trains are staffed with on-board service chiefs empowered to help with any problems or special requests. On shorter rides, train attendants see to details of your comfort.

Winning You Back

Amtrak has a computerized system of reservations. A toll-free phone call (1-800-USA-RAIL) will not only put you in touch with a reservation clerk, but also provides other sources of information about trains and tours. Motorcoach links are available at many train stations to transport you to hotels or to communities not served by the railroad.

Car and recreational vehicle rentals and hotel reservations can be made at the same time you make train reservations. Amtrak also sells packaged rail trips or train tickets to and across Canada on Via Rail, a Canadian counterpart, and can arrange connections with cruise ships departing from Canadian ports.

To lure passengers back to trains, attention has also been paid to fares. Special promotional and excursion fares ebb and flow with the seasons. One discount fare, however, remains constant. That's the "over 65 special," which offers a 25 percent discount on round trip tickets to anywhere on Amtrak's routes. Proof of age (a driver's license, Medicare card, etc.) is required to secure that fare. Excluded are certain "blackout" dates. If you have time and flexibility, you can save money. Senior citizen fares don't apply to club car travel, sleeping car accommodations, or discounted fare tickets. The rule is that you can't get two discounts.

Excursion fares or other special fares frequently are less expensive than the senior specials. Ask for the most advantageous fare when you speak with a railroad representative.

For people who are enterprising, energetic, and who can keep their luggage down to a minimum, there's a big bargain in the 30-day Circle Tour. Via a system called Optional Routing, an adventurous traveler can see the United States by train and save hundreds of dollars on rail fares to boot. The Circle requires changing trains, perhaps carrying your own food and luggage, and getting off at small towns for overnights to make the next connection.

An example of a Circle Tour starting from Chicago might include stops in New Orleans, San Antonio, San Diego, Los Angeles, San Francisco, Sacramento, Portland, Seattle, Spokane, St. Paul, and back to Chicago. The fare would be about $500. If you had to pay for this rail trip in segments, the fare would be more than $1,000. An Amtrak route map will help you visualize other possibilities.

The easiest way to travel the rails is to plug into an already planned trip. More than 200 packaged rail trips are now available to every interesting part of the U.S., Mexico, and Canada. These excursions are discussed in the chapter on tours.

Class Distinctions

Trains offer two classes of accommodation, first and coach. For a day trip, most people find coach transportation adequate. You get a comfortable reclining seat with foot or leg rests and a tray table for reading, writing, or snacking. That's usually enough comfort. If you want to upgrade your seat just a touch, there are first class club cars.

Overnight accommodations are a little more varied. In the coach car, you'll get a pillow and a comfortable reclining seat. On long distance trains the coach section will have a large dressing room where you can change your clothing for nighttime.

Sleeping accommodations start with the least expensive slumbercoach, a tiny private room with toilet and washbasin, which can sleep one or two. The second person would have to sleep in an upper berth.

The roomette is a slightly better accommodation. The best sleeping car arrangement is the bedroom, but here, too, one of you would have to use an upper berth. The alternative is to make up a pallet on the floor beside the lower berth to avoid climbing. The cost of sleeping arrangements is determined by the route.

Baggage

The scarcity of redcaps (baggage handlers) have turned many a would-be train traveler to other modes of transportation. Most large stations have redcaps and even baggage cars; smaller ones do not. Check with Amtrak before you start on a trip to determine if there is baggage handling at the station you are destined for.

To avoid carrying luggage from the train to the taxi station, check your luggage through. Bring your well-tagged bags to the baggage department at least one hour before train time. You can check as many bags as you like free, as long as they do not add up to more than 150 pounds. At your destination, you can pick up your bags from the baggage department. Your carry-on, with medications and toiletries, should accompany you on the train.

Tips on Train Travel

- ☐ If you're traveling in summer, take along a sweater or jacket in case the air conditioning is too cold.
- ☐ Try to start your journey when stations are less crowded; you stand a better chance of getting that rare commodity, a redcap. Before and after rush hours and never on holidays would be a good rule.
- ☐ Trains can provide special meals for those on restricted diets. Make reservations 24 hours ahead to request a special meal.
- ☐ If you need special assistance for whatever reason (perhaps porter or wheel chair), advise the stationmaster in advance by calling 1-800-USA-RAIL. That number can provide information about a multitude of services.
- ☐ Women might wear low heeled shoes, slacks that are not confining, and an overblouse. Men would be comfortable in slacks, a sports jacket or sweater, and a knit shirt.
- ☐ A pair of houseslippers might be helpful if you are planning to overnight in a reclining coach seat. Trains provide pillows but no blankets in coach class.
- ☐ When going to the snack or dining cars, do not leave valuables on your seat. Men should be sure to take their wallets with them and not leave money or important papers in coat or jacket pockets at their seats.
- ☐ Put luggage tags on your bags whether they are checked or not, and keep a list of the things you have in your bags with you, just in case they get lost.

For tour brochures and timetables, write Amtrak Distribution Center, P.O. Box 7717, Itasca, IL 60143, or phone 1-800-USA-RAIL.

Plane Facts

When you were growing up, it took a lot of courage to get on an airplane. Today, we often take planes for granted. It is a major form of public transportation.

The biggest virtue of air travel is its ability to telescope travel time from days into hours. That's important for people who don't want to spend time getting there.

But getting there isn't too bad either. Life aloft can be very pleasant. You can see a movie, listen to music, buy a drink or two, have lunch, dinner, or breakfast, read a book, play cards, talk to your seatmates, or take a nap.

Reservations and Tickets

Getting a plane reservation is rather simple. Decide when you want to go, and find an airline that goes there. The do-it-yourselfer can call a major airline and ask if it serves a particular destination. If not, they'll tell you which carrier does. When calling about flight information, always ask for the cheapest fare, and be prepared to answer a number of questions. Pertinent questions might be how long you plan to stay, whether you'll be at your destination over a Saturday, if you can leave in the middle of the week, if it is possible for you to buy your ticket in advance, etc. Hopefully, your answers will help the reservation clerk find you the lowest fare.

You could make your reservation on the phone, in person at the airport, or at an airline office in town. By making reservations in advance you may be able to lock in special low-fare seats that are sold in limited numbers, like Supersavers. Protect the low fare by buying your ticket as soon as your reservations are confirmed, preferably with a credit card. Once you are ticketed, the airline can't charge you more, even if the fare goes up.

The airline ticket itself is fairly straightforward. Your ticket carries your name, your destination or destinations, the numbers of your flights, dates, and times of departure. These are all clearly typed or written in in small boxes. Airlines use the 24-hour clock on international flights. That means that 1 P.M. will be 1300 hours and 9 A.M. will be written 0900. One of the most important boxes on your ticket is Status. If *OK* is written in it, your reservation is confirmed. If it reads *RQ*, it means you are "wait listed." You will have to wait until a reservation is cancelled, relinquishing a seat. There are usually a number of people wait listed. Keep checking the airline until your seat is confirmed. If there's enough traffic, sometimes a carrier will put on a larger plane, allowing more wait-listed people to get seats.

The ticket also carries the price you paid, plus the $3 international departure tax if you are traveling over international waters.

Each airline ticket has a serial number. It's printed at the bottom. Keep a record of that number and the date and place of issue. If you lose your ticket, you will have a record to facilitate a refund.

Losing an airline ticket is like losing cash, especially if it's for a domestic flight. Anyone can use your lost ticket. A ticket for an international flight requires that a passport be presented. Finders can't use those tickets.

Inform the airline immediately in person about the loss of your ticket, and provide the airline personnel with whatever information you have. If the airline can readily confirm that you had a reservation and were ticketed, it will issue a new ticket. There is usually a fee of $20 or $25 for this service. You may also have to sign an indemnity form, which obligates you to pay for the flight if your lost ticket was used. Some special low-cost fares are not refundable at all.

Your Seat

First class passengers don't worry too much about where to sit. Their ticket price assures them of a wide seat with plenty of leg room and only one seatmate.

Economy class passengers have more constricted seating arrangements, so do your best with what you're offered. Some airlines allow you to select your seat in advance. Ask about that.

Aisle seats afford you the greatest ease and most leg room. For people who have to make frequent visits to the washroom or who want to get up periodically to stretch their legs, these are the seats that offer the most convenience.

Try to avoid the middle seat in a three-in-a-row configuration. It's the worst seat in the house. You are literally hemmed in. If you want to get up and take a walk, you have to disturb the person seated next to you.

Window seats are fine if you don't wander too much. On a long flight you can prop your pillow up against the window and rest your head against it. You'll be most comfortable in this seat if you can sleep on a plane. Seats next to the emergency exits usually have more leg room, as do bulkhead seats, the ones with partitions in front of them.

If it's stability you want, you will get it in the midsection of the plane, over the wings.

Smoking and non-smoking seats are also choices to be made. Those who want to puff away during the flight will be relegated to the rear of the plane. Try to avoid the last row. Washrooms are located just behind those seats, and a line of traffic may form there. In addition, the last row of seats doesn't recline back far enough. The back part is the noisiest place on a plane, and if there's turbulence, you will feel it most there.

Dining Aloft

Airlines do a credible job of feeding passengers, despite the moans and groans of elitists who constantly decry airline food. Major airlines include meals, snacks, and non-alcoholic beverages in the price of your ticket. No-frill airlines often charge for these amenities.

If because of health, religion, or your own idiosyncrasies you cannot eat the standard foods served aloft, carriers will oblige with a variety of special diets: salt free, kosher, diabetic, etc. Arrangements for these meals must be made in advance, when you make your reservations. When it's a major concern, you should double check with the airline 24 hours before your flight to be sure your meal is planned.

First class passengers get the full treatment. All wines, hard liquor, and other beverages are offered free, as are gourmet meals. Business class passengers aren't treated too badly either. Their seats are more spacious, and cocktails are usually served gratis, too.

Amenities Aboard

Pillows and blankets are usually put aboard longer flights for passengers who want to snooze. They are stored in overhead baggage racks. Ofttimes airlines don't put on enough pillows to go around, so if you want one be sure to get your pillow before you settle down in your seat.

Longer flights offer movies. In economy class there's a charge for the headset that will allow you to hear the sound track. If there's a movie you want to watch, request a seat with a good view of the screen. When there's no movie, there's usually music.

Playing cards, newspapers, and magazines may also be available.

Luggage Allowances

In London before Christmas, an American woman impetuously bought 12 large jars of plum pudding and a variety of jams to bring home as Christmas gifts. She never thought how she was going to take those heavy glass jars home. When repacking for her return flight, she realized they would have to be hand carried or they might break. At the airport, she checked her luggage through, and then dragged two huge Harrods department store shopping bags to the departure gate. An airline official asked about the shopping bags. "Oh these," she said airily, struggling to lift them, "they're my carry-ons."

"If you can't lift them, madam, they are not carry-ons," the rep said rather dryly.

Free checked luggage allowances on airlines are variable. First and economy class allotments can be the same. On overseas flights, many airlines count pieces rather than weight. Two or three bags may be checked free of charge. When it's by the piece, each bag allowed can weigh up to 70 pounds, or 32 kilos, and must conform to certain dimensions. Your larger bags should not measure more than 62 inches (figuring one length, width, and height), your second bag, no more than 55 inches. Your carry-on luggage could measure between 40 and 45 inches; it varies with each airline. Some foreign countries require airlines to adhere to weight rather than the number of pieces. Your carry-on luggage may be weighed in as part of your total weight allowance. On flights within foreign countries, baggage allowances are more restrictive than they are on international flights.

On domestic flights, three bags can usually be checked free, though this may be changing on some carriers. Each can weigh up to 70 pounds. Dimensions are the same as on overseas flights. An airline tote bag can be substituted for the third piece. Umbrellas, cameras, and purses are not counted as carry-on luggage.

Safeguard Against Loss of Luggage

Use identifying tags. Luggage tags must be securely fastened to your bags. They should include your name, address, city, state, and phone number. It's a regulation.

Provide inside information. Put the same identifying information inside your bag, taping it to the lining, in case the outside tag is ripped off.

Use special tour tags. On a group tour, you are usually given special luggage tags that name the tour. If you don't have such a tag, type a mini-itinerary, listing hotels and dates, and slip it into the sleeve of your luggage tag. If a bag is lost, you can be traced.

Use your own marker. If your luggage looks like everyone else's, put some distinguishing mark on it so you can spot it easily. How about "Fly me" in colored adhesive tape?

Remove old tags. While it's fun to keep luggage tags as a reminder of all the flights you have taken, keeping them on the bag only confuses baggage handlers. Take used tags off.

Guard claim stubs. Take good care of your baggage claim stubs when the airline checks your bag through. They provide proof that the bags are yours and that you checked them with the airline. In case of loss, damage, or misdirection, you need these claim checks. At some airports you must show your claim stubs to retrieve your bags.

Carry it on. If your bag is small enough, you can take your luggage on the plane with you and stash it under the seat.

Check your bags through. It's always easier to check your bags through to your final destination. However, there's an inherent problem of loss or misdirection with connecting flights. Some carriers, too, will not transfer bags to another airline. If your luggage has to be transferred and you only have a half hour between flights, ask if you can take your suitcase with you on the plane. When there's one or two hours between flights, you can be confident that they'll be transferred. Airlines have a minimum connecting time, dependent on the carriers and on the size of the airport.

Claim luggage first. Do not go off and make a phone call or something until you have collected your bags from the baggage claim area. There are too many look-alike bags around, and if you're not there to look after your own things, someone might take your luggage by mistake (another good reason to have itinerary and hotel information taped inside the bag). If your bag is missing, report is immediately.

List the contents. Remember to carry a list of what you packed in each bag.

Security

Security checks are a fact of life at airports everywhere in the world, and it's a good thing, too. No one wants to fly with a potential terrorist or a fellow passenger who is carrying guns, knives, or other dangerous weapons.

Everyone who gets on a plane is subject to scrutiny by special security officers, metal detectors, x-ray machines, and personal inspection of hand luggage. Even interviews may be conducted in the interest of trouble-free flights.

Some airports and countries are more vigilant than others. In some airports, a Swiss-type army pocket knife would be considered a dangerous weapon. The more troubled the area, the more touchy the security officers are. To speed your way past security, keep suspect items like hunting or fishing knives out of your hand luggage. Pack them with your checked luggage. Combustible spray cans, too, should not be in the cabin with you. Put hair and insect aerosols in a checked suitcase.

Much has been written and said about the effect of x-rays on undeveloped film. Most security x-ray checks have a low level dosage, not enough to damage film. If you're worried, pack your exposed and unexposed film in your checked luggage. It is not likely to be harmed there. If your camera is loaded with high speed film, ask the security guard to hand-inspect your camera. High speed film is more sensitive to x-rays than other film, and multiple entries through security could be damaging. Be prepared, however, to meet with resistance in many countries, notably some Eastern European nations.

Tips on Air Travel

Use direct flights. Look for direct flights to your destination. Changing planes necessitates waiting around airports, heightens the possibility of losing luggage between flights, and often necessitates walking long distances to another gate.

Select wide-bodied planes. When you have a choice of aircraft, select a wide-bodied plane; it is more comfortable. Ask the reservation clerk to identify such aircraft for you.

Avoid heavy traffic times. Avoid traveling on holidays or the day before, and especially on Monday mornings and Friday evenings. Traffic to and from airports is very heavy, the airport itself is very crowded, porters and taxis will be scarcer than ever, and there's a good possibility that your plane may be delayed because of heavy air traffic.

Get on a wait list. If you can't get a reservation because the flight is completely booked, get your name on a wait list, and call the airline periodically to see if someone has canceled a reservation.

Try a standby seat. If you're willing to be a standby (to go to the airport and wait for the seats of "no shows") you may have a good chance of getting on the flight. This procedure is very iffy on a fully-booked flight over the holiday periods and to resort areas in season.

Check TV monitors. If you don't know the departure gate for your flight and don't know who to ask, look to the TV monitors positioned all over the terminal. They show a listing of flights, hours of arrivals and departures, and their gate numbers.

Keep carry-on luggage light. Even though you have the privilege of taking carry-on luggage, keep it light with things that are important for you, like medications, toilet articles, and a sweater. Keep articles you don't need for the flight in your checked luggage.

Use airport buses. When you want to get to the airport inexpensively, take the airport bus. There's usually a huge difference in price between a bus and a cab.

Reconfirm your reservation. It's especially important on international flights. In some countries you will be bounced from the flight by computer if you don't advise the airline 72 hours ahead of flight time that you will be using your reservation. Domestically, too, you should reconfirm return reservations. An airline may cancel its flight and not tell you about it. Call the airline a couple of hours before flight time to determine if there's a delay.

Expect departure taxes. Don't be surprised if you have to pay an airport departure tax in a foreign land. It's a way of raising revenue. Some countries require that you pay taxes in local currency, others want dollars. Taxes vary. In Israel it's about $10, in Turkey $4, in Bangkok about $5, and in Tokyo about $8.

CHAPTER 6

Getting More for Your Money

Rich or poor, everyone likes a bargain.
Few can dispute that travel is one of life's most thrilling luxuries, but nowhere is it written that you have to pay full price for all its enriching experiences.

Watching small details, exercising a little restraint, and taking advantage of special offerings will keep you within budget. Go to the city, state, or country of your choice, but eat at less elegant restaurants, stay at more modest hotels and motels, look for discounts offered by club memberships, and travel off season.

You can also use your age for some special clout.

How old is older? A four-year-old boy was asked by another child how old his mother was. He thought a minute and said, "She's 36. No, 63. I don't know."

That's the way it is with seniorhood these days. How old a person is supposed to be for senior status is up for grabs. Healthy 60-year-olds look more like 50, and 70-year-olds, eight or more years younger than they are. Few can tell by looking who is a card-carrying, certified senior.

For practical purposes, 62 and 65 are the official ages according to the world of Social Security. But there are other worlds besides SSA. Hotels, motels, car rental agencies, airlines, theatrical enterprises, and other travel-related businesses, their consciousness raised by lobbyists for older people, have other age criteria. Some offer lower rates for people who have earned their half-century stripes, who are 45, or 55, or 60. The fact is that you don't have to be 65 before cashing in on some of the perks of seniorhood.

It would be impossible to list the thousands of special rates or free admissions offered by the travel industry. What is detailed in this chapter are the many ways you can travel while keeping your costs down. Asking questions and persistence will help you achieve your goal.

Probably the most efficient use of your travel dollars is to sign up for a packaged tour, with or without an escort. Through the bulk purchase of airline seats, a block of hotel rooms, seats on sightseeing buses, meals in certain restaurants, and more, a tour operator can bring in the cost of a complete trip much lower than if you bought each segment of an identical tour yourself.

By promising to deliver a high volume of tourists, operators can negotiate lower charges from businesses involved in moving recreational travelers. You as an individual traveler would have to search out every promotional gimmick and be on the alert for every air fare war to arrive at the same price as a tour arranged by an operator. (For more information on packaged tours, see Chapter 7.) If, however, you want to travel independently, apart from a group, this chapter will give you the information you need to get the most for your travel dollar.

In Quest of the Lower Air Fare

The most complex and confusing aspect of budget travel is the search for lower air fares. Even skilled professional travel agents, in business for years, have a difficult time finding the least expensive fare between two points.

Confusion is greater since airline deregulation. Airlines can do as they please. Fares can be lowered and raised like a child's yo-yo.

One day an airline announces a 36 percent reduction on its air fare to London. To qualify, you must begin your journey on Tuesday, Wednesday, or Thursday and put money up front 60 days in advance. The next day, another airline, not to be undersold, beats that offer by charging three dollars less to the same destination with fewer restrictions. You can travel on Mondays as well and buy your ticket only 30 days in advance. On day three, the battle heats up. A third airline moves in with its offer. This one serves free cocktails on its flight. The day after that, airline number four joins the fray.

Airline wars break out periodically, and if you're looking for bargains—and who isn't?—study newspaper ads with the same critical eye you would use in shopping for high interest rates on a money market fund. Keep your eyes and options open.

Get your travel agent involved, too. With the information you have, ask the agent to search for more possibilities in the office computer. You may be surprised to learn that there can be 29 different fares between two destinations and as many conditions and restrictions.

If bargain hunting is hard work for travel agents with all the tools of the trade at their command, it is even more difficult, and certainly aggravating, for a nonprofessional like you. Busy signals, answering machine messages, and long waits for a reservation clerk are the penalties for being a do-it-yourselfer. The lower fare, however, is your reward.

Competition and your travel agent can be your best allies in seeking low fares. Don't be irritated with your agent or the airline if you are quoted one fare today and another tomorrow. Almost as soon as a computer is programmed for one fare, another fare is certain to be entered by the competition. And computers, too, are not always the "honest" instruments of information they should be. Computers are only as good as the programs and information fed into them by error-prone mortals like us.

There also have been times when airline-owned computer systems have weighted information about fares and service toward their own carriers. Buried deep in that computer brain, and maybe four displays later, is information about another carrier that has a lower fare. Computers are also programmed for omission—that is, not providing all the information that's available.

For Bargains, Be Flexible

All kinds of restrictions come with special fares. You may have to travel on certain days, make reservations 14 days (or more) ahead of time, be required to stay a minimum number of days before your return trip, and not travel in "blackout" periods (especially designated times like Christmas and high seasons). But if you can fit your schedule to the regulations, you can get a terrific break.

Promotional fares are part of the competitive process. Air Canada, for instance, has been known to offer 66 percent reductions off regular coach or economy fares on certain routes. They call it a "seat sale," and it usually occurs twice a year. When economic forecasters predict slow business on certain routes, the airline will stimulate traffic by announcing a sale.

Every airline offers sale fares at one time or another, each with its own tricky name. Olympic Airlines, for instance, offers a Love-A-Fare. These sales, and the resulting air fare wars, make you the biggest winner. As you read this book, a "cease fire" in the fare war may be in effect, but be patient; it probably won't last long.

Other "fare friends" are the new airlines. This youthful generation of new carriers is anxious to establish itself in the market place. They will do anything to undercut their big brothers in the sky.

Lower fares are their biggest lure. Generally these carriers can slash existing fares because their labor costs are lower. You might be offered first class service at coach fare, or, conversely, the carrier may strip the flight of all amenities to lower the fare. The carrier may charge you for lunch, dinner, and soda pop or other refreshments, as well as for checking your luggage. If your expectations aren't too high and you can cope with frustrations, you can save $100 or more.

One of the recent popular new airlines is People Express, which has been giving economic anxiety attacks to the more established carriers flying the same routes. And no wonder when an airline can charge about $159 for a flight between Newark and London, from $27 to $40 for a flight between Newark and Buffalo, and $119 off-peak between Los Angeles and Newark. Those are hard figures to match for competing carriers with high overheads. Remember, however, on short flights there are no reserved seats. It's first come, first served.

There are a host of new airlines flying the skies these days and others waiting in the wings. Included among those now operating are Southwest, New York Air, American West, Midway, and more.

Be Cautious With New Carriers

Danger signals loom in booking on new airlines, and your caution has nothing to do with air safety. Many newer airlines are undercapitalized. Some have already been through bankruptcy and Chapter XI proceedings.

Because of threats of insolvency, many new airlines have created a problem that didn't exist before. Previously, there was cooperation among airlines. They would transfer baggage from one carrier to another when passengers made connecting flights, and they would accept each other's tickets for exchange if passengers wanted to change flights. Now some major airlines will not exchange tickets issued by new carriers. Their rationale is that if the new airline goes bankrupt, they would have to wait a long time before collecting that fare. A practical example might go like this—if you had a ticket on Airline X to fly from Florida to Puerto Rico and that flight was delayed, you couldn't automatically take your ticket over to Airline A, which flies the same route. Airline A might not accept your ticket in exchange. In that case, if you wanted to use that carrier, you would have to buy a new ticket and wait for a refund on your old one. Your alternative would be to wait until Airline X was ready to take off to your destination. That could be the next day.

To save on air fare, be prepared for comparison shopping, and keep your plans fluid so you can cash in on unexpected fare bonanzas.

Tips on Chasing Low Air Fares

Be up-to-date on fares. Read newspaper ads announcing promotional fares, off-season rates, in-between-season fares, weekend fares, advance purchase fares, and supersavers.

Use tour basing fares. Buy a combination hotel-air package to get a lower air fare. It's called a tour basing fare.

Book off-hours flights. Fly at off-peak hours or mid-week; it will save you money.

Consider alternatives. Anticipate some inconveniences, like taking off from out-of-the-way airports, changing planes, or taking circuitous routes to your destination. Nonstops can be more expensive. Be prepared for several stops en route to your destination.

Plan ahead. Make advance reservations to lock in savings when there are special fares. On supersavers and APEX fares the number of seats are restricted on each flight.

Be a standby. Be prepared to leave at the last minute on a cheaper standby fare.

Check on interchangeable tickets. Ask that new airline whether its ticket is transferable to another airline flying the same route in case of delays.

Stick to the rules. If your fare is conditional that you return on day 14, don't return on day 15. You will be charged the difference between your low fare and the regular fare.

Secure your fare. Pay for your ticket when it's a good fare. The airline can't raise the price of your ticket once you have received it. If the fare is lowered, you may get a refund. A group of travelers to Puerto Rico were thrilled when they got to the airport to find that their fare had been reduced to $99 from the several hundred they originally paid. They were given a refund on the spot. Airlines have varying policies relating to ticket restrictions. Always ask.

Use credit cards. Use your credit card to buy airline tickets. You may be given automatic free travel insurance, and your credit card protects you against loss of money on unused tickets in case an airline goes bankrupt. You are allowed up to 60 days after the date you were billed to write to the credit card company to inform them of the bankruptcy. No phone calls; you must write within that time frame!

Get cancellation insurance. Some discount fares carry a cash penalty if you cancel out. Be sure of your plans before buying these special tickets, and buy cancellation insurance from your travel agent to get your money back in case you had to cancel because of illness.

Low Fare Possibilities

To help you understand what to look for, here is a list of terms that have come to mean lower fares on both domestic and overseas routes. Some may be in effect as you read this, others have not been used for a while but are sure to pop up again whenever an airline feels it needs additional business.

Supersavers. An advanced purchase ticket, limited in number on each flight, which can cost up to 50 percent less than the standard fare. It requires a round trip reservation and is subject to a number of conditions. You may have to fly midweek, include Saturday in your travel plans, and stay for a set period of time—perhaps 7 or 14 days.

Unlimited mileage tickets. One fare will let you travel throughout the airline's system for a specific time period. Sometimes the passenger must travel with a companion, or may have to book flights some time in advance. You may be sure there'll be some conditions as a prerequisite for this fare.

Off-peak fares. A lesser fare allowed on travel before and after business hours. Usually these are restricted to very early morning or late evening flights. Discounts are also offered for travel in slow seasons. Airlines have their own criteria as to what constitutes off-peak hours. They vary, too, on different routings.

Weekend rate. Special low fares to a destination on Saturday, returning before 12 noon or other hours on Sunday. These usually run on typical business routes, like between New York and Washington, D.C.

Night coach fare. Usually a low, low fare if you travel 11 P.M. or later, arriving at your destination in the early hours of the morning.

Tour basing fares. Special airline fares, considerably lower than the standard fare, but contingent on the purchase of accommodations in special hotels and other possible ground arrangements, such as car rentals.

Excursion fares. Low fares based on round-trip planning, often conditioned by a minimum and maximum stay. No transfers are allowed to other airlines, and you usually must pay for your ticket at the time of reserving it. If you cancel this limited ticket, there's usually a penalty fee.

Group fare. A special rate based on a number of people traveling on that particular flight. Usually a travel agent will be able to add you to an existing group, but strictly for the purposes of getting you a special fare. You are not actually obliged to be part of that group.

Overseas travel APEX fares. Advance-purchase excursion fares on a reserved round-trip basis. You pay for your tickets well in advance and are limited to a minimum and maximum stay. These can cost about 50 percent less than the regular economy fare. The penalty for changing a return date is paying the next higher fare.

Super APEX fare. Same as the above, but there's a greater discount attached to it.

One-way APEX fare. Same as APEX, but it is not necessary to reserve the return portion. Yugoslav Airlines is one of the few offering this option.

Standby. You never know until departure time whether it's go or stay, but the fare is very low. Some airlines give you a break by allowing you to call ahead of time to find out the probability of getting a seat.

Senior Air Fares

Every once in a while an airline will introduce a special senior fare. Some are short-lived; others continue on for years and benefits improve. All these fares have restrictions of one kind or another—hours of travel, days of travel, holiday travel, etc. You can probably live with these restrictions if the price is right. Knowing when these windfalls occur is a matter of being alert to airline ads and keeping track of likely candidates.

Air Canada has had a long-standing policy of being generous to the 65-plus crowd within Canada. Last time around, the discount was up to 65 percent off excursion fares (with many conditions) and 25 percent off regular fares (with no restrictions) the year around.

Not to be upstaged by its fellow Canadian carrier, Canadian Pacific Air matches Air Canada's offer. Fares are good only for travel in Canada, though tickets may be bought in the U.S. Both carriers require proof of age—65.

Eastern Airlines has won a lot of friends in the U.S. and Canada with its unique year-long travel pass for 65-year-olds. The pass allows for almost unlimited travel in continental U.S. and Puerto Rico. The price—about $1,199—may seem steep, but you can get more than $5,000 worth of travel with it. What's more, the pass opens the way to 50 percent reductions at a number of hotels. There are restrictions and blackout periods. You can also buy one for a younger companion traveling with you. TWA, too, offers a new senior pass providing unlimited travel in the U.S. for a yearly fee of about $1,199. An extra supplement of $449 will provide the VSP Senior Pass for a round-trip air ticket to the Middle East with stopovers in Europe. A younger companion can accompany the 65 and older passholder at the same yearly fee.

Western Airlines clips its fares to Alaska, and sometimes to Hawaii, for 60-plusers with proof of age. In Hawaii, both Aloha and Royal Hawaiian Airlines have special discounts for seniors flying inter-island routes. KLM has recently introduced a low-cost round trip air fare to Amsterdam for travelers over 60. No advanced purchase is required.

In a major move to court the middle-to-older generation, Delta Airlines, in concert with Days Inns of America's September Day Club, is discounting peak air travel and tours for 55-plusers. Discounts are from 25 to 35 percent. Republic Airlines and U.S. Air computers are also programmed for bargain prices for seniors.

Over in Yugoslavia, the nation's airline is offering special rates to seniors on its tour program and also for independent older travelers.

While an airline may not be currently involved in a special program of discounts, look to their history of such offerings. American Airlines is one major carrier with no discounts presently, but who knows about the future? Airlines need passengers to fill seats in off hours, and passengers who qualify by dint of age and freedom to travel can use the savings. It's a perfect setup for both.

One word of caution, sometimes discounts don't provide as much of a savings as supersavers, excursion fares, or other promotional fares. Keep checking the possibilities.

Getting to and from the Airport

Most airports are located a long distance from the cities they serve. It's as true in New York as it is in Tokyo. A cab ride from Narita Airport to downtown Tokyo in Japan costs about $80, the airport bus fare runs about $10.50. In Denmark it's $13 by cab compared to $1.60 by bus. In Rome, a limo would cost $50, as compared with a $3-4 bus ride.

If you can manage your luggage, the airport bus or train will save you money. You should also inquire if your hotel provides free or less costly transfers to and from the airport. Your travel agent should be able to give you this information.

Charters

There is no question about it—charters are phenomenal money savers, whether you take a round-trip charter flight or buy the whole vacation package. The package is much like a regular group tour, often with a choice of hotels and sightseeing, but air transport is on non-scheduled flights. You have to be prepared, however, for "eventualities."

But first the good news! The savings are so sweet. You can literally chop hundreds of dollars off regular air fares and, with a package arrangement, trim your hotel costs to boarding house rates. You'll enjoy travel to places you always wanted to visit, but couldn't afford. Then, too, there's the company you will keep. You have much in common with your fellow travelers, who, like you, enjoy a good bargain now and then. Regularly scheduled airlines run charters, as do professional and social organizations, but the bulk of the business is in the hands of charter operators who do this work exclusively. You can find

charter operators by following the ads in your local newspapers or by asking your travel agent about them.

Now, the bad news. You may encounter exhausting
delays, unexpected fare increases, possible cancellation of
your flight—and *poof,* there go your plans! There's the
possibility, too, of the operator's substituting a smaller
aircraft for a larger one, changing airports with little
notice, and switching hotels from the convenient one in
the center of the city to one out in the boondocks. But
worse than anything is being stranded overseas by a
bankrupt tour operator.

These are the risks, but there are laws that can protect you. To better understand the whole concept of chartering and how problems arise, read on.

A public charter, as opposed to one operated by an
organization for its members, is open to one and all. It
usually includes air transportation to a favorite destination—Paris, Rome, London, etc., plus hotels and sightseeing. Some charters limit their service to just air transportation—and one way at that. The tour operator organizes
the trip on planes either owned by the charter company or
leased from an airline. When the operator schedules the
charter, he publishes the day of departure, but not neces-
sarily the exact time of takeoff.

There's a reason for this. The plane to be used is not
sitting around the airport waiting for you; it's out there
somewhere else in the world on other charter business. It
could be delayed by weather, airport traffic, mechanical
difficulties, or the lack of a pilot.

The reason for most delays, however, is lack of
equipment. When an international or domestic charter
flight is delayed, it causes backups throughout the system. If the wait is more than 48 hours, you have the right
to a penalty-free refund, but usually the charter company
will be looking to put you on another plane before that
time. They don't want to give up any revenue.

You as a charter passenger, however, can't just arbi-
trarily cancel your plans at the last minute without suffering a loss of money. Charter companies are required to
inform you about insurance coverage, and insurance policies can protect you if you have to cancel a trip because of

illness or other legitimate reasons. The fine print in each of these contracts will tell you the exact conditions for canceling.

Study the Contract

You must read the charter contract carefully. Know what you are buying, and don't pay for the trip until you fully understand the contract. It may be binding. Your rights and the tour operator's rights to cancel are spelled out. So is information on where you will be housed if you are buying a charter package. Determine if the operator can change the dates of the flight or the location of take-off. The contract will also give you the names and addresses of the companies that will guarantee a refund should the charter operator go into bankruptcy before or during your trip. (See also Chapter 12, Rights and Redress.)

Paying for Your Charter

Because there is a history of bankruptcies and defaults in the air charter business, laws have been written to safeguard passengers from financially unstable operators. One of these laws deals with payment.

Instead of paying the charter operator directly for your trip, you now pay into an escrow account, which the operator is mandated by law to open. Moneys for round-trip transportation and the other elements of the charter are held in that escrow fund by the bank and are not available to the operator until the whole trip is delivered. This escrow fund is in addition to a surety bond that the operator must purchase to protect the passengers.

If you are paying the tour operator directly, your check will be made out jointly to the bank and the tour operator. To make it even more explicit, write the date of the charter and the destination on your check.

When a travel agent is handling your charter reservation, be sure to insist that the agency makes out its check to the escrow fund. To be even more certain that your money is safe, you can call the escrow account officer in the bank and find out if the account for your specific trip is intact. In case the company goes out of business, your refund will come from the escrow fund.

A great many travel agents are not happy about booking their clients on charter flights. If flights are delayed, or hotel accommodations switched, agents don't want to be blamed.

Among the bigger charter companies who have been doing business for a number of years are International Weekends, Transamerica, Travac, Wainwright, and the Council on International Educational Exchange (CIEE). Their ads may appear in your local newspaper.

Because charters often make the difference between going and staying home, millions of people, including your friends and their college-aged children, have used them exclusively for years. While complaints have been lodged against the best of them, the majority of charters run smoothly and have been relatively problem free. There's no reason to think that the one you select may be fraught with difficulties. It's important, though, to be cautious about your choice.

Be aware that long distance flights can be exhausting, and the anxiety can be compounded by long delays in getting started. Program that into your consciousness when making charter plans. Also be aware that it is not likely that you can check your luggage through from a regularly scheduled airline to a charter. You will have to retrieve your bag and recheck it on the charter. Scheduled airlines usually don't transfer passengers' baggage to charter airlines.

Watch Their Language

Charter operators are no different from any other enterpreneurs selling a product. Their intent is to titillate you with promises of good times at bargain prices, sometimes at the expense of full disclosure.

The price you see may not be the price you pay. Watch for words like *restricted fares, good only on certain dates, good only for a limited number of passengers.* Somewhere in the small print (there's always that fine print), you'll find a line that may say *add percentage for taxes and services.* The amount to be added to the advertised low price could be 15 percent or even higher. Just keep your magnifying glass handy when reading the contract or the ads.

Also be aware that you may have a choice of hotels on a package arrangement. The price listed is for the cheapest accommodation, which is probably located far from where you want to be. When you contact the charter operator, ask for lists and room costs of other hotels they use.

Prices May Change

Unlike regularly scheduled airlines, which protect you against a fare increase once you've been ticketed, charters are allowed, by Civil Aeronautics Board regulation, to jack up their price 10 percent up to 10 days before departure time. (If fares are raised more than 10 percent, you can cancel your reservation and get your money back without penalty.)

Your original fare was based on the operator's high expectations of filling the plane. The operator may be unable to sell all the seats. The company will lose money if the plane goes half empty. To cut losses, the operator books a smaller, less comfortable plane. The original price could also have been determined by a favorable foreign exchange rate, which may have changed drastically since the trip was planned. Or the cost of fuel might have escalated. These factors make a difference in the cost of the charter. To make matters worse, not only has your charter price gone up, but the operator decides to have a sale to sell whatever seats remain. Latecomers get a bargain; they pay a price way below what you paid, and you can't do anything about it.

Tips on How to Pick a Charter

Compare rates. Look around first to see if a scheduled airline has a promotional fare lower than the price of the charter.

Reserve a safe date. To avoid the possibility of a canceled charter, pick a departure date during the busiest vacation period. A popular date leaves little doubt that the charter will be filled. Try not to book a charter at the

very beginning or end of the company's charter program.

Have firm plans. Before you sign up, be sure that's what you
really want to do. Changing your mind or canceling at
the last minute will cost you stiff cash penalties.

Check the operator's record. Ask your travel agent how long
the operator has been in business. Check with the
Better Business Bureau in your area to see if any complaints have been lodged against the operator.

Ask what is included. If you are buying an all-inclusive charter, find out specifically what you are paying for—
sightseeing, meals, hotels, transfers, etc.

Look for a charter specialist. Try to find a travel agent who
specializes in charter flights. They are in the best position to know who the good charter operators are.

Verify the carrier's reputation. Ask for the name of the air
carrier. It's only natural you would feel more confident
flying a well-established "brand name" airline than on
an unknown. All of them, however, must abide by
strict safety regulations, the same as regularly scheduled airlines.

Make connections. After you've made your decision, leave
enough time to purchase a special promotional round
trip fare to connect with your charter flight if needed.
Leave plenty of time both going and coming to take care
of delays. When you miss your charter flight, you lose
your money.

Clubs Have Clout

A membership in any good-sized, consumer-oriented club
or association can pay off in handsome savings. Even if
you're not a joiner, they're worth considering. The dollars
you invest in dues may bring substantial dividends in
lower prices for goods and services.

In the field of travel, the larger clubs can be effective
in securing lower rates on hotel rooms, car rentals, resort
accommodations, discounts on cruises, bus fares, fee-free
traveler's checks, free credit cards, half price on passport
photos, lower admissions to attractions, and much, much

more. Flashing a membership card on registering at a hotel or motel can be worth up to 25 percent off the established room rate.

The larger the association, the bigger discounts it commands. With the inherent promise of delivering volume business, large organizations are able to negotiate excellent dollars-off deals for members.

Some organizations are better at this than others. Best of all are the American Automobile Association, with its 24 million members, and the American Association of Retired Persons, with its 17 million. Both of these organizations offer an ever-increasing list of benefits. AARP's "Purchase Privilege Brochure" is constantly being revised and updated to make room for more services.

Although its major interest is public policy toward older persons, the Washington-based National Council of Senior Citizens, Inc., with four million members, has done its part for members who travel by securing discounts in selected motel chains and car rental agencies.

A fourth organization, the National Association of Mature People, with 400,000 members, was started in 1975 to alter negative attitudes on aging. In addition to this mission, it now also sponsors trips at reasonable rates and provides discounts for its membership at hotels and motels.

New on the scene is Mature Outlook, a member of the Sears Family of Companies. It already has more than half a million members. The $7.50 membership fee for people over 55 includes discounts on travel, car rentals, financial services, and a newsletter and magazine.

September Club, an organization of 304,000 members 55 and over, is a subsidiary of the motel chain Days Inns. It provides its membership 10 percent off accommodations at the chain's 320 motels, as well as discounts on car rentals. Hotel accommodations run from about $29 to $55. Airline tickets on Delta are also discounted.

In addition to these organizations, there are religion-oriented clubs like the Catholic Golden Age Club, with 800,000 members, and travel clubs, all engaged in getting special discounts for members.

Another kind of "last minute" travel club has recently

come into existence. This type capitalizes on tour operators' inability to fill all their space on charters, cruise
ships, and packaged tours. These clubs are for people who
can pick up and travel anytime at all, usually at the last
minute. Membership in one of these clubs could save up
to 50 percent off regular tour prices.

These clubs are located all over the country. Travel
agents wouldn't be particularly interested in telling you
about them because commissions are not paid. You can
check them out for yourself.

A recent example of the kind of reductions available
from one of those clubs was a seven-day package to Rio de
Janeiro from New York for $699, including hotel, trans-
fers, and air fare. With that price, travelers saved $335.
On a seven-day cruise to the Caribbean from Ft. Lauderdale, the cost of a $1,495 cruise became $999, and a
two-week package tour of four European countries sold
for $530, saving travelers $290.

Among these fee-charging membership clubs offering last-minute discount tours are:

Stand-Bys, Ltd., P.O. Box 2088, Southfield, MI 48037 (1-800-643-9466
in Michigan, elsewhere 1-800-621-5839)
Moment's Notice, 40 East 49th St., New York, NY 10017 (1-800-
253-4321; in New York State: 212-486-0503)
Encore Travel Card, 4720 Boston Way, Lanham, MD 20706 (1-800-
638-0930)
Discount Travel International, 7563 Haverford Ave., Philadelphia, PA
19151 (1-800-228-6500)

There are many more of these clubs located all over the
United States. Membership fees vary from $25 to $45.
Before you join and fly off with any of them, read their
literature carefully so you know what you are entitled to
should the trip be canceled or major alterations be made in
itineraries.

Club Discounts at Hotels

Budget hotels and motels provide very affordable
rates even without club discounts, but it's always nice to
be able to shave travel costs even lower.

Discount percentages vary with hotel chains and

with the negotiating skill of your club's management. Some hotels will accept proof of age if you don't belong to senior clubs, and others will honor only membership in your club and no others. *Show your card when registering.*

The following hotel chains are but a few of the many that offer discounts to seniors and other club members. All have toll free numbers, which you can get from information by calling 1-800-555-1212. Included among them are Travelodge, Best Western International, Econo Lodges, Econo Travel Motor Hotels, Friendship Inns International, Ramada Inns, Quality Inns International, Rodeway Inns, Scottish Inns, Sheraton Hotels and Inns, La Quinta Motor Inns, Howard Johnson's Motor Lodges, Holiday Inns, and Hyatt Hotels.

At the larger chains, discounts are available in properties in Canada, the Caribbean, Mexico, and Europe. When you call the chain's central reservation number, ask specifically about the individual hotel's policy toward discounts. Some hotels may not participate in the plan.

Club members also get discounts at car rental agencies. These, too, vary with locations, time of the year, special promotional rates, and other conditions. Major car rental agencies also have toll-free numbers, which information will give when you call.

Resources—Some Outstanding Senior Clubs

American Association of Retired Persons (AARP), 215 Long Beach Blvd., Long Beach, CA 90801 (1-213-432-5781). Membership open to people over 50; $5 fee covers couples or single membership.

National Council of Senior Citizens, 925 15th St., N.W., Washington, DC 20005 (1-202-347-8800). No age requirement; dues from $7 to $10, according to union or club affiliation.

September Days Club (Days Inns subsidiary), 2751 Buford Highway, N.E., Atlanta, GA 30324 (1-404-325-4000). Membership open to 55-year-olds and over; $10 dues.

National Association of Mature People (NAMP), 2212 N.W. 50th St., Box 26792, Oklahoma City, OK 73126 (1-405-848-1832). For people 40 and over; membership dues $7.50.

Mature Outlook, Inc. (Sears Family of Companies), P.O. Box 1205, Glenview, IL 60025 (1-312-291-7800). Open to 55-year-olds and over; membership fee $7.50.

When and Where to Cut Costs

You always want the most for your money, no matter where you go or when you take your vacation trip. But by choosing the right time and the right place, you can make your vacation dollars go even further.

Off-Season Travel

Off-season is the right season for a little penny pinching. It's the time when airlines, hotels, and car rental agencies in traditional winter-summer places find the flow of tourists has declined noticeably.

What do they do about it? They mark down their prices on tour packages, clip air fares, lower hotel rates, and call it off-season.

In the Caribbean, off-season is a long season. After the feverish rates of winter, there's a cool down in costs. It usually starts in May and ends about the day or week before Christmas. Caribbean countries call that time of the year "The Season for Sweet Savings," and not only do costs plummet, but bonuses flower. You might find a bottle of rum and coke in your room, courtesy of the hotel management, or discounts to local attractions. But one thing is sure—the islands' enterpreneurs want to please you. With less crowds, they have more time to devote to you.

Off-season rates are not confined to warmer climates. During a recent winter, Toronto's Hotel Association offered 50 percent discounts at member hotels for four winter weekends. Visitors were given "dollars off" coupon vouchers for a host of other tourist services—car rentals, sightseeing, and restaurant tabs.

Off-season are "go" seasons if you and the weather are compatible. Scandinavian countries offer superlow package trips in winter months, but if cold leaves you just that, and you don't relish mini-hours of daylight, you don't get much of a bargain.

There are trade-offs in everything. Extreme weather, however, is not exactly the right climate for a vacation. Study the weather maps of an area, which can be secured from travel literature in a library, and choose weeks during the off-season period when temperatures are at least moderate. Then you have a true bargain.

Weekend Specials

Weekends and holidays in big cities can be financial disasters to luxury hotels. The businessmen who wheeled and dealed all week long have gone, leaving empty rooms with no one to fill them. Holiday weekends are just as bad, or perhaps worse, for higher priced hostelries. Since staffs can't be furloughed, hotel managements have decided that the best way to keep occupancy rates up is to move room rates down.

Weekend packages can save up to 50 percent off regular rates in many luxury hotels. In addition to the room, you may also get such niceties as baskets of fruit, wine, champagne breakfasts, newspapers, and sometimes even theatre tickets as part of the package. When requesting hotel rooms for weekends, always inquire about the special weekend rate. Sometimes you can get two discounts, the weekend special *and* the discount you get with your club membership.

Lower hotel rates may also come with package plans put together by airlines or Amtrak. Ask about those, too.

Bargain Basement Countries

If you follow the financial news in your newspapers and magazines, you will find clues as to where the good travel buys are outside the United States. The key words are *a strong dollar* and *devaluation.* Devaluation often occurs when the currency of a country becomes so inflated that officials reduce the value of their currency in relation to the dollar. This means that your dollars buy more of their currency—pounds, pesos, rupees, cruzeiros, etc.

While it's a hardship for people who live in those countries, it's a bonanza for tourists with American dollars. Each time you cash a dollar or a traveler's check, you get more local currency than you would have before devaluation. If the country doesn't raise prices, hotels, food, and other purchases become cheaper.

In recent years, Mexico's hard-pressed economy reaped unprecedented travel bargains for American tourists there. Since then, prices on hotel accommodations and travel have risen somewhat, but Mexico is still a bargain.

Brazil, too, is now less expensive for Americans than it ever was before. Travelers report staying in first class hotels in Rio for about $40 double, paying $12 for dinner, including wine and tips, and spending $12 for an evening's entertainment in a night club. It will be a while before Brazil becomes expensive again, and in the meanwhile, the country offers travelers good value.

Apart from devaluation, there are some countries and some sections of countries where living standards are lower and travel is still a bargain. Portugal, Spain, Greece, Poland, Yugoslavia, and other Eastern European countries are less costly to visit.

There are also bargains to be had in wealthier countries. By staying out of the big cities, where costly real estate is reflected in hotel prices, you can keep your travel budget in line.

Seasons for Seniors

Whole communities, too, value the interest, enthusiasm, and business generated by the 50-plusers. They cooperate by discounting food prices, admissions, and hotel rooms during certain Senior Seasons.

The city of Williamsburg, Virginia, marks September as Senior Time for people 55 and over. Reduced admission fees, restaurant discounts, and other amenities are offered. In Colonial Williamsburg, colonial plays and operas performed during Senior Week are included in the reduced admissions plan. Greens fees are reduced 10 percent at the Golden Horseshoe and Spotswood golf courses.

Central Florida, too, has a special season for visitors 55 and over. Sponsored by the Greater Orlando Chamber of Commerce (P.O. Box 1234, Orlando, FL 32802), the season spans three months, from mid-September to mid-December. Popular attractions like Sea World and Cypress Gardens lower their admission prices for seniors. Car rental agencies, hotels, and restaurants also do their part to cut the cost of vacationing in the area.

Special Golden Age Games are held in Sanford during the second week in November for athletes 55 and over. Both spectators and athletes over 55 get the benefit of overall discounts during that period. Other areas of Florida, too, have special discounts for people past their 50s. The Florida tourism office in Tallahassee can fill in the details. (See Appendix A for address.)

Toronto and the whole province of Ontario have long been involved in looking after the needs of older travelers on fixed incomes. Discounts are on tap for theatre admissions, concerts, transportation, and even for the Shakespeare Festival at Stratford. As in all discount offerings, there are restrictions and blackout periods when these specials are not available. Discounts for Shakespeare performances, for instance, are only good for midweek shows.

Whole countries, too, are sensitive to the needs of the not-so-youthful set. Switzerland was one of the first nations to inaugurate "The Season for Senior Citizens." It's tied in with its half-fare rail pass. Swiss hotels by the hundreds cooperate in the program by offering discounts on rooms and sometimes on food.

Other Money Savers

There are plenty of ways to stretch your travel dollars. In addition to the tips offered in this chapter, you'll find more suggestions in the chapters on transportation (Chapter 5), tours (Chapter 7), cruises (Chapter 8), and foreign travel (Chapter 9). It's your money—get the most out of it.

Budget Accommodations

When you don't fit the age profile of certain hotel properties, there are other ways to effect savings on overnight accommodations. Chains of budget motels, hotels, and inns offer affordable rooms for travelers throughout the U.S., Canada, Mexico, and Europe.

There are scores of such hotels and motels in this country. The three described here are a mere sampling of what's available. To find others and alternative lower-priced lodging like B & Bs, check the references cited in Chapter 4.

In the northeast, Susse Chalet Motor Lodges and Inns offer accommodations for as little as $25 to about $35 per couple per night. In the upper midwest, accommodations at the Thrifty Scot Motels, Inc., average between $20 and $40. Super 8 Motels, Inc., has about 200 motels across the country charging an average of $20 to $50 a night per couple. These and others have toll free numbers. Just phone the 800 information number in your area.

Low-Cost Car Rentals

Florida is a big market in the car rental business. The state has Hertz, Avis, Alamo, National, Budget, and other well- and lesser-known agencies. If you are watchful, and planning to drive in Florida, you may encounter a car rental price war.

These price skirmishes break out in off-season months and usually revolve around a special model car. The weekly rates offered are something to be joyous about. Not only Florida, but any heavily traveled tourist area with a number of competing agencies can be expected to turn up some heady weekly rates. Even agencies in Hawaii will make you a deal. In scanning ads for these bargains, read the fine print carefully for time restrictions, advance reservations, and type of car offered. And plan ahead; the number of special cars offered at lower rates is limited.

Making Waves in Cruise Costs

For the next several years, cruise vacations may be one of the best vacation buys around. The reason is simple—competition and more supply than demand.

In 1980, practically every cruise vessel afloat sailed off happily loaded. It didn't matter whether the ship was the least or most expensive; people who wanted a cruise vacation in the winter had to book their cabins far in advance.

The cruise ship industry read this popularity as a sign of a new boom in sailing vacations and proceeded to build bigger and better ships. These brand new ships have come in—but the number of cruise passengers climbing up the gangplank are less than expected.

By shopping around you will find cruise lines quietly discounting prices for any number of reasons. If you make early-bird reservations, from two to six months in advance, you will get about a 15 percent reduction on your cabin, maybe more.

Latecomers, too, get price breaks if they act on the spur of the moment. There are standby fares. One California agency specializes in last-minute sales of available space on cruise ships. Travelers get 40-to-50 percent off. Contact Spur of the Moment Cruises, 4315 Overland, Culver City, CA 90230. Their toll-free number is 1-800-343-1991 nationwide. In California, phone 1-800-233-2129 or in area code 213, phone 839-2418.

Repeat passengers are offered discounts. Gather together 10 of your friends and some cruise lines will not only give you free passage, but may offer discounts all around.

The more expensive cruise ships would never deign to call what they are doing discounting—nothing that crass. Luxury liners call them price incentives. To attract you, they will pay air fares, even if it means free flights on the expensive supersonic aircraft, the Concorde.

Other air incentives are less grand but just as helpful. If you live far enough from the port of embarkation, these free or discounted air fares can save you a lot of money. Passengers who live near the port of embarkation should ask the cruise line for discounts on cabin prices since the lines do not have to pay for their air passage.

Another way of luring you aboard is by offering cash credits for future cruises. With each cruise you take, you are given a substantial credit toward the next cruise you book on the same line. This can be a convincing way to encourage the cruise habit. Cash credits are sizable—$400 to $500 off cabin prices, perhaps more.

One line offers a one percent discount on your next cruise for each day spent on your current cruise. If you take a 14-day voyage, you get 14 percent off the next one.

The Bahama Cruise Line offers senior citizen fares at certain times of the year.

There are even incentives for single travelers. Princess Cruises charges only a 10 percent premium for a single room on all their cruises. Not on deluxe accommodations, however. Other lines have much higher single supplement rates. Just remember to study the conditions carefully when buying a cruise in advance.

For more about cruises, see Chapter 8.

Trimming the Fat Off Food Prices

Eating is one of the great pleasures of life. Trying out local and regional specialities, dining at famous restaurants, and pampering your taste buds with new foods are as important to your trip as seeing the famous sights. It's all part of the total travel experience.

Gourmet meals, however, come with high price tags. Have your food fling, but economize at other meals. Breakfast is a good time to start. Avoid breakfast in your hotel room or even in the hotel dining room unless it's prepaid. An early morning walk is not only good for you, it's an opportunity to explore the neighborhood and discover a wonderful inexpensive cafeteria or coffee shop where your eggs are scrambled and your toast buttered for at least two or three dollars less than the price charged by your hotel.

And don't think that because the hotel is located in a rich neighborhood there are no inexpensive restaurants available. Remember that hotel employees, shop workers, paper vendors, and even the unemployed have to eat, too. A good example is the posh Union Square section in San Francisco. Right across the street from the elegant St. Francis Hotel is a cafeteria serving good food at reasonable prices. Every morning you can find some of the hotel's guests, businessmen with their leather briefcases and $400 suits, saving a little on their expenses.

While a steady diet of fast food fare is certainly not to be recommended, don't turn up your nose to the discounts some of the food chains offer.

When traveling by car, pleasant picnic areas en route

can be just the right locale for the barbecue chicken bought at the supermarket. Deli sandwiches are nice, too, when dining al fresco with the birds, and hopefully not the bees or ants.

Some days you might want to take advantage of a restaurant's "early bird" specials. Your dinner check for a meal served at 5 P.M. instead of 7 will be considerably less, even though the courses are identical. Restaurants offering this money-saving opportunity are usually found in resort areas catering to people who don't want to drive at night, but they can be found everywhere. It's good for the restaurant, too. It keeps their staff busy.

Dining out costs can decline if you order the blue plate or table d'hote specials, complete dinners at a set price. Steer clear of a la carte restaurants where each dish is charged separately. Over in Europe, your restaurant checks will be considerably less if you order the tourist menu of the day. Many foreign governments require restaurants to offer tourist menus—a fixed price meal— every day. Prices run from $8 to $10. The special meal will include a number of courses, plus taxes and tips. Belgium, Holland, Ireland, Spain, France, Germany, and Scandinavian countries are some countries which mandate that restaurants do this for tourists.

Europe also has its share of snack bars, pizza parlors, pubs, trattorias, tavernas, coffee houses, and other lower-cost eateries where light meals are served at light prices. In England, for instance, you can get a pub lunch. It will probably be cottage pie—ground lamb with vegetables, topped with creamed mashed potatoes, or "bangers and mash," sausages and mashed potatoes.

One word of advice about hard liquor in foreign countries. It is costly. Scotch, rye, bourbon, gin, and vodka are exorbitantly priced in most countries. If you have any doubts, check the prices of spirits in their liquor stores. When you want an alcoholic beverage, drink wine or beer in Europe; it is less costly, and it's probably the country's specialty.

Saving on Purchases

Any shopper worth his or her "cents off coupons"

knows how to find a bargain in the United States. Sales, outlet stores, discount houses, flea markets, stores specializing in "seconds," and factory outlets are the usual sources for bargain hunting.

What's true in the United States is also true abroad. Hong Kong has its "factories" where luxury clothing is made. Contractors there sell this clothing to tourists as well as to locals.

In Thailand, Star of Siam, a famous silk store in Bangkok, and Jim Thompson, an equally well known one, hold periodic silk clearance sales. In London, the open-air street markets and the super bargain department store Marks and Spencer draws the budget wise. Reject China shops in England are popular with shoppers who don't really care if there's an imperceptible flaw in bone china; they'll buy "seconds" and gift them off as "firsts." Paris perfume sellers, too, have their discount shops. Michel Swiss and other similar perfume discounters do a brisk business among people who don't want to spend high prices on French perfumes.

And then there's bargaining, the mode of business in the Middle East, the Far East, Africa, and all Latin American nations. Bargaining can really cut the cost of your purchases if you know how. The strategy begins with a highly inflated price. Then you make your offer, half of what it's worth. Eventually, you arrive at a compromise, a fair price. There are plenty of variations on this theme. You can adopt a no-nonsense attitude, mix the game with a little humor, or exhibit a touch of toughness; but, above all, you have to know what you want.

Your strongest position is knowing what the merchandise is worth. From then on, it's a matter of give and take and courage. Can you bluff a little and leave your prize behind? If you do, will the seller realize you are bluffing, or will he run after you with a counter offer? The next part of the serial is in your hands.

Duty-Free Shops

The majority of duty-free shops at airports around the world have lost their attraction, and with good reason.

Airport merchandise is usually more expensive than that of city stores. The only advantage for travelers is that items are for sale for last-minute purchases, and it's helpful when you've forgotten to buy a present for your next door neighbor who was kind enough to water your plants and take in your mail.

Additional Money Saving Tips

Take proof of club membership. Always take your club membership card with you. "Never leave home without it."

Show your card. Present your club membership card when you check into a hotel and ask for the discount then. Or, when you phone in your reservation, inform the clerk of your membership in the club and ask for the discount rate.

Bring along proof of age. You may be asked to prove that you are really 55, 60, or older, even when you have a club membership card. A Medicare card, your driver's license, or your passport should provide proof of your entitlements.

Ask about phone surcharges. Check with your hotel about the price of phone calls from your room. Some tack surcharges on phone calls. Your best bet may be a pay phone.

Look for free traveler's checks. Take advantage of free traveler's checks and free credit cards.

Use toll-free numbers. Use toll-free numbers whenever you can in the U.S. Before dialing that long distance number, call 1-800-555-1212 to find out if the hotel or tourist facility has a toll-free number.

Bargain a little. If it's the style of a country to bargain, join in the fun. It's worth money to you.

Do your own light laundry. Wash your own linen. Hotel laundries charge a lot for washing your underwear. Take along some washing soap and inflatable plastic hangers and do your own.

Investigate free attractions. Look for free attractions. A band concert in the park, a street fair, art shows, a free guided tour are some of the things you may encounter in your travels. These events can be very rewarding.

Stay out of cabs. Whenever possible, use the local transportation systems. The subways and buses will not only put you in touch with local people but save you money on cab fares. Many European countries have special passes for unlimited use of subways and buses.

Look for specials. Keep alert for promotional discounts on air fares, train rides, motorcoach trips, and other special bonuses.

CHAPTER 7

All About Tours

Group tours are as old as the story of Moses. Travel writers would tell the story this way. Moses organized a desert tour out of Egypt on short notice. Since there was no time for planning, there were plenty of problems. Water and food were scarce, there were long delays, and the tour was oversold—600,000 joined that trek. No provisions were made for ground transportation, so thousands walked. Tour leaders heard nothing but complaints for 40 years. Misrepresentation was the biggest gripe. No cancellations were permitted. It was all one way, there was no turning back.

Today's tours are a marvel of safety, comfort, variety, security, efficiency, intelligent planning, and fun.

Whatever your goal—adventure, education, art, history, golf, tennis, archaeology, sitting on a beach, or beating a path through a jungle—tour programs neatly package dreams and deliver them to you, often at down-to-earth prices.

What exactly is a group tour? It can be an intimate gathering of 10 of your own friends or convention meetings of 500. The common denominator is that it is prepaid and all parts of the trip are assembled. The tour operator or producer looks after your lodging and sees to it that you are transported from place to place, shown the sights, admitted to famous attractions, and perhaps fed and entertained.

The cost, the schedule, the hotels you sleep in, and the sights you see are determined before you leave home. Whatever else you enjoy doing—having cocktails, going off by yourself to some special restaurant, attending an opera or a theatrical performance, shopping, etc.—comes out of the pocket money you set aside to enhance your trip.

In addition to saving you money, a group tour relieves you of the details of planning a trip, provides companionship, attends to your luggage, and, should you get sick, has someone on hand who can arrange medical care.

Group tours are not all alike. Some do everything for you; others offer limited service. Before deciding on a tour, you ought to know what's available.

First, the Package

Your trusty old Webster's will tell you that a package is a bundle of things made up for transportation. That's exactly what a package tour is. All the elements of travel—the means of getting there, the place to sleep, meals, transportation to and from the points of arrival and departure, transfers, tips, most taxes, sightseeing, perhaps car rentals—are tied together and sold to you as a package. You go from one arrangement to another. It's all there for you to enjoy.

The package theme has many variations. Some packages include an escort to accompany you, others just provide the bare essentials. Some provide all your meals, others omit them entirely. Some show you all the sights, others give you the option of selecting what you want to see.

Packaged tours are organized by tour operators, airlines, railroads, motorcoach companies, hotels or motels, religious institutions, clubs, museums, banks, or anyone else who can organize a group to travel together.

Types of Tours

Tour packages vary considerably. In all of the following packages, you get what you pay for.

Escorted, All-inclusive Tours. These tours usually include both air and land arrangements. The price will include all or most of your meals. If it's very deluxe, you may have a free choice from the menu.

A tour escort will be with you for the entire length of your trip. Local guides will be hired to fill in the information gap. If it's a deluxe trip, the guide may have special expertise. Some guides, notably those on tours organized by museums and educational institutions, have advanced degrees in history, botany, archaeology, art, or whatever subjects are appropriate to the nature of the tour.

In addition to experts, special entertainments—such as gala welcomes and farewell banquets, balls, or folkloric evenings—will probably be featured.

Escorted Tours. Again, someone will be with you on your tour. Transportation to and from the destination may or may not be included. Transfers, baggage handling, tips, and hotels are all promised for sure. Differences are determined by the style of travel you select—deluxe, first class, or tourist class. The hotel and number of persons on the tour will be reflected in the price and classification of your tour.

Hosted Tours. Independent tourists enjoy this type of tour because they get the advantage of a lower group rate on hotel accommodations but are free to do what they want with their vacation time. A host, the tour operator's representative, will be on hand or a phone call away to provide counsel on sightseeing possibilities, restaurants, and stores. The host is also available to help when there are troubles.

Some hosted tours include a welcoming cocktail party, one sightseeing trip for orientation, perhaps a meal or two, and a program of optional tours, which the traveler can buy or reject.

Carefree, Freelance Tours. Tour operators have their own names for this plan. They aren't too different from hosted tours, except there is no host right on hand. A representative will be available for help and guidance. Since you have prepaid, vouchers are supplied for transfers, car rentals, hotels, and other services in your tour.

Foreign Independent Travel (FIT). These are customized tours made up for you especially. A travel agent will make all the arrangements, including guides and hotels. It's the expensive way to go.

Group Inclusive Tour (GIT). A tour operator arranges a group rate on a plane. Members of the group need not travel together after they deplane. Sometimes certain land portions of the trip must be purchased to qualify for the group rate. A minimum stay may also be required.

Independent Tours (IT). You are on your own, but your prepaid tour includes a hotel, car rental, or perhaps a train ride. These are often fly/drive holiday packages, which include the price of a car rental, hotels, and air fare. They could also be a rail/drive tour, including the same elements but with a train included.

Air/Sea Packages. These are prepaid cruise voyages with air transportation fully or partially absorbed. These packages often allow you to sail one way and fly the other.

Charter Packages. These include charter flights plus regular group tours, with hotels, sightseeing, and other options spelled out by the charter organizer.

Stay-put Tours. People who want to travel to one destination and stay for a time in an apartment, condominium, or villa can choose this option. Operators who arrange these "tours" will reserve a number of apartments or condominiums, possibly arrange lower-cost air fare, and provide transfers and luggage handling to and from your home away from home. You'll probably get some maid service, but no meals.

Hotels, too, arrange packages. Weekend packages are discussed in Chapter 6. Longer package tours are available with transportation companies. Some might include bus fare to and from the airport, taxes, service charges, and some meals.

Singles Pay Double

No discussion of package tours can be complete without mentioning the "single supplement." If you are traveling alone on a package tour, you will be charged extra for your single room. Tours are arranged for twosomes sharing a room, each paying half of the double room cost. If you want to occupy a room by yourself, you're going to have to pay extra. The charge is more than one and a half times the double rate. Some tour operators and cruise lines will try to match you up with another single so that each may save a little on room rates.

Why an Escorted Group Tour?

Apart from good value, why should anyone take a group tour? Travel can be hard work. There are those burdensome details, unfamiliar customs, confusing and maybe frightening crowds, ambiguous directions, and scores of other problems you don't want to deal with on your own.

Escorted group tours are convivial movements of travelers. There's always someone to talk to and share experiences with. If there's any trouble, an experienced escort will know what to do. Escorted groups have even won over experienced travelers who once hated the very idea of a group trip.

One well-traveled couple, fiercely independent, wanted to go to China. A group trip was out of the question, but when they looked into the costs of going alone it was beyond their means. They finally relented and took a tour.

Their tour group included people of various backgrounds, each providing some expert and interesting input into the overall experience. The energy and enthusiasm of the group was so contagious that everyone had a wonderful time. The anti-tour tourists came back exhilarated. "It's the only way I'll ever go again," one of them said. "It was really a vacation—everything was taken care of."

There are other advantages to group travel. If luggage is delayed, you don't have to wait around the airport or your hotel until it arrives. The tour manager will follow through on luggage problems.

Hotels honor reservations of group travelers. There is little chance that your room won't be waiting for you. Hotels count on business generated by tour operators. If you are alone, there's always the possibility of your room being sold.

Transportation will be waiting to pick you up going and coming, without the hassle of getting a cab and possibly being overcharged.

If the country you are visiting requires visas, tour group organizers often get a group visa, which covers the whole tour. It eliminates writing and waiting for both your passport and visa.

Despite the advantages, group tours are not for everybody. Strong personalities who cannot adjust to the team spirit are poor tour candidates. They are not flexible, nor can they be tolerant of others' weaknesses. And when it comes to complying with the simple discipline of getting to the bus on time, they rebel and become trip spoilers. For their own sake, and for the sake of others, people who recognize these traits in themselves should not join a tour. Chronic complainers are also bad news on tours.

There are others, too, who would not make good tour companions. High-powered executives, who have had a lifetime of perks, have a rough time traveling in a group as just a tour member. They should organize a very small group of 10 compatible friends and custom tailor trips to their needs.

Structure of a Group Tour

While prices, destinations, and size of groups may differ, all escorted tours are essentially structured the same way. You travel with the same number of people every day. Your escort will manage all your tour services and can be counted on to collect your passports, preregister you at hotels, hand out your room keys when you arrive, see to it that you get your wake-up calls, and check the number of pieces of luggage that get on and off the bus. The escort also makes arrangements for your luggage to be picked up outside your hotel room door on

departure days. You won't have to lift a thing. Your job is
enjoyment. It's a good idea, though, to double check that
your luggage is in the lobby with the rest of your group's
bags. It's also a good idea to see that the baggage handlers
put your luggage into the bus.

Another sure thing about a group tour is that you
and your companions, perhaps all strangers at the beginning of the trip, will be friends by the end of your journey.

Tour Escorts

There are no guarantees, of course, but if you deal
with a well-established tour operator, chances are good
that the leader of your tour will be intelligent, charming,
diplomatic, informed, witty, capable, fun, and experienced. You hope!

The personality of your escort often sets the tone of
your trip. Tour operators are very much aware of the
impact escorts have on a tour, and they try to get the best.
A tour escort can make the trip so memorable that tourists will want to come back to the same company for their
next tour.

Escorts are the field representatives of the tour
operator and, as such, act as trouble shooters, advisors,
consultants, and a communication center. They are not
guides; they see that things run smoothly and you get
your money's worth.

If you are not satisfied with your room or are being
charged for food and services not ordered, your tour
escort will intercede and solve the problems. While it may
not be the escort's responsibility to stay behind with an ill
tourist, escorts on first class tour operations do what is
necessary to protect members of their group.

On the sightseeing portions of group tours, local
guides and drivers are provided. The guide may be with
you for one day or for the whole journey. The guide is
responsible for answering your on-site questions. Sometimes the driver wears two hats and acts as a guide also,
but not on a deluxe tour.

Cutting "Classes"

Just because you've paid for a tour doesn't mean you

have to climb every hill, see every church, eat every morsel of food, and go to every event. It's perfectly permissible not to do something if you are not up to it or it does not suit you. No one will fault you; you'll probably be admired for your convictions.

On a recent trip to Germany, officials of a gem-like medieval town invited a special group of tourists to climb the 365 stairs up to the town's centerpiece attraction—a 700-year-old town hall. Once on top, the special guests were to be feted with beer, white sausages, and a spectacular view of the walled city below.

The group of tourists included middle-aged and older people. Among them were two men who had had heart attacks within the last few years and who were not doing their exercises, a woman subject to angina attacks, and several others who were overweight and not in good physical condition.

The travelers who knew their limitations declined the invitation to visit the tower. The woman with angina went right up those stairs. An hour or two later she developed severe angina pain. A physician was called, and the good news was that she was able to continue with the trip, though her activities were limited for a day or two.

The woman's fellow travelers were sympathetic but critical of her for not being realistic about the state of her health. She could have put a pall on their trip.

Tipping on Tours

Escorts. The usual tip for the tour manager who is with you for the length of your trip is about $2 daily. If the escort does something special, add something extra.

Tour Guides and Drivers. On motorcoach trips of a day's duration, local guides get $1 a day, the driver about 75 cents. On tours of several days to a week or more, the guide's tip goes to $2 a day; and the driver's to $1 or $2. Some tours recommend that the driver get the same as the guide.

Host. On tours that "stay put," the host or hostess on call at your destination who has done a lot for you—arranging day trips, getting medications for you—should be tipped about $2 a day. If services to you were limited, $5 to $10 at the end of your stay would be a nice gesture.

Boning Up

A high school tennis coach was telling a friend about her forthcoming trip to Scotland. "What have you read about the country?" the friend asked. "Oh, I don't have time to do any reading. I just look for people who have done the research and stick with them." This hit or miss approach to a trip will never get that high school coach credits for getting the most out of her trip.

While the hope is that the tour guidebook is going to be a font of exciting and interesting information, you may not be that lucky. A poor guide, compounded by poor preparation on your part, will cheat you of the full value of your trip. When you know where you will be going, read books on the place or country you will be visiting. If you don't care about all the churches, museums, and monuments, don't buy a tour guide, but do find a book that provides a background on the way people in the area or country live and play.

Being a tourist doesn't mean you have to see everything in sight. Some people would rather walk the streets, browse in shops, sit around outdoor cafes, and watch or talk to people. It would help to learn a little about the people to better understand their ways.

Evaluating Group Tours

With so many tours available, what makes one trip more attractive or a better buy than another to the same destination?

Your travel agent can help make a determination, but don't leave it all up to the agent. Read the brochures with a critical eye, and read between the lines about things that are said and not said.

Gather together a number of different tour brochures covering the same area and do a little comparison shopping. Price should not be your only criteria, though you should cost out the price on a daily basis.

Divide the price by the number of days you are on the tour. If your tour starts at noon or dinner time, is that counted as a day? If it ends after breakfast, does the operator regard that as a day? Some operators count nights, not days.

Food is an essential element when computing the price of a tour. How many meals are offered? Do you have the choice of anything on the menu, or are you limited to selecting a table d'hôte menu (the blue plate special)? Is dinner a group event, or can you dine separately from the rest of the tour? Are you offered the option of dining around if you wish—that is, being given a choice of restaurants on an American plan (includes three meals)?

Keep in mind, too, that if the tour includes meals in Paris, New York, or San Francisco, food prices in big cities tend to be higher.

And what about the hotels and motels? What quality of accommodations are being offered? Are the hotels centrally located, or are they at a distance from where the action is? If you don't want to use public transportation, will it be too costly to take a cab to the sites you want to explore? Check with one of the hotel rating guides (AAA, Mobil Travel Guides, etc.) to get an idea of the quality of the accommodations.

The pace of a tour is very important. Are you going full speed ahead every day? Does the itinerary have you leaving at 8 A.M. daily to a new destination? If you're flying overseas, are sightseeing events scheduled as soon as you get off the plane, or is time provided for you to get some sleep and catch your breath? Reading a Lindblad Travel Inc. tour folder to the Far East, I noticed that two days were allotted for Tokyo at the outset of its tour so that tour members could recover from time zone jet lag. This is not wasteful of a tourist's time, but a good way to rest after a long plane journey. Experienced travelers know that rest at the beginning of a trip will assure you of plenty of energy for the rest of the trip.

Determine ahead of time how many people are taking the tour. Will there be two or three buses? If a tour is overly large, there are delays checking into hotels and getting into tourist attractions. When there's just one busload, there's more flexibility and greater ease. Deluxe tours usually limit the size of groups to about 20 people.

It's easier to travel with people of like interests, but it is interesting, too, to have a diverse group on a tour. Different backgrounds add an extra dimension to the experience.

Evaluating the Operator

How do you know if the tour you like is run by a reputable tour operator? You don't, unless you do some checking.

Membership in the United States Tour Operator's Association offers some assurance about your choice. Membership in the American Society of Travel Agents should, too.

The USTOA has very high eligibility requirements. An operator must be in business for at least three years and have no less than 18 references! In addition, the organization sets stringent requirements on insurance, liability, and financial responsibility. A million dollar Errors and Omissions policy pays the tourist in the event that a mistake was made in booking. It is akin to malpractice insurance for the medical and legal professions. If a tour operator promises a room with an ocean front room, that tourist had better get that room with a view, say officials of the USTOA.

Another determinant is how long the company has been in business. It's a safe assumption that firms delivering travel for many years will continue to do so. When it's a newer company, look to its auspices.

The usual link between you and the tour operator is your travel agent. What does your agent know about the tour operator and that company's ability to deliver its promises? If your travel agent is a knowledgeable professional who keeps up with the literature, you can count on his or her counsel. When you're not so sure how much your agent knows, continue your research.

Another clue as to reliability is a referral from a satisfied customer. Check, too, with the Better Business Bureau in your area. Ask if any complaints have been lodged against the tour operator. If the operator is a member of the American Society of Travel Agents, you can check with them, too.

Some tour operators don't belong to ASTA or USTOA. A list of members of the United States Tour Operators Association can be secured from USTOA, 211 E. 51st St., New York, NY 10022.

Fantasy for Sale

Anybody with something to sell is going to try to glamorize a product. It doesn't matter if it's cosmetics, a fur coat, or a frost-free refrigerator. A little hype is good for business. Tour operators with travel packages do the same thing. They have fantasy on their side.

Beautiful color photographs and exciting and glowing adjectives spark their copy with positives and obfuscate negatives. As a traveler, be wary of all those claims. Your hard-earned money and your vacation dreams are at stake.

As a general rule, look for the omissions, and read beyond the headlines. When an all-inclusive tour is advertised in a newspaper for a price that seems incredibly low, look twice. The tour operator isn't lying, but the price only includes the land portion. The real heavy of that tour is the air fare, which is barely mentioned. In the ad, "air fare extra" is in very small print. In a brochure, it's on another page.

Apart from the destination, the biggest come-on of any advertised tour is price. When you see one that looks exceptionally low, look for the asterisk right beside the price and find the small print (probably well-hidden) that explains it. "Per person based on double occupancy" means you must travel with a partner, each paying that low price and sharing the rooms. If you have no one to travel with, the price will be a lot higher. "Subject to availability" may mean that they have only five rooms at the advertised price. By the time you call, those rooms may be gone and you'll be asked to pay a higher rate. Other catch phrases are "valid on specific dates," "prices subject to change," "room tax not included," and— sweetest ploy of all—the effective date. It's good two days after the ad appeared and valid until a week later. Could you get your act together in such a short time?

For tours that tout the sun and warmth of the Costa del Sol in Spain, watch for the supplemental charges. You can be assured that the weather will be better when they charge a supplement.

When a tour brochure says a place is "easily explored by public transportation," the translation is, "you're on your own."

Exactly what do they mean when they say "tourist class"? Ask if tourist class means a shared bath.

Don't be impressed when they offer "meals and beverages aloft." Unless you're on a no-frills flight, these come with your ticket anyway.

When an ad for a cruise says "fly free," compare the price of the cruise with another like it. That free air fare is probably buried in the whole price of the package.

As a general rule, if conditions listed on the back of a tour brochure are so small that you require a magnifying glass to read them, and a law degree to interpret them, try another tour operator. My feeling, and I admit I'm prejudiced, is that a tour operator who puts conditions and disclaimers in fine print has something to hide. He or she owes it to the traveler to spell out conditions in a readable and understandable way. And on the subject of disclaimers, if you have a friend who is a lawyer, ask him or her to read the conditions of your tour contract. Tour operators may disclaim all responsibility for wrongdoings of suppliers (hotels, sightseeing buses, etc.), but it may not hold up in court, according to Thomas A. Dickerson, a New York attorney who has become a specialist in travel law, and has written the definitive book on the subject, *Travel Law*, for the legal profession.

Evaluation Checklist

Before you select a tour, evaluate it in terms of your own health, financial ability, personal preferences, and even prejudices. After reading the tour brochures, compare what is offered with the questions raised on the following checklist.

HEALTH CONSIDERATIONS

- ☐ If the trip involves a long transcontinental or trans-oceanic flight, does the tour allow time to recover from jet lag, or does the program commence immediately?
- ☐ Is the itinerary so fast-paced that you are in a different hotel each night? Packing and unpacking every day can be tiring. Two or more nights in one place will be easier on you physically and will allow you the time to absorb the atmosphere. You'll gain a clearer perspective on your travels.
- ☐ On the daily itinerary, when do events start? If you have to have your bags out and be ready to move every morning at 6 or 7 A.M., it's exhausting.
- ☐ If you have walking disabilities or heart or respiratory problems, study tours from the point of view of altitude, rough terrain, uphill attractions, or long stairways.
- ☐ Is there anything about the destination that might jeopardize your health—climate, sanitation, lack of medical facilities, etc.?
- ☐ Is your energy level up to the program offered?
- ☐ What arrangements can be made if you become too tired or ill to continue with the tour? Perhaps nothing, but ask.

VALUE FOR MONEY CONSIDERATIONS

- ☐ Is air fare included? If not, does the operator try to get you the lowest possible air fare?
- ☐ What's offered? Does the tour include fares, meals, taxes, transfers, sightseeing tours, special attractions?
- ☐ If you cancel, will you get your money back, or will you have to pay a penalty?
- ☐ Is the price guaranteed? Can the tour operator raise the price after you've paid?
- ☐ Compare different tours to the same destination. Which offers the best value? Count the number of sightseeing tours, special bonuses, meals, etc.
- ☐ If you're traveling alone, will the operator provide a roommate (if you want one) to spare you the expense of a heavy single supplement?

☐ Is trip insurance included in the price of the tour?

☐ If you are getting meals, do you have the run of the menu, or will you be limited to "blue plate specials"? Are meals included in big cities, where food prices are higher?

☐ If the trip goes awry, does the operator have insurance coverage to refund your money?

☐ How many optional sidetrips are there in the itinerary? How much extra will you have to pay for them? Are all admissions included?

☐ How far from home is the tour gateway (the place where the tour begins and ends)? How much extra will you have to pay to get there?

GENERAL CONSIDERATIONS

☐ Does the itinerary excite you? Does it go to the places you always wanted to see? Will you get what you want out of the trip?

☐ Will you be comfortable? Are the amenities offered compatible to your life-style?

☐ Will there be sufficient opportunities to shop and meet people?

☐ Does the tour operator give you tips on what clothes to take and what kind of weather you may encounter?

☐ How many bags are you allowed to take? Do you have to pay extra if you bring more?

☐ Will the tour operator provide free or low-cost additional equipment you might need—e.g., binoculars at an African game park, golf or tennis equipment?

☐ Do you know anyone who has recently taken the same tour or a similar one with the same operator?

☐ Are you familiar with the operator? Have you checked the company out with the Better Business Bureau or professional travel societies?

Types of Tours

The world is your oyster when it comes to finding a packaged tour. Pick a place at random, and chances are there's a tour already arranged waiting to escort you there. If you want to be specific and pinpoint a special interest, an in-depth travel experience is yours, too. All you have to do is name your subject.

Special Interest Tours

Tour operators, working closely with museum operators, food consultants, historians, archaeologists, and other specialists create itineraries for highly refined interests.

On special interest tours, not only do you see the broad outlines of the subject in its native locale, but you are taken behind the scenes. Local curators will guide you through a museum exhibit not yet available to the general public. On a music festival tour, you could be invited to all the rehearsals of orchestras and famous soloists. On special interest tours you may find yourself dining at a banquet in a centuries-old city hall or museum.

If a museum, zoo, or wildlife association organizes the trip, it will be more costly, but part of your payment is a tax-deductible contribution to their good works. Check your local or national non-profit organizations to see what trips they have on tap, or else ask your travel agent to find you a special interest tour. Check newspaper ads and travel literature for offered tours. Look for books and pamphlets that list operators running such tours. One such is the booklet, "Specialty Travel Index," updated twice yearly and selling for $3 a copy. Write Specialty Travel Index, 9 Mono Ave., Fairfax, CA 94930, or phone 1-415-459-4900.

Health-Related Tours

Some tours are keyed to special health problems of tourists. To avoid high mountain passes, you can find rail tours in Switzerland between Zurich and Geneva, a distance of 167 miles, which never go above 3,250 feet. The Swiss even make special arrangements for checking your luggage at a train depot to be delivered to your hotel. At the end of your trip in Switzerland, they can have your luggage accepted at train stations to be checked through to your U.S. port of entry. Services like these are not free, but they are part of tour services in Switzerland.

There are other tours designed for travelers who want more leisurely paced trips. Study the offerings of trips run by AARP, SAGA, Grand Circle Tours, and others. Carefully read tour brochures and see how long you stay in one place. Avoid one night stands. They are not relaxing.

U.S. Motorcoach Tours

The most popular of all tours are conducted by motorcoach in the United States. According to industry estimates, more than 10 million people took group tours by motorcoach in the U.S. last year. The popularity of motorcoach travel is understandable. So many places in this country have something special to offer. If it's not knockout scenery, then it's old-fashioned appeal, quaintness, ethnic vitality, homespun charm, nostalgic architecture, or even the razzle-dazzle of gambling meccas.

Motorcoaches can take you right into the heart of all this in relaxed comfort. From the large tinted windows of air-conditioned or heated buses, you watch the passing scenes and listen to the stories and legends about the more interesting places from your guide.

When you stop to see the sights you will find that Americans are all different close up. As the landscape changes, so do the people. And so does the food. The U.S. has its own brand of haute cuisine, a blend of native and imported styles. In Louisiana, French Acadians (originally from Nova Scotia), along with Spaniards, West Indians, and local Indian settlers, each tossed a little something into the pot to create unique Creole and Cajun cooking.

States close to the Mexican border serve up pots of tearful, five-alarm chili and bean dishes, and lunch or dinner out west from a chuck wagon beats eating in any five-star restaurant. Tour operators try to introduce travelers to regional fare.

Limited only by unfinished roads, motorcoach tours go just about everywhere. New England is an extremely popular tour objective, especially in the fall, when the leaves turn. The South, of course, is the most traveled of all. Almost everyone wants to see Florida's Disney World Epcot Center, Miami Beach, Palm Beach, and maybe even try the waters of the fountain of youth in St. Augustine. New Orleans is a magnet for motorcoach tourists, as are the great old plantation houses along the Mississippi. Other popular motorcoach destinations are the national park areas, California and the Northwest Pacific coast, desert oases in Arizona, and other places throughout the West.

Motorcoach trips are not all operated alike, alas. Some operators are not as skilled at offering the small touches that make a trip great. But there are a number of very good companies on the road. They pay attention to details. Because so many tourists like sitting in the front seat, thoughtful tour operators rotate seating so that all passengers get an opportunity to sit there. It's not only equitable, but mixing up the seating arrangements makes for a friendlier tour.

Another thoughtful bit of planning is the time tours begin in the morning. When there are long distances to travel, it may be necessary to get an early start. At other times, free mornings are not only restful but give travelers a chance to pursue local interests.

One tour operator, Tauck Tours, is particularly sensitive to guides who steer passengers to special shops. The company has a strict rule against that kind of conduct.

Selecting a U.S. Motorcoach Tour Operator

The motorcoach industry is not what it used to be. People used to go by bus because it was the cheapest way to travel. There were no frills. These days, motorcoach travel has become very upscale. Fashionable and rich folk can be found on motorcoach tours. There's a good reason for this. The equipment and ambiance are so much better now. Riding in a motorcoach is like being in a parlor car of a first class train. Seats are wider and more comfortable. Sometimes there are footrests and adjustable headrests, and carpeting covers the floor. In the very newest tour coaches you may find some seats that can be swiveled around so that four people may face each other for conversation or a game of cards.

Deregulation of the industry has spawned a whole generation of new operators anxious to get a piece of the

profits. Today there are about 2,500 companies operating
buses for charters and group tours from the U.S. to points
in Canada and Mexico. Some of the new people chartering
these are "Mom and Pop" tour operators. The Interstate
Commerce Commission no longer has any jurisdiction
over the licensing of these tour brokers. It's up to you or
your agent to check on their reliability. Some don't carry
insurance and are financially tenuous. If they have a cash
flow problem during your prepaid tour, guess who's left
holding the bag? You. It's important that you select a
reputable operator.

Travel agents should be able to help you, but if they
can't or won't, a good sign of reliability is membership in
the National Tour Association or the American Bus Association. Their logos, NTA and ABA, are signs of membership compliance with strict fiscal and ethical standards set
by the associations. Each member of the National Tour
Association must maintain a million dollar professional
liability insurance policy to cover errors and omissions.
The ABA, with almost 1,000 bus companies and 150 tour
operators, has its own set of protective insurance standards.

Tourists with legitimate complaints against member
companies should write to The American Bus Association, 1025 Connecticut Ave., N.W., Washington, DC
20036, or to the National Tour Association, 120 Kentucky
Ave., Lexington, KY 40502.

Motorcoach companies that run group tours are still
under the aegis of the ICC, and they must take out performance bonds.

Give some thought to the style and amenities of your
motorcoach tour. Here are a few tips to help in your
selection.

- Some motorcoaches are equipped with a refrigerator
  for cold drinks.
- Toilets on board come in very handy.
- Crowded bus trips are no fun. Ask how many pas-
  sengers will be on the bus.
- Rotational seating is a big plus. It's fairer.
- Frequent bus stops aid your comfort.

☐ A tour mix of people from all parts of the country can make the trip more interesting. Large operators tend to draw variety.

☐ Consider your own comfort and ease in evaluating a tour. Inexpensive tours may omit desired conveniences.

European Motorcoach Tours

Hundreds of different charter motorcoach companies crisscross Europe daily with busloads of holiday-bound Europeans. These comfortable motorcoaches are not only a very pleasant way of seeing a country, but they represent good value. There are many chartered buses with American travelers, too, such as those chartered by American Express, TWA, and the American Association of Retired Persons Travel Service. But if you would like to mix with Europeans, you can find an unlimited number of bus companies in this service. Reliable operators with inexpensive tours may be reserved in the U.S. through your travel agent.

Europabus is a semi-official motorcoach tour operator affiliated with a number of European railroads. It has been providing a variety of short and longer motorcoach tours since 1951, principally for the European market. It now has service to 18 countries from Scandinavian destinations down to Italy, and as far east as Hungary. Tours average about $50 a day, which in many cases includes board.

Because of its multinational makeup, Europabus has tour guides who speak a number of languages. That in itself should make it interesting for Americans who join their tours. Here's a chance to see the country, meet the Europeans, and pick up a few words in a foreign language, too.

Cosmos is another company with bus tours originating overseas. Its escorted tours average about $40 a day, higher in some countries, lower in others. Rates are also subject to seasonal variations. This company spells out in detail what you get for your money. American travelers who book Cosmos for overseas touring can take advantage of specially arranged low trans-atlantic air fares from a number of gateway cities in the States. Other com-

panies may do the same. Check them out with your travel
agent or write for more information.

Europabus, c/o Germanrail, 747 Third Ave., New York, NY 10017.
    Written inquiries about Europabus overnight tours will be an-
    swered; phone queries not encouraged.
Cosmos, 69-15 Austin St., Forest Hills, NY 11375 (1-800-221-0090; in
    New York State 1-718-268-7000).
AARP Travel Service, 5855 Green Valley Circle, Culver City, CA
    90230 (1-800-227-7885).
SAGA International Holidays, 120 Boylston St., Boston, MA (1-800-
    762-3413; in Massachusetts, 1-800-462-3322)

Special Note About Smoking

The growing militancy of American tourists about
smoking on public vehicles has resulted in the banning of
smoking on many U.S. tour buses. Tour operators who do
this provide more frequent rest stops to permit smokers
to light up. Most European motorcoach tours, however,
don't seem to care if passengers smoke, so when traveling
on motorcoach tours run by European operators, don't
expect smokefree buses.

Tours by Rail

One impediment to rail travel is the need to carry
your own luggage up and down stairways and across long
corridors and station platforms. There are still some porters around, but few people in the United States or in
other developed societies look forward to a career as a
baggage handler.

People who love train travel no longer have to stay
away. Escorted rail tours include baggage handling. Rail
tours are available in the U.S., in Europe, South America,
South Africa, India, and China, as well as other places.

There are very few tour operators conducting rail
tours in the U.S. Four Winds Travel, Inc. has been escort-
ing first class "rail cruises" into Mexico and Canada and
through the most scenic parts of the United States for a
number of years. These tours are almost completely all-
inclusive, providing about 77 percent of meals, as well as a
choice of sleeping acommodations on trains, first class
hotels, sightseeing, taxes, and even most tips.

Don't get the impression that rail tours use railroads

exclusively; they don't. Parts of the journey make use of motorcoaches, cruise ships, and even sightseeing from helicopters or small planes.

Solo travelers who want to avoid single supplements can join Four Winds' matching roommate service. If no suitable roommate is found, the double room is yours at half the double occupancy rate.

Riding the Rails Overseas

Even if Agatha Christie hadn't immortalized it in her book *Murder on the Orient Express,* that train would have carried off honors anyway for glamor, intrigue, and splendor.

In its time, the 100-year-old Orient Express train transported them all—royalty, spies, fancy ladies, millionnaires, political refugees, revolutionaries, and power brokers—to and from the various capitals of Europe. The aura of that glorious past still remains, and today's travelers looking for a little nostalgia are making the Orient Express one of the most popular train rides in Europe.

Society Expeditions, Inc., charters the vintage cars of the train for escorted tours. The 98 or so who take the 10-day tours between Paris and Istanbul can't help but be caught up in the train's special atmosphere of style and elegance. The train's appointments, Lalique glass, and mahogany and teak paneling set an opulent tone. Travelers sleep in comfortable rebuilt Wagons Lits cars dating back to the 20s and 30s. Gourmet meals are served throughout the "voyage."

"Happenings" describes what goes on at train stops in Reims, Salzburg, Vienna, Budapest, Brasov, and Istanbul. If it's not a special show or event, then it could be a private ball in a baroque palace, a performance of the Vienna Boys' Choir, or other classical entertainment. Glamor doesn't come cheap; the nine-day tour is about $4,500, the ten-day tour almost $5,000, double occupancy!

Society Expeditions, the same company that runs the Orient Express, runs other epic escorted train journeys, as exotic and deluxe as the vintage European trains— including the 19-day Trans-Siberia Special between Moscow and Mongolia, a 24-day trip from Paris to Peking, and the Imperial Peking Express Train through China. You can contact Society Expeditions at 723 Broadway East, Seattle, WA 98102 (1-800-426-7794).

By no means in the same class, but still a train tour, is TWA's Getaway two-week rail trip of Italy. Programmed for travelers who want a railroad experience, the tour provides rail transportation, hotels, baggage handling, and transfers from hotels to trains and planes. In between, however, the traveler is free to tour local stopovers on his or her own.

Shorter Rail Tours

It's not necessary to take an extended rail journey to experience the classic elegance of Europe's most celebrated trains. In Britain you can book at least seven different day trips on the Venice Simplon Orient Express. They are not inexpensive, from around $120 to over $150. This company, incidentally, is not affiliated with Society Expeditions, which runs the Orient Express from Paris to Istanbul.

Reservations may be made in the U.S. through a travel agent or by contacting Venice Simplon Orient Express, Suite 2841, One World Trade Center, New York, NY 10048 (1-212-938-6830; outside New York 1-800-524-2420).

For information on Japan's Bullet Train, contact the Japan National Tourist Office, and to learn about The Blue Train tours in South Africa, contact the South African Tourism Board. (See Appendix A.)

CHAPTER 8

Cruises—Leisure Afloat

From Ulysses to Eric the Red to Christopher Columbus and on through history, great adventures often started with a sea voyage.

For millions starting out on their own personal travel adventures, a cruise is the easiest, most relaxing, and most comfortable introduction to the wonderful world of travel. And now, cruising is all one-class.

The Joy of Cruising

Once you've unpacked your bags, you're set. Your stateroom becomes home sweet home for the duration of your voyage. Cruise ships have all the refinements of a deluxe resort hotel, and it's the combination of luxury resort living and the excitement of seeing exotic ports of call that make cruise vacations so special. When you are not visiting new ports, you are pampered and indulged by the ship's staff.

Eating is one of shipboard's preeminent pleasures. Food is abundant, enticing, and artistic. Even breakfasts get special treatment. Lamb chops and hamburger steaks often nudge out puffed rice and shredded wheat as early-morning choices.

Like Scarlett O'Hara, you'll never go hungry aboard today's cruisers. The next feast is never more than a few hours away. Between big meals there are little repasts, and should you get hungry at bedtime, there's another eye-appealing buffet awaiting you with cold cuts, salads, fruits, cheese, and pastries.

Room service is also included on most cruise ships. If you want breakfast in bed, or a midnight snack in your cabin, all you have to do is ask.

If for medical reasons you can't take advantage of all this abundance, luxury liners can produce special diets for you—low sodium, diabetic, whatever. Inform the liner about your dietary needs when you book passage.

A Small Town at Sea

Once you've paid for your cruise, all the big expenses have been taken care of—your stateroom, all meals and snacks, nightclub dancing, movies, plus the run of the ship's myriad facilities. Out-of-pocket expenses will be for tips, cocktails or wine, purchases on board the ship, and other personal needs. The cost of shore excursions and port taxes are also your responsibility.

Life aboard a cruise ship is like that in a small town. A daily newspaper provides news of the world in brief, weather reports, sports scores, and stock market quotations. Fancy boutiques sell clothes and luxury gifts at prices comparable to shops at duty-free ports of call.

For your tonsorial needs there's a barbershop and a beauty parlor. There's often a gym on board to work off the extra pounds gained in the dining room. Group calisthenics or aerobic exercise classes are arranged for people who want to stay fit.

If you want to post a letter, send a telex, or even call home, the communication center will connect you to your land interests. There's also a bank, a drugstore, and a library.

People nervous about their health can relax. Medical assistance is just a few cabins away. Every oceangoing vessel carrying more than 12 passengers is required by law to have a doctor on board. The physician will be an experienced doctor, probably on a year's sabbatical from his or her own practice.

In addition to regular office hours, the ship's doctor is on call 24 hours a day—and, yes, he or she does make cabin calls, and there is a charge. Ships also carry a nurse, and on longer journeys even a dentist. The longer and more deluxe the cruise, the larger the complement of medical personnel and facilities. All ships are equipped with apparatus for medical emergencies, and some even have an operating room. Chances are your only medical problem will be a cold or overindulgence.

And to Entertain You

Entertainment and education are very much a part of life on the high seas. Author-lecturers, historians, social scientists from think tanks, and money specialists are booked for talk sessions, and if you want to take classes there are a variety to choose from. Liners have been known to schedule classes in bridge, dancing, foreign languages, and even napkin folding.

Before disembarking at each port of call, a travel specialist will usually lecture you on what to see, do, and buy.

Evenings are filled with music and entertainment. Often celebrities from Broadway, television, and the nightclub circuit showcase their talents on the ship's big stage and off in lesser rooms. In addition to big bands, there are smaller combos to play for dancing or just listening.

Just so you don't miss anything, a daily calendar of events is slipped under your door. It not only tells you what's going on but suggests suitable attire, in case you aren't sure. Tipping, too, is the subject of a tactful directive.

You Are Never Alone

People traveling alone have no worries about being friendless. Companionship is built into the structure of shipboard programming. Cruise directors, with mission-ary zeal, mix and match passengers with such skill that sometimes on-board acquaintances flower into lasting friendships.

The dining room chief, too—called chief steward on some vessels, maitre d'hôtel on others—tries to seat compatible people together at mealtime.

Destinations

Cruises come in all lengths, styles, and themes, and they go to all places. You can sail away for a year and a day, or just two days. You can go absolutely nowhere (there are cruises to nowhere) or everywhere, travel by sea one way and come back by air; anything is possible.

Tourists take ships because they are fun and promise constant activity, others go to watch whales. The main attractions, however, are the destinations and getting there in the most comfortable way possible.

There are voyages on the high seas or on languid canals, on the mighty Amazon River or on calm lakes. You can sail off for a week or a weekend in Bermuda or Nassau for a short fix of tropical beauty, cruise the Mediterranean or the coasts of Europe, go transatlantic or transpacific, sail in and out of the Hawaiian islands, to Bora Bora or Mooréa in Tahiti, voyage up the Yangtze River, or go on a freighter, not knowing for sure where you will land.

The More Popular Destinations

The Caribbean and the west coast of Mexico are probably the most popular of all deep-water destinations in the wintertime. Alaska's Inland Passage attracts luxury ships in the summer, and cruises to Bermuda and the Bahamas are popular the year around.

If you choose the Caribbean, you'll find that almost every island is a different foreign country. Curaçao stands as a miniature Holland with better weather; Puerto Rico and Dominican Republic are the Spanish señoras; Barbados, Jamaica, Antigua, and the British Virgins are British-mannered with island overtones; St. Martin and Sint Maarten are a two-for-one bonus—one half French, the other Dutch; Haiti is French; and the U.S. Virgin Islands are U.S.A. with more than a dash of Danish.

Most of the island ports have beautiful fine white beaches with calm warm seas, making them ideal for swimming. Caribbean waters are unique for crystal clarity and turquoise-blue-sapphire colors.

Purse strings loosen naturally in this type of clime; even non-shoppers go shopping in Caribbean ports. Luxury merchandise comes to market on these islands from all over the world, and the buys are so good that people can't resist them.

Caribbean ports are served by many cruise lines from the East Coast. Included among them are Carnival Cruise Lines, Costa Cruises, Cunard, Norwegian Caribbean, Royal Caribbean, Princess Cruises, Holland America, Westours, and others. Some ships carry as few as 200 passengers; others as many as 1,400 or more. On a single day in St. Thomas you might count six different cruise ships in port!

Caribbean ports also include Gulf of Mexico destinations and the Yucatán peninsula of Mexico, gateway to the archaeological wonders of the Mayan civilization, which flourished around 600–900 A.D.

The Panama Canal, too, is a popular destination. Some ships cross the Canal, carrying passengers into the Pacific and along the west coast of Mexico, stopping at "Mexican Riviera" resorts like Acapulco and Puerto Vallarta before going on to Los Angeles and San Francisco. Cruise lines serving trans-Panama Canal destinations include Costa, Cunard/NAC, Sitmar, Royal Viking, Home Line Cruises, Royal Cruise Line, Princess, and more.

Cruising to Canada and Alaska

What Caribbean ports are to the East Coast, Canada, Alaska, and the west coast of Mexico are to travelers on the western side of the Rockies. From late April through September, luxury cruise vessels ply the waterways from Los Angeles and San Francisco to western Canada and Alaska. This northern routing passes through the protected waters of the Inland Passage. Cruise vessels stop at far northern ports of Ketchikan, Sitka, Skagway, and Juneau, and pass around the waters of the Glacier Bay National Monument.

Ice floes are an everyday occurrence on these Alaskan trips. It's not unusual to see a bald eagle "bumming" a ride on a mass of ice. Seeing a piece of glacier break off from the cliffs of ice that hug the shoreline of Glacier Bay National Monument is another matter. It could be the most dramatic moment of your trip.

Ketchikan's special attraction is its ornately carved totem poles, as tall as hemlock trees. Sitka exudes an atmosphere of old Russia. The city was Russian-held territory until 1867. At any of the ports, fashionable frontier types in their fringed cowhide jackets add to the ambience of the Old West-Alaskan style. Towns near the sea have wooden sidewalks, and it's obvious all along the northern route that oil, not gold, is the new economic force.

Because Alaska is so far north, temperatures are moderate during summer. Days are cool, and summer evenings are chilly enough for sweaters. As for sun, you get more than your money's worth. The sun sets at 10:30 P.M. and later as the summer progresses, and it rises again at 3:30 A.M.! The midnight sun is a reality in this area of the world.

Many lines ply the Alaska route. Royal Viking, Sitmar, Cunard/NAC, and Princess are just a few of the most luxurious ones.

Cruises to Mexico

In the winter, some of the same luxury class ships that voyage to Alaska and Canada turn around and sail south to Mexico for short cruises. Mexico is the new hot attraction in cruise destinations. Mexican resorts along the west coast from Baja California down to Puerto Vallarta and Acapulco are well developed with good hotels, restaurants, and beautiful boutiques; and Mexico's prices are reasonable compared with those at other destinations.

The Baja peninsula is especially interesting to whale watchers, since the gray whales have chosen this area to spend their winters, playing and breeding. More than 15,000 migrate annually from Alaska to this region.

A Little More Exotic

With more than 70 percent of the world's surface covered by ocean water, it's easy to see why so many exotic lands are served by ship. You can sail to China or voyage in and out of Aegean and Mediterranean ports. Voyages through the fjords near the North Cape of Norway and cruises between the Hawaiian islands are extremely popular with people past 50.

You can travel by ship just about anywhere—to South American ports or Indonesian ports. Not all ships will provide "resort" services, but you are sure to have an interesting time, and perhaps unique experiences.

Closer to Home

It's not necessary to venture out into the deep blue of the Atlantic or the Pacific to enjoy a cruise. Cruise vacations are now offered within the immediate sphere of North America. Smaller ships, yachts, clipper ships, paddlewheelers, and other vessels are now taking tourists into areas once accessible exclusively by autos, motorcoach tour, and trains.

On the East Coast, opportunities for cruises have never been greater. Cruise service extends from Miami up to Maine, and then inland from Baltimore down the Intracoastal Waterways to such interesting ports as Savannah, Yorktown/Williamsburg, Morehead City, Charleston, and Hilton Head Island. The Chesapeake Bay, waters off the coast of Maine, the Hudson River, and even New England have been newly charted for cruise passengers.

If you wanted to travel even further north into eastern Canada, cruises are available for those destinations, too. The St. Lawrence River, the Saguenay Fjord, and little-known areas around Halifax and Nova Scotia are all served by cruise ships. Wherever there is a waterway big enough, there's a cruise company eager to try the waters.

The American Canadian Line operates cruises to Canadian ports as well as voyages on the Intracoastal Waterway from West Palm Beach to Warren, Rhode Island. Ships can accommodate from 70 to 80 passengers. Inland passage voyages from Baltimore to Savannah as well as to southern destinations and also New England can be booked on American Cruise Lines. Their ships take from 49 to 128 passengers. The Clipper Cruise Line yachts, with room for 102 passengers, offer a variety of itineraries out of Boston, Baltimore, Fort Lauderdale, Savannah, and the Virgin Islands.

River Cruises

Even if you're a confirmed landlubber, you can get in on the luxury and excitement of a cruise vacation. If you're the type who gets nervous when the land disappears over the horizon, how about considering a trip on one of the world's great rivers?

Quiet Flows the Mississippi

Although its banks are never out of view from either side of the paddlewheelers, mid-stream on the Mississippi is as far removed as you can get from reality. Fantasy plays a large part in cruising on the Mississippi. Huck Finn and his pals probably had a lot to do with that.

Two paddlewheelers offer Mississippi River cruise service—the famous old *Delta Queen*, with accommodations for 192, and its more modern sister ship, the 406-passenger *Mississippi Queen*. A third ship, not a paddlewheeler, has joined the Mississippi service. The *Savannah* (American Cruise Lines) is a new sight on the muddy Mississippi.

History book destinations—Baton Rouge, Vicksburg, Natchez, and New Orleans—are featured stops. Your most difficult decision on these cruises is which Creole dish to select. The rest of the daylight hours in between port excursions is yours to watch the river traffic, count the number of barges, watch people fishing off the levees, and glimpse the remains of old plantation or ante-bellum homes half hidden by moss-heavy trees.

Cruise prices range from about $115 to $370 a day per person. Your travel agent can provide more information on these cruises.

Romantic Rivers in Europe

While many in the United States are just discovering the pleasant adventures of cruising on a river, Europeans have been enjoying this kind of vacation for years.

Some trips are on 200-passenger luxury liners on the Rhine, Moselle, and Danube rivers. Others are on small canal barges with room for just 6 to 24 passengers.

The Rhine is in the heart of romantic Germany, and from the river boats you can see centuries-old towns and villages, castles of twelfth-century vintage, complete with moats and drawbridges, and lush vineyards that produce the best wines of the country. Passengers won't miss a single fairy-tale castle at meal time; the windows of the dining room are extra large just for that purpose.

On all cruises, passengers can get off the boat at frequent stops, walk around the town, drink some of the local wine, and even have time for a sightseeing trip to a nearby castle.

The winding Moselle River, between Koblentz and Trier, is another cruise possibility. This river is also in the heart of Germany's wine country.

The KD German Rhine Line operates a great many of these river boats. Four- or five-day cruises run about $590 to $715 per person; shorter cruises from $320 to $440.

Over on the Danube, a new 215-passenger ship, the *Danube Princess*, is plying the not-so-blue 1,776 mile river from Bavaria, through Austria, Czechoslovakia, and Hungary. The ship, run by the Exprinter Cruises and the P & O Cruises of London, operates one-week cruises. Rates are from about $755 to $1,665 per person.

Barge About Europe

Floating trips on the tranquil small rivers and canals of England, France, Belgium, and the Netherlands provide a scenic waterway tour through some of the most historic and beautiful regions of Europe. These riverways, too, small for larger vessels, are the perfect size for house barges and their limited numbers of passengers. Included among the many companies offering such cruises are:

Floating Through Europe, Inc., 271 Madison Ave., New York, NY
    10016 (1-800-221-3140; in New York State 1-212-685-5600).
Horizon Cruises, 7122 West Main St., Belleville, IL 62223 (1-800-
    851-3448). Offers barge and ballooning cruises in France.
Salt and Pepper Tours, Inc., 200 Madison Ave., New York, NY 10016
    (1-212-692-9644 in New York City or collect from Canada; 1-
    800-522-6558 in New York State; 1-800-223-1222 in rest of
    U.S.).

These luxury barges can tie up anywhere, permitting
passengers to roam the streets of tiny hamlets, browse
through village shops, sip coffee or cognac with locals,
and really absorb the ambience of small European towns.

Meals are taken on these boats, and necessary supplies and fresh fruits and vegetables are brought to the
boats daily by a car that follows the meandering routes of
the barges. Each tour usually has its own chef.

Barge cruises cost about $230 per day, based on
double occupancy. Prices vary with the seasons and the
length of the cruise. All meals and wines are usually
included.

Nile River Cruises

One of the more exotic cruises is found in Egypt,
which in the last few years has become a very popular
destination. Traveling up the Nile on a river boat is a
convenient and comfortable way of seeing the best of
Egypt—the tombs and temples of the Pharaohs. Fantas-
tically-carved stone walls tell the stories of ancient
civilizations.

The boats themselves, a far cry from Cleopatra's
royal barges, are air conditioned and have swimming
pools, television, and private showers in each room. Hilton and Sheraton both operate boats on the Nile, with
passenger capacities ranging from about 96 to 150. Other
companies, less well-known in the U.S., also run Nile
cruises. The price range for a five day–four night cruise is
about $372 to $940, double occupancy, depending on
season.

At each stop, you'll get plenty of local color, including
hoards of small boys selling shards of pottery (which they
claim to be ancient, of course), scarab rings, carved

turquoise-like necklaces, caftans, and "treasures" right from King Tut's tomb or some other royal tomb. These children are very sharp traders and play the game extremely well. If you see something you like, buy it; you'll never see it anywhere else. But don't expect to pick up any genuine treasures, and never accept the first price.

Adventure Cruises

The Amazon and Yangtze rivers, the waters of the Red Sea, the Galápagos Islands, and the Great Barrier Reef are becoming popular cruising destinations for a growing number of travelers seeking adventure. As people gain more travel experience, they want to extend their horizons to some of the more remote parts of the world.

Some travelers who look for these adventures are well past their 50s, even into their 80s. Tour operators who cater to them emphasize exploration, wild life, nature, history, and culture. Experts are often hired to lecture on the fine points of what's to be seen and experienced on these off-the-beaten-path cruises.

Society Expeditions and Lindblad Travel use smaller vessels for some of their cruises, while others, like Sun Line Cruises, provide passengers with a super deluxe cruise ship environment. On Amazon River cruises, the 620-passenger *Stella Solaris* is used. From the decks of this vessel, passengers see the lushness of life along the Amazon and the not-so-unusual sights of 70-pound fish leaping out of the waters.

Cruises to these unusual destinations can run from $2,500 to more than $20,000. It varies with the length of the cruise, the cost of getting to the ship, and the kind of accommodations.

Tramp Steamers

Travelers who are fearless, healthy, free spirited, and content with a book or their own company might enjoy the adventure of sailing aboard a freighter.

While cargo ships with passenger service are slowly

being phased out, there are still about 80 vessels continuing to provide this service. Staterooms are air conditioned and have private bathroom facilities. Cargo ships provide laundry rooms (you do your own), reading rooms, a library, free deck chairs, and simple fare for meals. The lines will not accommodate passengers on special diets. Only up to 12 passengers can be accommodated.

At one time freighters were the least expensive way to travel. Today, you can't expect the same kind of price break; freighters are just a shade less costly than a cabin on a regular luxury cruise liner. The daily cost runs from $60 to $135. There is no entertainment, except movies, and very few amenities. Some ships, like those of the Ivaran Lines, have small swimming pools.

While everyone else is lifting age barriers because older people are healthier, freighters still have a cap on age. Some will not carry passengers over 82; others set a lower age limit. All require a medical certificate attesting to the good health of passengers 65 and over. There are no physicians assigned to cargo vessels.

And to make things even more difficult, you will not get a firm commitment from the line about ports of call or even a day of arrival. The first priority of a cargo line is cargo, not passengers.

If you can stay loose, the ports you stop at may be surprises. Subject to the vagaries of their business, crowded ports, weather, and changes of schedules, freighters can end up in places you never dreamed about visiting. These trips could truly be an adventure.

Opportunities for freighter voyages are shrinking every year. With profits in mind, cargo lines have taken to containerizing cargo. It now takes a day or two, or even less, to discharge or take on containerized cargo. So little time in port makes these trips less desirable.

Because there are so few freighters available, long waiting lists exist. Companies suggest you send a letter telling when you are available to travel. If someone cancels out at the last minute and you are free to go, you can book passage. Voyages can be from one to three or four months.

Companies offering some passenger service on cargo vessels include the following.

☐ American President Lines Vagabond Cruises (out of West Coast ports)
☐ Delta Line (from Philadelphia to the west coast of South America)
☐ Ivaran Lines (from Baltimore and Gulf Coast ports to the east coast of South America and Caribbean ports)
☐ Lykes Lines (with 40 ships; from New Orleans and other Gulf ports to the Far East, the west coast of South America, eastern and southern Africa, and the Mediterranean)
☐ Polish Ocean Lines (from New York or Baltimore to Gdynia)
☐ Prudential Lines (New York to Romania and Mediterranean ports)
☐ Yugoslav Great Lakes Line (Montreal to Mediterranean and Adriatic ports)

Travel agencies specializing in freighter travel include the following.

TravelTips, P.O. Box 188, 163–09 Depot Road, Flushing, NY 11358 (1-212-939-2400)

General Steamship Corporation, 400 California St., San Francisco, CA 94104 (1-415-772-9200)

Pearl's Travel Tips, 175 Great Neck Rd., Great Neck, NY 11021 (1-212-895-7646)

The TravelTips agency also sponsors a club for interested travelers. The $25 annual membership fee includes a bi-monthly magazine. Another club, Freighter Travel Club of America, publishes *Freighter News* and sponsors club cruises. For details, write the club at P.O. Box 12693, Salem, OR 97309.

Traveling in Class

With about 84 luxury ships now in cruise service from the United States, it's difficult for a newcomer to cruising to know which ship and which cruise would be more enjoyable.

Ships, like people, have different personalities, different styles, and different ethnic makeups. Some attract the very young, others the more affluent, while some appeal to a combination of both. Ships, too, reflect the crews' nationality, be it Italian, French, English, Spanish, Portuguese, or Scandinavian.

Some ships are very formal, others casual and light-hearted. While ambience is important, cost, ports of call, and port of origin are the important factors in choosing a cruise.

Since no one but a professional travel agent or a ship buff could keep up with the constant buying, selling, and refurbishing of the many ships in service, rely on the experts to help you make a choice. Travel writers who cover ships are in a good position to help if you follow their stories in newspapers, magazines, and books. A free booklet, *Answers to the Most-Asked Questions About Cruises*, is available from Cruise Lines International Association, 17 Battery Pl., New York, NY 10004.

Here are some questions you might ask yourself or your travel agent before selecting a cruise.

- ☐ Do all the ports of call appeal to you?
- ☐ What is the ratio of staff to passengers? The higher the ratio, the better the service you will get on the ship.
- ☐ What kind of seas will you encounter at the time of the year you select for your cruise? Even if the weather is warm, might the seas be rough?
- ☐ Will your ship tie up at a dock at ports of call, or will it be necessary to transfer to a tender to go ashore? (While burly seamen hold you steady as you climb into the tender, it's not too much fun for the less agile, especially in rough seas.)
- ☐ Can the ship accommodate people on special diets if necessary?
- ☐ Do you have to take shots or malaria pills for any of the ports of call?
- ☐ How much will shore excursions cost? What port taxes can you expect? Does the ship have a no-tipping policy?
- ☐ What special facilities does the ship have—gym, medical equipment, etc.?

□ Is there a dress code on the ship?
□ What nationality is the crew? (It will determine the kind of food served.)
□ Will the cruise line absorb your air fare to the port of embarkation and back? Will the ship provide transfers from the airport to the dock?
□ Are there any discounts available? Specials for seniors?
□ How is the ship's sanitation rated by the Public Health authorities? If your travel agent doesn't know, find out yourself by writing to U.S. Miami Public Health, Chief of Sanitation and Vector Control Activity, Quarantine Division, 1015 North America Way, Miami, FL 33132 (1-305-350-4307).
□ If you should have to cancel, what is the cruise line's policy about refunds and penalties?
□ On ocean-bound vessels, ask about tonnage. It may make a difference to how queazy you might feel on the open seas.
□ How long do you stay in each port?

When Cost Is an Object

The accommodation you choose, the season you travel, the luxuriousness of the vessel, and the length of your voyage will determine the price of your cruise. Minimum, or least expensive, staterooms are the first to be sold out. There's a good reason for this. There are very few minimum accommodations. Book your reservations early. Standard cabins are also limited in number. If, for economy's sake, you are thinking of choosing an inside room (without windows), give it more consideration. Some people get claustrophic in rooms without windows.

Cruises vary in cost from a low of $65 per person per day to $4,000. As a rule of thumb, you can expect to spend about $160 to $220 per person per day on an average cruise. If you're computing costs, don't forget to add port taxes and your shore excursions. These are not absorbed by the line.

Lower cruise fares are available through clubs and organizations. The American Association of Retired Persons and the AAA are among those offering members discounts on cruises. Cruise consultants Landry and

Kling, Inc., 232 Madison Ave., New York, NY 10016, offer "Cruise Advantage" fares, available by or through prearrangement with organizations. Discounts can amount to 10 to 25 percent off cabin prices.

(For additional suggestions on how to get lower cruise fares, see the section on "Making Waves in Cruise Costs" in Chapter 6.)

Selecting a Stateroom

Ocean-going cruise passengers today don't have to worry about which side of the ship their cabin should be on. All cruise ships are air conditioned. Other factors, however, should be considered in requesting a stateroom— cost, convenience, and layout.

Study the ship's deck plan and cabin layouts to see how rooms are furnished and equipped. Some rooms have a lower bed and an upper berth you have to climb up to. Others have double beds, twin beds, two lower beds, and sitting rooms convertible to bedrooms.

The majority of staterooms have showers. Some of the more expensive cabins come with private tub baths.

With comfort still on your mind, consider which part of the ship your stateroom should be on—bow (forward, or front), aft (stern, or back), or mid-section. From the point of stability, the mid-section is probably the best. In rough seas, you might feel the sway in both forward or aft sections and on the top deck, which, incidentally, is the most expensive; it's where the view of the sea is the best from your porthole or window.

If you want complete privacy during daytime, don't select an outside stateroom on a deck with a wraparound promenade. Passengers on that deck can walk by and peer into your stateroom through the porthole. (Portholes do have curtains, however.)

Noise is another factor that might influence your choice of stateroom location. Some ships are not well insulated. You might hear the disco music if your room is located directly under the dance floor.

Convenience to Facilities

If walking long distances is not exactly in your game

plan, ask for a stateroom near the elevator or close to the dining room or other public rooms.

Some people like taking a dip in the pool every day. If that appeals to you, request a cabin in the aft section of the ship close to the swimming pool. It would eliminate the need for walking through the ship in your swim togs.

People who like to be first off the ship when it comes into port might choose a cabin on the lobby floor to almost guarantee a quick getaway.

Each ship is different, but minimum, standard, deluxe, and superior cabins on ocean-going cruise ships are the usual classifications as to the space and location of your stateroom.

Minimum-priced staterooms are the least expensive and may come with or without portholes or windows. The cheapest, of course, will be without portholes.

Standard rooms, too, come with or without windows. Outside rooms will cost more than those without portholes.

Deluxe is the top accommodation on some ships. When it is the best the ship has to offer, it will be an outside room amidships, usually on the top deck, with portholes or windows and a tub and a shower (equivalent to the superior stateroom). Inside rooms also come in deluxe class, but staterooms are larger.

Superior accommodations could have both a bedroom and a sitting room, with windows, tub and shower, plus features of deluxe staterooms.

When Do You Eat?

One of the things you do when you board your luxury cruise ship for the first time is to make your dining room reservations. (On some ships you can pre-book your seating.) Most large ships have two seatings because they can't accommodate all the passengers at the same time. The more luxurious ships have only one seating. On two-seating ships, the first shift is for early birds. Breakfast is usually served at about 7:30 A.M., lunch at 12:15, and dinner at 6:30 P.M. The early dinner seating will get you out of the dining room in time to catch an early show or take part in other early evening activities.

Passengers who want to stretch out their dinner with cocktails first, or who prefer to dine late, will be more comfortable with the second seating. They won't miss any activities, because shows are repeated for the late crowd. Second-serving meal times are about 8:30 A.M., 1:30 P.M., and 8:15 or 8:30 P.M.

Special Dining Room Tips

☐ Choose a large table if you're alone. You'll have a better chance of finding compatible people. Stay away from tables for four unless you know and like the other people.

☐ If you want to be a twosome, ask for a table for two.

☐ When you find you don't like your seat companions, ask the maitre d' to change your table. Do it very early in the cruise.

☐ If you are having a birthday or anniversary and want some special cake or dessert, you can arrange it free of charge just by asking.

Shore Excursions

Shore excursions are not usually included in the price of your cruise. Four-hour sightseeing tours can start at about $10 per person. If you can get together a few people, you might think about hiring a cab and doing your own tour with the cab driver's help. This alternative is good for people who have done some reading about the destination and can ask the driver questions. Renting the cab will give you a little more liberty in stopping where you like.

Getting the Most Out of Your Cruise

The choice is yours. Will it be simple pleasures, like sitting in a deck chair watching the sea, or would you prefer taking part in the manifold activities offered aboard? You can go either way and have a good time, but a combination of both is best.

If you can, take part in the activities aboard the ship. Whether it's shuffleboard tourneys, Ping-Pong, or taking advantage of the educational features, participation will enhance your journey. Come out into the night, too, even

if you don't dance. (Dance lessons are often given on
board a ship.)

Who's Who on a Ship

With so many employees aboard a ship, it's difficult
to know what each of the officers does. Some ships com-
bine functions; others separate them. For example, one
ship may have a bank, while on another, the purser's
office handles money. Differences exist, but here's a list
of some of the personnel you will notice on board the
vessel.

The Captain. This is the one person in charge of the whole
ship, responsible for getting it safely through all kinds
of seas. Your happiness and welfare are the captain's
responsibility and primary concern.

Staff Captain. This person takes over when the captain is
not available and is also in charge of operational
officers.

Chief Engineer. This person's office is the engine room
where the responsibility for getting the ship underway
and back is managed.

Ship's Doctor. He or she is a licensed physician, and may
have a staff of nurses as assistants.

Chief Radio Officer. The communications chief handles
overseas calls, telegrams, and other overseas communications for passengers as well as for the ship's officers
and crew.

Hotel Manager. Yes, that's right. Ships are referred to as
floating resorts. The hotel manager is involved with
the resort aspect of the ship—your stateroom, meals,
and entertainment. When there is no hotel manager,
there's a chief steward who assumes these responsibilities as well as seating you in the dining room.

Chief Purser. This officer is all things to all passengers
because he or she handles money on the ship. The
purser is in charge of changing your traveler's checks
and keeping valuables in a safe deposit box. The
purser's office also assigns cabins, issues informational
messages to the passengers, takes care of mail, and is
the complaint bureau.

Cruise Director. In charge of all the entertainment and fun and games, he or she is often assisted by a host and a cruise staff.

Captain of the Dining Room (or maitre d'). This person is responsible for the smooth running of the dining room. Sometimes there are also sectional captains, each one in charge of one section of a large dining room.

Who's Who—to Tip

Here comes that old problem again of how much and who to tip. It's much easier on larger cruise ships because the guidelines are usually spelled out. The lineup is as follows.

Room Steward or Stewardess. Fancy names for houseman or maid. They will make up your room, change the towels, clean the bathrooms, etc. These people may also be called Cabin Stewards or Cabin Attendants. The usual tip is $2.50 a day per person.

Dining Room Stewards. A sea-going waiter. The tip is about $2 per person per day, plus half of that for the busboy.

Wine Steward. When the steward brings you the bottle of wine you order, the tip should be about 15 percent of the price of the bottle.

Night Steward. Since you're not paying anything extra for the ice cream, cookies, or sandwiches you order in your room at midnight, you could tip a dollar or more for the services provided.

Deck Steward. First day out, ask the deck steward to save you a deck chair near the pool area or wherever else you might want to relax. A $2 tip at the outset is fine. With that show of generosity, the steward might see to it that others don't occupy your chair. The steward also serves drinks on deck. If the services are pleasant and friendly, $10 would be nice at the end of a 14-day trip, $5 for a seven-day cruise.

Bartender, Hairdresser, Masseuse, etc. Use the same guidelines you would at home. If the ship is very deluxe, add a little extra to your tips, especially if you come from a town where tipping is less generous.

Take sneakers or crepe-soled shoes. Not only are they comfortable, but they are helpful in walking up and down the ship's outside stairways. They are also easier on the feet in walking on cobblestones on shore.

Inform the ship about special diets. Remember to advise the ship before booking of any dietary problems you may have.

Take sunscreens. Sunburn can be especially severe on the high seas. Take a hat that won't blow off and plenty of suntan lotion. Some drugs make the skin more sensitive to the sun's rays; ask your doctor about that. Also ask your physician about sun, medications, and alcohol.

Get advice on mal-de-mer. Don't forget to ask your physician what to do if you get a little queazy on a rolling sea. Ships do have an ample supply of motion-sickness medicine.

CHAPTER 9

Traveling Overseas

A visiting group of American teachers was greeted on arrival in China by a delegation of their counterparts. The leader of the teachers' group introduced his spouse to the chief of the delegation by saying, "This is my wife, Sylvia."

Beaming, the Chinese leader turned to his group and said to them in English, "This is Mrs. Wife."

Language misunderstandings and misinterpretations occur all the time between peoples of different tongues, but it's these little mistakes that often color overseas travel experiences with warmth, friendship, and humor.

No matter how much you love your country, the ultimate travel experience is visiting a foreign land, where culture, history, people, and even food are different enough to create an interesting and exciting adventure.

Whether your dream is to see the Eiffel Tower you've heard so much about, to track lumbering rhinos in an African game park, to explore the mysteries of the Far East, or to be serenaded by a mariachi band in Mexico, a foreign trip requires some extra thought, preparation, and paperwork.

To fully appreciate your experience, you'll want to learn a little in advance about the destination and its

154

people. Reading newspaper stories and magazine articles about the country's political and social conditions will help you understand and have empathy with the problems of its people. A phrase book of the country's language will help you learn some words that could enrich a chance encounter.

Getting to know different foods will please your palate, learning the different currencies will make daily negotiations easier, and knowing the local traditions and customs in advance is the surest route to friendship.

Sending flowers when invited to dinner, taking your shoes off when stepping into temples and mosques when appropriate, covering bare shoulders in churches are just some of the things you should learn about customs in countries before going there. People respond positively to your respect for their customs.

Passports and Visas

Your passport!

The very words signal a glamorous flight of fancy, a beginning of a great adventure. Even the most sophisticated are not inured to the excitement and thrills of that first step toward a far-off adventure.

The United States requires U.S. citizens to have a passport to leave and to reenter the country after a visit to most foreign lands. Mexico and Canada are exceptions, as are some islands in the Caribbean. Most foreign countries require visitors to have a valid passport.

So how do you go about getting one?

If you've never had one before, apply in person to a passport agency with some proof of citizenship—a birth certificate, a baptismal certificate, or any affidavit stating that you were born in this country or became a citizen. If you changed your name through marriage, bring your marriage certificate, too.

People born outside the United States will need naturalization papers or proof of citizenship, plus other proof of identity. A driver's license with a photo and a signature, present or former work identification with a photo, or any other identification that describes you and has your signature must be brought with you.

If you don't have this kind of documentation, bring a witness who has known you for no less than two years (a spouse is acceptable). Your witness, too, must carry identification. You should also bring a voter's registration card, a credit card with your signature, or any other signed document that identifies you.

When applying with your witness or identification documents, you must bring two identical photos measuring 2 by 2 inches. They should be close-up photos of your face, from your chin to the top of your head. Pictures can be in black and white or in color—and, yes, you can smile; you don't have to look like you're in a police lineup. All the passport agency wants is a photo that looks like you. Don't wear a hat, dark glasses, uniforms, or anything that obscures or alters your physical appearance. Vending machine photos are not acceptable. Get a photographer to take your passport pictures, and while you're at it have additional copies made. You'll never know when you may need them. They'll come in handy if you need photos for visas. Should your passport be lost, having extra photos will expedite the process of replacement.

For a first passport, the fee is $42. Apply at the passport agencies in any of the following cities: Boston, Chicago, Honolulu, Houston, Los Angeles, Miami, New Orleans, New York, Philadelphia, San Francisco, Seattle, Stamford, Ct., and Washington, D.C. Look in the phone book under U.S. Government Offices, State Department.

In other places, ask local post office authorities where you can get an application and where it can be processed. They can tell you which federal and state courts of record are authorized to process passports.

If you had a passport and it expired more than eight years ago, you will have to go through the same procedure as someone applying for the first time. More recently expired passports can be renewed by mail. The cost is $35. To renew, you will be required to fill out another application, which you can obtain from any of the passport agencies. Get another set of photos and submit these with your expired passport. Send it to the Passport

Agency, U.S. Department of State, Washington, DC 20524, or the passport agency nearest your home. (The addresses are on the back of the application.) Send it by certified mail, and request a return receipt. Take heart, the $35 or $42 you pay will keep your passport valid for 10 years!

When you start thinking about overseas travel, apply for your passport. It's not necessary to have exact plans, unless, of course, you are applying to visit countries that have no diplomatic relations with the U.S. It takes time to get a passport—up to a month or more, so don't delay. During winter months, when travel is somewhat down, you stand a better chance of getting it faster. If you get your passport early enough, you'll have ample time to get all your visas should you require them.

For further information about foreign travel in general or travel to Eastern European countries, write to the Bureau of Consular Affairs, Department of State, Washington, DC 20520.

Your American passport is the most important document you carry when you leave the country. It identifies you as a citizen of the United States, and it eases your way in traveling from country to country. With this document, you have a call on the U.S. diplomatic service abroad for help in times of threatening political unrest, wars, earthquakes, and other disasters. That navy blue document can help in other ways, too. If you use your credit card for large purchases or seek additional cash, your passport serves as your best personal identification.

Hotels in some countries ask that you leave your passport overnight when you register. They submit the passport data to the police or other authorities. If you're traveling with a tour escort, he or she will be sure you get your passport back. When you're on your own, remember to pick up your passport the very next day. You can't travel without it.

Visa Requirements

A visa is another little complication for travelers. It is a foreign government's official permission for you to enter and visit their country. Comparatively few countries now require visas of American citizens, but some still do, including Japan, Egypt, Nepal, India, and Eastern European countries.

Getting a visa is easy for those who live in large cities like New York, Washington, Chicago, Los Angeles, New Orleans, and San Francisco, where foreign governments maintain consular offices that process visas.

If you are on a group tour or your trip is being arranged by a travel agent, sometimes the agent will get your visas for you or tell you how and where to obtain them. Independent travelers, however, have no such option; they must get the visas themselves. If you don't live in a city where a consular office is located, send for a visa application, fill it out, and then mail it along with your passport and whatever photos and fees are required to the nearest consular office. (Addresses of foreign consular offices are in the Congressional Directory in your library.) Certified mail is best. If your trip entails getting visas from a number of countries, begin this process at least three months before your planned departure. It all takes time!

Along with visa requirements, foreign governments sometimes oblige you to have certain immunizations to protect their nationals from communicable diseases. Governments also want to prevent any health risks (malaria, cholera, etc.) you might encounter in their country. See Chapter 10 for a full explanation of the health aspects of travel.

Countries That Require Visas

An up-to-date list of countries that require visas is available from the U.S. Department of State, Bureau of Consular Affairs, Washington, DC 20520. That office will direct you where to apply and tell you what fees and supporting documents you need.

Visa fees are often waived for U.S. citizens. When there is a charge, fees usually cost from $6 to $10, but could be as high as $24.

A less formal, but no less official, document is the tourist card, used in lieu of a visa. An airline or official office of the country will inform you when you need one.

Mexico requires a tourist card. Usually airlines, bus companies, etc., will supply them, as will the country that requires them. There's a minimal fee of $1 or $2.

The High Cost of Staying in Touch

Phoning Home

Staying in touch from abroad by telephone can be a very costly luxury. Hotels around the world have been known to impose a huge surcharge on overseas long distance phone calls from your room. Some charges are more than 30 percent over the actual cost of the call itself!

A traveler from New York State called home from his Munich hotel, and the $64 phone call ended up on his hotel bill as $352. German and Swiss hotels are the worst offenders, followed by France and Italy.

Because of customer complaints, AT&T worked out a Teleplan agreement with a number of hotel chains and telephone companies to reduce those surcharges. As a result, the number of hotels guilty of this communications overkill has declined. One thousand hotels and chains have agreed to the plan and reduced surcharges to as little as $1 and no more than $10, regardless of the length of the call.

You should ask your hotel if they have a Teleplan agreement. If your hotel has not agreed to this plan and you want to call home from your room, dial home, give them your phone number and room number, and ask them to call you back. The phone call from the U.S. is much less expensive, and there is no surcharge. Your one-minute exchange to the U.S. to establish contact will not be too costly.

You could also call from a phone booth in the lobby of your hotel or make your call from phone centers or post offices. Another alternative is to make a phone arrangement before you leave home and have your relative call you at an appointed time. Don't forget the six or more hours time difference when setting up that call. You may be getting your call in the wee hours of the morning.

Using telephone credit cards or making collect calls

are other alternatives to cut the cost of overseas phone calls.

What to Do About Mail

For receiving mail from home, your best bet is to have it sent to your hotel marked "To Be Held for Arrival." With the state of mails these days, have mail sent well enough ahead to arrive before you check out of the hotel. When registering, don't forget to ask at the front desk for your mail.

Another alternative is to have it sent to "Poste Restante" (the universal term for General Delivery) at the main post office in the city or community you plan on visiting. Have it marked "To Be Called For." Mail will be held for at least two weeks. Tell the writer to address it the same way your name appears on your passport.

At one time, American Express offices abroad were mail drops and meeting places for all Americans. With so many people traveling these days, the company isn't so anxious to continue the practice. But they still do to a limited extent. The service is available only to card holders, or traveler's check customers. Others have to pay a fee. Letters must be marked "client hold." Your American Express card or your traveler's checks serve as proof of your being a client.

While U.S. embassies and consulates don't encourage travelers to use their offices as a mail drop, they will, in limited cases, accept mail for Americans who are staying more than a month in a foreign country and who have no fixed itinerary and can't be reached any other way. You must register first at an embassy or consulate before it will accept any mail for you.

Helping Hands—Overseas Emergencies

Losing a passport, being robbed of money and credit cards, or getting sick overseas can be frightening, but kindly Uncle Sam's overseas reps—embassy and consular officials—can help an American in distress.

Passports are lost daily, but it's still a serious matter to lose one. The situation is not hopeless. Remember those extra photos you had made? Here's where they come in handy. With those photos and a driver's license, credit cards, or other identification proving who you are, the process of getting a replacement passport becomes a little easier. Under certain circumstances it may even be managed in several hours.

Traveler's checks and credit cards lost through negligence or theft are another matter. Consular officers can direct you to the banks or credit card offices that issue these documents, but the State Department can't advance funds. They will assist, however, in getting private funds transferred from back home. The consular office will allow a collect call to relatives so you can arrange a transfer of funds to the Citizens Emergency Center at the U.S. State Department in Washington. When the transfer is made, the center will authorize the consulate or embassy to give you money. Keep the Citizens Emergency number with you in case you need it. The direct line number is 1-202-632-5225.

The most serious problem of all is getting sick abroad, especially if you are traveling independently. A tourist on a group tour has an escort who can assist in an emergency and round up medical help. Travelers on their own must seek other assistance. If you require hospitalization or evacuation from your hotel, the local U.S. consulate will assign a staff member to assist you. Other emergency services may also be available. Ask your travel agent for an evaluation of Assist-Card, Near, Inc., and other services that function in foreign countries.

Credit Card Emergencies

Losing your credit cards is not only a nuisance but very disruptive if you're completely dependent on them and have no other backup funds. When you discover their loss, call the company or bank emergency numbers immediately and block further use of the cards. Where does that leave you once the cards are canceled? American Express claims it will issue another after a 24-hour check. If you don't have your card number, they can computer check your name and address. Your new card will also get you needed cash.

Diner's Club will issue a new card within 24 to 48 hours if your credit rating is good. It will also issue you up to $1,000 in cash overseas and may even exchange the cash for traveler's checks without a fee.

Bank cards like Visa, Mastercard, and others have different policies determined by the issuing bank. Before your trip, visit the bank that issued your credit card and find out what they are prepared to do for you in an emergency. Bank credit cards with a bigger line of credit may advance you some cash. It's up to the individual bank.

Credit card holders can take out special insurance against loss. Many of these insurers make money available and cover the cost of your ticket home.

Under certain conditions, foreign banks can help. If your bank is an international one, with branches overseas, go to the foreign branch and talk to an officer. With the right identification and enough money in your home bank, you might be able to get replacement funds. All cases are treated individually.

Loss of Traveler's Checks

Loss of traveler's checks should be reported immediately by calling the emergency numbers companies maintain for such purposes. Be ready to provide the numbers of the checks lost and the name of the bank that issued them. Your records can facilitate a same-day refund. Companies will have to verify your claim before reissuing you other checks. When you buy your checks, find out the company's procedures in case of loss. Read instructions carefully and keep a list of check numbers separate from your checks.

Don't count on a personal check to get you through a cash emergency in foreign countries. If necessary, call home (you can call collect) and have your family send money in the form of an international money order or wire you money via Western Union. It is just now becoming possible to get cash from foreign banks with your home bank cash machine card, your Visa, or American Express card. Ask your bank about these services before you go on your trip.

Be Prepared

A little advance preparation will help you meet emergency situations, or maybe even avoid them. Here are a few tips.

Keep records. Make a list of the following: the number of your passport, its date of issue, its expiration date; credit card numbers and expiration dates; airline ticket serial number; traveler's checks serial numbers, amounts, and name of issuing bank; and other important documents you carry. Keep this information apart from the original documents, cards, etc. Your hand luggage is a good place to keep the list.

Make copies of your itinerary. Make at least two copies of your travel itinerary. Keep one copy with you at all times, and tape a second copy to the lining of your luggage. Should you get lost in a foreign country while taking a walk and forget the name of your hotel, you can refer to the itinerary. It can and does happen. As for the copy in your luggage, it might help track you down if your luggage is lost.

Be prepared in case you lose your passport. Take extra passport photos and some proof of your American citizenship. A voting card or a driver's license will do. If you speak English with a heavy foreign accent, make a special effort to take these extra precautions; they will expedite getting a replacement passport.

Carry family phone numbers. Take along the name, address, and phone number of a close relative back home in case of illness.

Ask about replacements. If you carry a bank credit card, visit the bank that issued it and ask what they can do for you should you need money or a card replacement in case of loss.

Don't presign checks. Only one signature should be on your traveler's checks until you're ready to use them.

For the Love of Shopping

Love it or hate it, shopping is as important as sightseeing to travelers. Part of the fun of visiting foreign countries is bringing back some tangible memento of the exciting and interesting time you had there.

Whether it's an antique treasure, pink coral sand, or a fake artifact sold by some enterprising boy on the banks of the Nile, those treasures can give renewed life to your travel experiences long after the trip has ended.

By now you've probably amassed more possessions than you know what to do with, but that shouldn't stop you from collecting things for others. Why shouldn't children, young and older, benefit from your trip and shopping forays?

Small tots, especially, will cherish costumed dolls, regional toys, unique boats in miniature sizes, or unusual headgear and clothes. What little girl wouldn't delight in a hand-smocked dress or a tartan skirt, and what mother of a small boy wouldn't be thrilled to see her youngster in an Eton jacket?

The most reasonably priced gifts are items that originate in the country you are visiting. Stay away from imported luxury goods. They are subject to the same import taxes you pay here.

Before you take off, learn the special "buys" of the country you are visiting and note prices on these imported items so you can compare them with what you find in the country of origin.

Gifts for the home are very popular. A young couple, newly married, would be thrilled with an additional place setting of their English china, sent from London or from a free port in the Caribbean.

Practical purchases, like fabric from a country noted for its textiles, are also welcome gifts, as are inexpensive hand-loomed carpets.

If clothing is on your gift list—handmade sweaters, silk shirts, all wool socks, and slippers are nice gifts to consider—take along sizes or measurements or both in your travel notebook. Jot down sleeve and neck sizes and pack a tape measure. When buying cottage industry (handmade) knits—the right size sweater may have sleeves four inches longer than they should be. Be cautious.

Handicrafts from Latin Neighbors

Good buys in Latin American countries might include semiprecious stones and leather goods from Brazil, or perhaps a pound or two of their home-grown coffee. Peru's clever artisans make wonderful handmade alpaca wool sweaters, wool wall hangings with Inca designs, warm furry alpaca slippers for children, and interesting silver pieces. Leather, wool, and fur items are good buys in Argentina, and Mexico's colorful handwoven cotton ends up as inexpensive clothes for men, women, and children and other decorative items with Aztec designs.

Gifts from the Far East

Exotic and luxurious gifts are sold inexpensively in Far Eastern countries. Thailand's lustrous silks are made into decorative pillowcases, ties, stoles, both men's and women's shirts, and other clothing. A Thai silk jacket could cost about $50. Gem stones are excellent buys in Thailand. Bali offers incredible opportunities to buy batik fabrics, wood carvings, primitive paintings with Balinese scenes, puppets, and other handcrafted gifts. And if Tahiti is your destination, don't forget the French connections. Perfumes are a good buy, and so are Polynesian prints, shell jewelry, and paintings done on black velvet.

Treasures from Europe

Americans on the prowl for gifts will find hand-embroidered clothes and household items in Hungary, Romania, Poland, Yugoslavia, and other Eastern European nations. Czechoslovakia's crystal beads and bowls are worthy gifts. Denmark is noted for heavy silver, England for its antique silver, tea, woolen goods, Scotch whisky, and sweaters. In France, it's perfume, cognacs, and crystal. Portugal is noted for its linens, knits, crochet work, and ceramics, while Spain is good for leather goods. Heavy Greek handmade sweaters are always welcome. If you don't want to spend a lot of money in Austria, buy a Sachertorte, that rich chocolate cake from Vienna.

The list of gift possibilities is endless. Information on each country's specialties is available from their tourist offices in the United States.

Closed for Lunch

Shopping hours in many foreign countries differ from those in the United States. Many stores, especially those in warmer climates, close for a long lunch at around noon or so and remain closed for two or three hours, reopening when the heat of the day has dissipated somewhat. They remain open at night until about 8 P.M. In Paris, most stores are closed on Monday mornings.

Store hours vary from city to city. Travelers on tour who look forward to shopping should check store openings and closings. Stores in Spain, Italy, Portugal, Greece, Israel, and most South American countries close for a long lunch. Department stores, however, usually remain open all day. In the Far East, especially Hong Kong, storekeepers don't miss a beat. They stay open and make money.

Tour guides often steer groups to a large store that sells everything. The guide gets a commission on your purchase. Time to look around is limited, and the quality of the merchandise is often substandard. Ask the tour leader whether there are other opportunities for browsing in shops. If there are, save your money and taste for other shopping opportunities.

The stores in your own hotel often have good, even superior, merchandise, and their prices are not too far out of line.

Flea Markets for Bargains

Normally you don't bargain in established stores, but there's no harm in asking for a discount "for dollars." Storekeepers may agree, especially if you've purchased a number of things.

Bargaining is not the American way, but there are places in the world—the bazaars, souks, or markets in Mexico, Morocco, Tunisia, Turkey, Greece—where it is the established practice. Some merchants even set the stage for negotiation by offering a cup of coffee or tea before the game begins.

You don't have to travel deep into the Middle East for the trading scene; European flea markets, too, are scenes of this commercial give and take. El Rastro in Madrid, Portobello Road and Petticoat Lane in London, the Monastiraki in Athens, and the Feira da Ladra in Lisbon are some of the more famous bargain marts.

You should have an idea of how much the item is worth before you offer a price. As a wedge, find fault with the merchandise and capitalize on a flaw.

If all this is too much for you, look for government stores. They are very reliable shops, and the merchandise is often superior. Mexico, the "dollar stores" of Eastern European countries, Tunisia, India, and Sri Lanka are just a few places where governments maintain these kinds of stores.

Fly Away Prices at Airports

For last minute gifts, there are the airport shops. Don't be cheered by "duty free" signs; these stores usually carry no bargains. Your best buys in most of them are liquor, cigarettes, perfumes, and candy. If you're buying liquor, don't forget to bring your boarding card and passport. Your boarding card shows you're leaving the country and entitled to buy these items duty free. You can pay in American money.

Some duty-free shops do give you a fair deal. At Schiphol Airport in Amsterdam, cameras and jewelry are priced fairly. The airport at Athens has good prices on the expensive gold jewelry made by Lalaounis and Zolotas. In Tel Aviv, the duty-free H. Stern jewelers offer jewelry and diamonds at lower-than-town prices. Hong Kong, Bangkok, and Rio de Janeiro duty-free airport shops are also less expensive.

Food items make an interesting gift, but not fresh meats, sausages, or other meat products. They will be confiscated by U.S. Customs. Which brings us to two booklets you should have—*Know Before You Go* and *U.S. Customs and Tips for Travelers.* These booklets detail what you can and cannot bring back to the United States. (See reading list in Appendix B.)

The Mechanics of Sending Things Home

Before you buy that marvelous inexpensive Korean chest for your daughter or yourself or that intricately carved teak desk in Thailand, find out how much it's going to cost to ship it home. The price can often be three or four times as much as the cost of the item, and that doesn't include customs.

Furniture and large objects require special handling. That means the purchases must be crated. Then you have to pay for insurance, pay for a customs broker, pay duty, spend more money for repacking the crate, and then get a freight company to send it home.

Is it worth all this trouble and expense? At the moment you're doing all this, perhaps not, but later on, when you have the unusual things installed in your house, a resounding YES. I should know, my home is filled with such treasures.

Small purchases should be mailed, and if the value is under $50 it will be exempt from customs. Mark the package "unsolicited gift." More expensive purchases must be carried by you to include in your exemption. Mailed items of value are subject to duty.

A woman was browsing through a shopping arcade in Hong Kong when she spotted the ultrasuede suit of her dreams. It was only $250, custom made, and a real bargain. She couldn't resist.

The tailor assured her that he could finish it in three days if he started on the project immediately. She put down the required deposit. The next two days she returned for fittings, but the suit was still not completed when her tour was leaving.

"Don't worry," the tailor soothed. "I'll mail it, and you'll get it the same week you return home." To make his point he produced a sheath of letters from satisfied customers who received their merchandise through the mails.

Her suit arrived the week she returned, but before she could claim her new treasure, U.S. Customs imposed a duty of $68.75. She was furious. The price had now climbed to $318.75, and a discount store near her home was selling ultrasuede suits for $325.

If you want something made, leave extra time for the tailor to finish it. While U.S. Customs has liberalized the duty-free allowances on purchases you carry with you, duties on more expensive purchases mailed home remain the same. Purchases sent from the U.S. Virgin Islands, Guam, or American Samoa are the only exceptions. They can follow you duty free if you claim them on the $800 exemption allowed only on these islands.

Sales taxes take the fun and bargain out of shopping. That's especially true in Europe, where so many of the Common Market countries have adopted the value added tax (VAT). This is a vertical tax imposed on every step of manufacture, from raw material to the finished product. All taxes along the way are included in the price. Nothing is exempt. Car rentals and hotel bills are also subject to VAT.

The tax can be as high as 33 percent of the price of the item, but it is usually lower. In many cases the tax money is refundable to foreign visitors. You usually have to spend a minimum in the same store. For example, the minimum is about $100 in France, $75 in England, and a low of $50 in Austria.

Purchases worth more than $50 that are sent home from a store may automatically be exempted from the tax at the source. You'll be paying customs duty in the United States instead. So what should you do? If you can, take your purchases to the airport in your hand luggage, along with the VAT exemption form given you by the store. Take the purchase, your passport, airline ticket, and the VAT form to the customs officer. Once they see that you've paid the VAT taxes, they'll stamp the form. It is possible you may get a refund at the airport, but more likely you will have to send that stamped form back to the store for a refund.

Do all this before you get on the plane and leave plenty of time for this transaction.

Getting money due you from VAT may actually cost you money. Some stores mail your refund in their currency. A bank will charge you a foreign collection fee to exchange that check into American money.

When a country does not give you your VAT refund in dollars, your best bet is to use a credit card rather than cash for such purchases abroad. When the tax refund authorization is received by the store, they will credit your credit card account for the tax—and it will be in dollars.

Customs—It's a Cinch

If you have nothing to hide, you have nothing to worry about when going through U.S. Customs.

Customs agents are not looking for you; they are out to nab the cheats, the drug smugglers, and the people who threaten our agricultural industry by bringing in fresh farm products that might carry insects or disease. Remember the Mediterranean fruit fly?

Big Spenders Get Breaks

Along the way, of course, they're going to charge you duty if you were an overly big spender. Current regulations allow each individual who has been out of the country more than 48 hours $400 worth of duty-free purchases. If you bought more than that, you pay a flat 10 percent fee on the next $1,000 worth of goods. For purchases over that amount, regular rates of duty will be charged. Percentages vary according to the specific items. Gold jewelry is taxed at one rate, silk at another, and so on.

Traveling with a family member who lives with you provides an extra advantage. You can pool your purchases, and lessen your tax.

If you've been out of the country less than 48 hours, or returned from a foreign land 30 days before and claimed your $400 exemption, duty-free purchases are limited to $25 worth of goods. Over that, regular rates of duty prevail.

Travelers planning extensive shopping forays in developing countries should write for *GSP and the Traveler*, available from the U.S. Customs Service (see reading list in Appendix B). GSP (Generalized System of Preferences) is a special duty-free arrangement the U.S. has with developing nations. U.S. Customs exempts or charges minimum duty on purchases made in those countries. It's an attempt to bolster the economy of these nations. Many luxury items from Hong Kong, Sri Lanka, Brazil, India, and more than 140 other countries are admissible with little or no duty under GSP. Jewelry, furs, furniture, and unset precious and semi-precious stones are included.

Tips to Breeze Through Customs

☐ If you have a foreign camera (German, Japanese, etc.) with a serial number, register it with U.S. Customs at the airport before you leave. Keep the certificate of registration with you, as proof that you didn't purchase it overseas on your trip. Insurance on the camera taken before your trip will also serve as proof.

☐ Other valuable imported items, like jewelry, watches, etc., that have identifiable markings should also be registered before you leave the U.S. This must be done in person at the airport or at border crossings.

☐ Leave your foreign original gowns at home. If you return from Europe with a French designer's dress in your luggage, you'll have to prove to U.S. Customs that you didn't buy it abroad. You'll need to carry a receipt with you, or even a descriptive letter from your dry cleaner. Your best bet is to leave it at home.

☐ Honesty is the best policy. Chances are good that customs won't open your bag. It's not worth the anxiety to drastically understate purchases or sneak in forbidden items. You may be fined and your property confiscated. Worse still, your name will be entered into the computer as a violator of the law. Next time you come through customs you may be subject to a more thorough search.

☐ Put all your purchases in one bag, and keep your receipts with you to show customs if they ask.

☐ If you bought a piece of clothing and are wearing it, declare it. People don't fool officials too often. They know all the tricks; they were trained to outsmart you.

☐ Art works and antiques are admitted duty free. Get a receipt documenting the age of the antique.

☐ You can pay your duty by personal check, traveler's checks or U.S. currency, but not in foreign currency.

Getting Around Overseas

Buzzing Around by Bus

Long distance bus service is available in Europe as it is in the United States, though there's very little publicity about it here, and few travelers realize it's available. Point-to-point bus service makes it easy for independent travelers who don't want to drive to take full advantage of bed and breakfast accommodations, guest houses, and other types of low cost lodging possibilities.

In Britain, for instance, travelers who yearn to see the beautiful green English landscapes and savor the small charming villages of the Cotswolds, Yorkshire, or other quaint areas can get on and off buses at will.

In Germany, the medieval towns of Rothenburg, Dinkelsbühl, and Augsburg and other picturesque Bavarian places are on the bus route from Weisbaden (outside of Frankfort) to Munich. You can get off anywhere on this "Romantic Road," stay at dollhouse cottages, walk through the small towns, and then get on a bus to the next picture postcard village.

Europabus is the bus system that connects 16 countries of Europe; the bus company name changes in each country. What does not change, however, is that Europabus is linked to the Eurailpass system, and in many instances your Eurailpass will provide free transportation on buses.

Europabus also offers prepackaged tour programs in Austria, Belgium, France, Germany, Great Britain, Italy, Portugal, Scandinavia, and Switzerland. (See Chapter 7 for further information on bus tours in Europe.)

Riding the Rails

While planes are quicker and motorcoach travel cheaper, there's nothing like a European train ride to capture the excitement and thrill of cross-cultural experiences. Passing a border with passport control conducted right on the train makes you feel like you're participating in some international plot.

The makeup of many passenger cars—six seats in a compartment—adds to a European train's uniqueness. The dining car, too, with its old world flourishes, intensifies your sense of a pleasant strangeness. And the company you'll keep will make your journey even more pleasurable. Your seat companions will most certainly be Europeans, but they could also come from South America, the Middle East, Australia, and—oh, yes—even from your own town.

One place you know you'll meet people is on a European train. If you don't know their native tongue, somehow congeniality manages to break through the language barrier.

On a train from Switzerland to Austria, an American couple, with three cameras between them, were constantly getting up from their seats and moving into the corridor in pursuit of the perfect picture. An 80-year-old Austrian seated next to them decided to take over. He knew the route well. Each time a good shot was in the offing, he indicated on which side of the train the couple should be.

The Americans knew no German, the man no English, but by the end of their trip, they were sharing bread and wine. Both parties learned a few words of each other's tongue. When the couple returned home, they had pictures to show their friends, but their experience with a European on a train was an even better memento.

Apart from the friendly atmosphere on board, the new European trains are noted for their speed and comfort. Views are spectacular, and many of the most famous trains are scheduled so that passengers can travel over the most scenic routes during daylight hours.

Europe's top trains speed along at over 100 miles an hour, and there's a network of the super-fast, first class Trans European Express (TEE) trains now covering the continent's rail system.

In addition to the TEE trains, there are now brand-new Intercity (IC) trains that accommodate both first and second class passengers. These trains travel at about the same speed as the TEE's—90 to 125 miles per hour. Because of the mix of first and second class, dining cars have been replaced with cafeteria-style cars offering buffet service.

European train travel requires a little extra planning. At most stations, porterage service can't be counted on. There may be baggage carts, but the trick is finding them. Take as little luggage as possible—only as much as you yourself can carry. Luggage with wheels will help, or you can take along a luggage cart that's lightweight and collapsible. There are a few other things you should know about trains. (1) You can choose smoking or non-smoking cars. (2) If your seat is not reserved, be sure to look for the sign on the side of the car that lists your destination. Some cars are dropped en route. (3) Major railroad terminals have multilingual agents who can point you in the right direction. Keep your tickets in hand, and remember the name of your porter (if you're lucky enough to get one). (4) Many stations now have pictograph signs, with symbols for shops, police, customs, toilets, lost and found, and snack shops. If you don't know the language, you can read the pictures.

Rail Discounts Overseas

All European countries except those in Eastern Europe (Soviet Union, Bulgaria, Czechoslovakia, etc.) have special senior citizen half-fare discounts for train travel. Age eligibility varies for women—60, 62, or 65— but for men the standard age is 65.

While these discounts certainly sound like bargains, they are not always as good as they seem. Senior fares were developed for the European. Usefulness for foreigners is limited. In Switzerland, the Senior Citizens Half Fare Card costs around $55 and is good for a year of travel on Swiss Railroads. During Switzerland's special Season for Seniors, the card also entitles its holder to a 10 percent discount at specified small hotels.

What's the matter with that, you ask? Nothing, except that if you're spending only two weeks in Switzerland, you're paying for a card that is good for a whole year of travel. A better bet is to purchase a half-fare travel card for $25. Another option is the Swiss Holiday Card offering 15 days of unlimited first class travel on Swiss trains for about $131; $90 for second class.

France's Carte Vermeil (translated, it means mixture of silver and gold) can be purchased by men over 65 and women over 60 for about $8 at any French railway station. With the card, you can travel anywhere on French railways for half fare. Its disadvantage is that there are limitations on the days and times you can use it. (See Chapter 6 for more details.)

The same restrictions and price differentials may be found on the railroads of the other European countries.

Bargain hunters who want to travel European railroads should forget about age and opt for a Eurailpass, but not before doing some homework. First get the rail fares between the places you intend visiting. Add them up, and compare the total with the price of the Eurailpass. The pass is for first class travel without restrictions. The advantage, apart from price, is that you don't have to stand in line to buy your ticket. Fifteen-day Eurailpasses cost about $260, 21-day passes about $330, and one-month passes $410. Prices have remained the same since 1983.

Travel on British trains is not included in the Eurailpass. The British have their own pass, BritRailPass, which comes in both first and second class. Costs are: for first class, $155 for 7 days, $230 for 14 days, $290 for 21 days; for second class, $115 for 7 days, $175 for 14 days, and $220 for 21 days.

Japan, too, offers rail passes for foreigners. They must be purchased before arrival in the country. The seven-day pass is just a little higher than the round trip fare between Tokyo and Kyoto on the super-fast Bullet Train.

Tips for Rail Travel

☐ The Eurailpass, BritRailPass, or Japan rail pass must be purchased in the United States or Canada. They can be used on the extra-speedy trains.

- ☐ The concierge of your hotel will reserve your seat. Eurailpass does not guarantee seats unless they are reserved.
- ☐ Travel agents or the U.S. offices of national railroads will sell passes. You get a free map of routes with the Eurailpass.
- ☐ Make reservations for rail journeys two months in advance for late spring and summer trips when tourist traffic is heavy.
- ☐ Eurail Aid offices in major cities and rail stations will help in replacing a lost ticket. Show your signed receipt.
- ☐ Tap water on trains is not potable. Drink bottled water.
- ☐ Europeans use the 24-hour clock on timetables.
- ☐ Keep luggage in the corridor next to your compartment. Racks above the seats are too narrow to hold most luggage safely. Even if you lift weights daily, it's a struggle to get your bags up there.
- ☐ Porters are more likely to be found in southern European countries like Italy, Spain, and Portugal. In Germany, you'll find baggage carts at the station—hopefully.
- ☐ European trains have two types of railroad cars. Some have compartments with two facing rows of three seats each. Others have center aisles, much like U.S. trains. If you like the idea of a private compartment, say so when making a reservation.
- ☐ Service charges are included in the price of meals in dining cars. There are usually two seatings; a representative will come through the cars asking which you prefer.
- ☐ Seat reservations are required on TEE trains.
- ☐ To find your train track, look for the TV monitors in the depot. To find where your car will be located, check the diagram on the platform. It will indicate where you should position yourself.
- ☐ The cheapest sleeping car is the couchette—it's coed. People sleep in their day clothes.

For a free *Through Europe by Train* (timetable), Eurail map, and Eurailpass brochure, write: TRAINS, P.O. Box M, Staten Island, NY 10305. BritRail brochures are available from BritRail offices in Los Angeles, Dallas, Chicago, Vancouver, Toronto, and New York City: 630 Third Ave., New York, NY 10017.

Car Rentals

If you're planning on renting a car overseas and you are over 60, check car rental agencies in the U.S. about age maximums.

There are actual age restrictions on who can or can't rent an automobile in some places in the world. Those vary from country to country and agency to agency. In Aruba, Netherlands West Indies, for instance, if you were 61 and tried to rent an Avis, you would be turned down. Their maximum age for renting a car is 60 years old! National Car Rental Service has no such restriction in Aruba. In Antigua, though, the National Car franchise sets 65 as a maximum age for car rental customers. Some agencies in London, Singapore, Indonesia, Jamaica, Ecuador, Barbados, and the Dominican Republic have restrictions for people in their 60's.

Car rental agencies that normally offer discounts to certain organizations in the U.S., sometimes do not honor those discounts overseas. It has nothing to do with the parent organization; it's the franchise.

Special bargains are often available to lessen the cost of a car rental. One international company offers a seven-day advance rental plan with unlimited mileage that reduces the weekly cost of renting a car in Europe by about $100. You can pay in European currency! With a strong dollar, that might make a seven-day car rental in London cost about $133 less. Booking the same car in London from the same company might cost you more. Check the rates of a number of auto rental companies before you go.

It's probably better to rent from an international company before you leave than from a local private car rental service. With an international company you have the security of knowing that if anything goes wrong with the car, they'll exchange it and pick you up. Also, car rental franchises of the larger corporations adhere to certain standards of maintenance and service, and their cars are usually newer than those available from a local dealer.

Many do-it-yourself packaged tours provide car rentals as part of the price of the tour. Ask your favorite international airline about their auto tours. Some airlines offer a free car rental, tax included and no drop-off fees.

Brief yourself about the driving habits of different countries. In Britain and the Virgin Islands, they drive on the left side of the road. Germans are notorious for their high speeds on their expressways. Countries have different regulations about speed limits, seat belts, directional signals, headlights, right of way, etc. Get all the information you can about driving idiosyncracies and customs before you go so you'll be confident and safe behind the wheel in an unfamiliar environment.

And for extra security, check with your auto insurance broker about your coverage for driving out of the country. Chances are you will have to buy insurance overseas, but check it anyway.

Checklist on Car Rentals

If you're planning on renting a car overseas, there are some questions to ask the agency, whether you rent it here or there.

- ☐ Does the car have automatic shift? Automatic shifts are more costly to rent but easier to drive than stick shifts.
- ☐ Is there a drop-off charge? If so, what is it?
- ☐ Is the car large enough? Is there enough room for you and your luggage? European cars are smaller and less roomy.
- ☐ Can the trunk be locked?
- ☐ Is a spare tire provided?
- ☐ How old are the cars available?
- ☐ Is air conditioning available?
- ☐ Will the agency give you help in planning your trip, provide free maps, make reservations, etc.?
- ☐ Are VAT taxes included in the price? In Europe, value added taxes are often a hefty extra.
- ☐ How much extra is collision-damage waiver insurance? If you don't take it, will you have to leave a cash de-

posit? Is liability insurance a must, and how much does it cost?
- ☐ Does the company have 24-hour service?
- ☐ Do you have to pay for the rental in advance?
- ☐ Can you get a written confirmation of your reservation for a car? It assures you of getting what you asked for.
- ☐ Will you need to get an International Driving Permit, or will your own state automobile license do? If you do need one, check with your local American Automobile Association for an application. Membership is not required. You'll need two passport-sized photos to apply. The fee is $5, and it's good for a year.

Car Rental Agencies to Start You Off

Avis International, 6128 E. 38th St., Tulsa, OK 74135 (1-800-331-1212)

Hertz International Reservations Center—10401 N. Pennsylvania Ave., Oklahoma City, OK 73120 (1-800-654-3001; in Oklahoma 1-800-522-3711)

National Car Rental (Europcar in Europe, Tilden in Canada), 7700 France Ave. So., Minneapolis, MN 55435 (1-800-328-4567; in Minnesota 1-800-862-6064)

Handling Foreign Currency

An American traveling in a rural section of Italy couldn't understand why the small storekeeper wouldn't accept American money for the cigarettes and snacks he bought. Wasn't the American dollar good all over the world?

Yes it is, but what would an Italian peasant in a small town do with a five-dollar bill? It would be a nuisance to exchange it for Italian currency.

While the dollar may be almighty, you can't expect foreigners to adopt it as their own. What's theirs is theirs, and it's up to us to learn their currency when going abroad.

Admittedly, when our dollar is worth hundreds or even thousands in their money, it's difficult to comprehend. We are not used to dealing in such high figures. Thousands of lire seems overwhelming for paying a restaurant bill.

The most painless method of dealing with foreign currency is to get an inexpensive hand calculator or a currency converter for an immediate translation. Converters are often given to you when you change your money at money exchanges, in gift or souvenir stores, and in some banks. These converters can also be bought in book stores before you leave the U.S.

There's been much discussion about whether you get a better deal on foreign currency for your dollars from foreign exchange specialists in the U.S. It's doubtful, because American currency does fluctuate on foreign markets. It's a good idea to buy just what you need to get you through the early hours of your arrival in a country.

If you buy too much currency, you may find you have shortchanged yourself. The rate may have changed since you bought the currency. If the foreign government decides to devalue its currency while you are traveling, you will have lost a big advantage.

Money Management Tips

☐ Avoid changing money in hotels and restaurants. Rates are usually less advantageous there.

☐ Buy enough foreign currency before you leave for your immediate needs—tips, taxis, a soda.

☐ If you are arriving on a weekend, don't count on a bank to exchange your traveler's checks for cash. There's usually an exchange bank at the airport when you arrive.

☐ Get traveler's checks. Many are now available free from banks and through club organizations. They often yield more foreign currency than cold cash. Don't forget to count the checks before you leave the counter.

☐ Black market currency exchanges on the street will get you a higher rate, but it's a risky business. It is illegal and may be an invitation to arrest. In some countries, it's an invitation to theft. When it is an open practice and winked at by the government, do what you think is right.

☐ In general, do your purchasing with credit cards. If you need cash, you can get an advance on them but you do need to take other identification with you. There is one word of caution on the blanket use of credit cards for purchases. Some countries have different exchange rates, one for credit card purchases, another for changing dollars at a bank or foreign exchange office, and a third rate on the black market. When purchasing with a credit card, you may spend more for the item because your dollar amount will be exchanged at the lowest rate.

□ If the country has a fluctuating exchange rate, divide your funds into cash, traveler's checks, and foreign currency. Change enough money daily or every two days rather than a large sum at once.

□ Have at least $20 in single dollar bills handy. It avoids having to change a large traveler's check.

Tipping in Foreign Countries

Extending your hand with a palm full of foreign change is not the ideal method of tipping. Not only could you be taken advantage of, but tipping is a gesture of thanks, not "here, kid, buy yourself a cigar."

Tourists often do just that because they don't take time out to learn the value of currency. To remedy this rather amateurish method of tipping, remember to ask the moneychanger at the airport or at the bank to give you the equivalent of a dollar's worth of change. Study what you have in your hand so you know the worth of the coins.

My own experience is that people in foreign countries rarely seem to have small change for tips. To assure that you get money in smaller denominations, cash a $10 or $5 bill. It might be a good idea to accumulate small change daily just for tips.

Tipping is frowned upon in the Soviet Union, but if you want to be nice to your local guides and drivers, they'll be happy to accept presents. Women like lipsticks, fashion magazines, and other American magazines. Drivers might enjoy American cigarettes. In other Eastern European countries, like Poland, Czechoslovakia, Hungary, and Romania, tipping is acceptable—about 10 percent is right.

Service charges are included in hotel rates. Additional tipping is not required. If you feel, however, you should give the porter something additional, you can. Customs on giving money vary around the world. In Japan, for instance, if you want to leave the chambermaid a little extra money, you leave the money under the pillow.

In restaurants where the service charge is included, it is customary to leave small change as part of the tip.

In foreign countries there are some services for which tips are expected. These include ushers who show you to your seat, washroom attendants, the concierge, and even gasoline attendants. Here are some tipping guidelines not covered in other sections of this book.

Washroom Attendants. Tip the equivalent of about 20-25 cents. At an expensive club, make it about 50 cents. Both sexes tip.

Ushers. Fifty cents is more than adequate.

Concierge. The all-knowledgeable person at your hotel who gives you directions, tells you which bus to take, and gets you tickets to the ballet, etc., usually gets a special tip. The equivalent of $5 is about right for a medium amount of special services. Tip more if she or he mails packages or heavy books home for you.

CHAPTER 10

Medically Speaking

by Norton M. Luger, M.D.

There are few health reasons today to prevent anyone from enjoying the pleasures of travel. Altitude or tropical heat may not be wise for some people, but everyone can find some interesting places to visit where health is not a problem.

When you are planning your trip, consult your doctor regarding your objectives and ask for advice. Physicians travel extensively for professional study and for pleasure. A medical insight can be helpful to you.

Use this visit, also, to have your periodic checkup. Arrange to do this far enough ahead of time to correct any medical problems without having to revise your departure date.

During this consultation, have your immunizations brought up to date, if necessary, and get prescriptions for medications you will need for your personal medical kit. Ask your doctor for the generic or chemical names of those medications, so that you can identify them for foreign physicians should you need medical care abroad. Ask for a brief summary of your significant medical history, your current diagnosis if pertinent, drugs and biologicals to which you may be hypersensitive or allergic, and a photocopy of your most recent electrocardiogram, whether or not you have heart disease. Your doctor's phone number is useful; in emergencies, a long-distance call can be completed in minutes, even from the other side of the world.

Arrange a time schedule for needed immunizations. Even the most complicated set of immunizations can be completed within four to eight weeks.

Check your current health insurance policies to be certain they will cover illnesses abroad (see below— Medical Insurance).

Individuals differ physically and medically. Should anything in this chapter appear contrary to your personal physician's advice, you must be guided by his or her counsel, since it is based on knowledge of your personal medical condition.

Immunizations

There has been much confusion in recent years about which immunizations travelers should take. I believe in maximum protection and minimum risk. It may surprise you, but "shots" are not only for kids. Many adults lose the immunity they acquired during childhood and adolescence. Therefore, it is advisable to check your immunizations, even if you are limiting your travels to the United States.

All immunizations, including those not required for overseas travels, should be recorded by your doctor in your yellow International Certificate of Vaccinations folder, and those that may be required have to be validated by your local governmental health officer. Without validation, the certificate will not have the legal status needed during epidemics abroad. This vaccination form, which may be obtained from your travel agent or your local Department of Health, is an excellent personal record.

Travel in United States and Canada

Flu. Each year the vaccine changes slightly to protect against new strains of the virus as they appear. One shot is taken each year unless you are allergic to eggs. Occasional mild fever may result. I recommend this for all over 50 years of age.

Tetanus and diphtheria toxoid. Many in the over-50 group have not had the initial immunizing series of these injections. It is worthwhile having this protection because travel accidents cannot be foreseen, and lockjaw is a fearful disease that is preventable. Tetanus toxoid can be given alone or combined with diphtheria toxoid in a single injection, which costs about the same as tetanus alone. There is still diphtheria in many foreign countries.

Pheumococcus vaccine. Pheumococcal pneumonia was the great killer until penicillin and other antibiotics appeared. In older people to this day, the disease can develop so rapidly and be so overwhelming that death can occur before antibiotics can become effective. This immunization is advised for those who have chronic heart and lung disease, diabetics, people undergoing cancer chemotherapy, or those who take cortisone. One injection is given, and the immunity lasts for at least five years.

Travel Abroad and South of the Border

There are no immunization requirements to enter any country or to return to the United States. The following immunizations are recommended primarily for your own protection and to avoid the possibility of being stopped at the border of countries where there may be an outbreak of a disease.

Smallpox. This immunization is *not* needed and you should not take it.

Typhoid. This is advised for travelers to countries where sanitation is poor. This includes most of the world except Canada, Great Britain, Europe from Austria northward, Australia, New Zealand, Ireland, and Japan. The initial immunization requires two injections separated by a 4-8 week interval. Local soreness and even a low-grade fever may occur, but this responds to aspirin or acetaminophen. Annual boosters are recommended for those who travel abroad frequently.

Cholera. This is a constant threat in underdeveloped areas of the world, especially in southern Asia, Malaysia,

Indonesia, Bangladesh, Afghanistan, Iran, Turkey, the Middle East, and Africa except for South Africa. The initial immunization consists of two injections with a 2-4 week interval. The immunization is valid for six months. Single boosters are taken prior to further visits to cholerous areas.

Yellow Fever. Immunization consists of one injection of a live, but weakened, virus. Only specially designated centers can give this shot. These are U.S. Public Health Service Clinics and clinics that specialize in international travel and tropical health. Your travel agent or local health department can guide you to an authorized center. Travelers to southern Mexico, Central America, northern and central South America, northwest Brazil, eastern Peru, Ecuador, and central Africa should be immunized. For those going into jungle areas, it is an absolute necessity. This immunity lasts at least 10 years. This vaccine should not be taken by a pregnant companion or by people with immunodeficiency due to cancer chemotherapy or lymphomas, or those who are taking cortisone for any disease.

Poliomyelitis. While this disease sounds like ancient history in the United States, it is still prevalent in many areas of the world where childhood immunization is not practiced. In older people, polio can assume the severe and often fatal bulbar form, and for this reason immunization is advised. Two vaccines are available. The Sabin vaccine is a weakened live virus vaccine, which is given to children. Some physicians prefer that unvaccinated adults be given the inactivated polio vaccine (Salk). This requires three injections at least one month apart (i.e., this can be accomplished in 8 weeks) and a fourth 6-12 months after the third injection. Boosters should be taken every five years.

Hepatitis. This disease is caused by several viruses. Hepatitis A is spread via food and water contamination. Before a long trip to anywhere but northern Europe, I usually advise 5cc of gamma globulin injected into the buttock. This should be given the week before departure. It affords some protection for 1–2 months. Hepatitis B is spread by intimate personal contact, contami-

nated syringes, or injections. Routine immunization is
not advised.

Malaria Prevention. There is as yet no vaccine against malaria. However, most human malaria is prevented by
taking one chloroquin (Aralen) tablet weekly starting
one week before arriving in the malarious area and
continuing for eight weeks after leaving the area. Your
doctor, a health department, or a travel agent can identify malarious areas on your itinerary.

The exception to this rule are strains of Falciparum
malaria, a killer, that have become resistant to the
preventive and curative effects of chloroquin. At the
present time, these strains occur in East Africa and in
eastern Thailand, Cambodia, northeast India, and Bangladesh.

The current preventive for these areas consists of
one tablet each of chloroquin and Fansidar weekly a
week prior to, during, and 8 weeks after being in these
areas. These medications are not a foolproof prophy-
laxis but are strongly advised. Malaria is transmitted by
anopheles mosquitoes. Keeping them away is the best
preventive (see below).

Vaccination Scheduling. All vaccines can be taken together.
However, yellow fever and Sabin polio vaccine are live
virus vaccines whose effectiveness may be decreased if
they are taken along with gamma globulin. Therefore,
they should be taken as early as possible. Gamma globulin is most effective when taken the week of departure.

Keeping Healthy Away from Home

Rule 1—Get Adequate Rest

Travel is stressful as well as pleasing. You know
yourself. Once you arrive at your destination, be reasonable about your activities. Do not press too much activity
into any one day. A tired person doesn't see as much,
absorb as much, or enjoy as much as a well-rested person
in good humor. If you are tired, rest!

For long distance travelers by plane, jet lag produces
a special problem. Your body has its own natural sleep-

wake cycle. As you travel rapidly across time zones, your own body cycle is not synchronized with the time and light-dark cycle of your new location. Your timing and sleep-wake cycle is deranged, and it will take about one day for each time zone to become accommodated to your new sleep-wake pattern.

Limit your touring for the first few days. When you feel tired, rest. When you feel sleepy, sleep; but try to accustom yourself to the local time by sleeping at night. To sedate yourself, take a beer, a glass of wine, a mild tranquillizer, or even a sleeping pill. You will find that sleep is not a waste of time. It is the best preparation for a relaxed holiday.

Each traveler has his or her own special remedy for jet lag. The consensus is that excessive alcohol and food may delay accommodation to new time zones. Sleep on the plane is helpful, the more the better. Use eyeshades to keep out the light and have a nap.

Dr. Charles Ehret, who has studied the body's natural rhythms for over three decades, has developed a jet lag diet, which he believes is helpful. The diet instructions, which are very complex, are available through the Office of Public Affairs, Argonne National Laboratory, Argonne, IL 60439. Enclose a stamped, self-addressed envelope with your request.

Rule 2—Be Careful About Water and Ice

If Americans are concerned about drinking local water abroad, it is for good reason. Outside of northern Europe, Australia, New Zealand, Britain, Ireland, Canada, and Japan, the water systems are not as safe as they are in the U.S.

In some of the larger cities of the world, the water supply is excellent, but since you don't know which cities have up-to-date water systems, my advice is: don't drink tap water. Despite well-intentioned reassurances from tour guides and seasoned travelers, locally installed filtering systems are not to be trusted. Water is clearer, but bacteria or parasite eggs are not filtered out in a reliable and predictable fashion. Water boiled for one minute is bacteriologically safe anywhere. My own preference for carbonated water prepared in a factory is safest. Bottles of "still" water are known to have been refilled from the tap by hotel personnel and then recapped. Beer, hot tea, and coffee are safe.

When you have to drink the local water and can't boil it, add either two drops of liquid laundry bleach (like Clorox), Halozone tablets (obtainable at your pharmacy), or five drops of ordinary tincture of iodine to a quart of water and mix. In thirty minutes this should be safe to drink if you can taste either the chlorine or the iodine. If you can't taste it, add a little more, and wait a while before drinking it. For cold or cloudy water, double the dose.

Typhoid fever, paratyphoid, polio, hepatitis, bacterial and amoebic dysentery, "turista," intestinal parasites, and other forms of diarrhea are spread by contaminated water. That's why these precautions are so important, even for brushing teeth. When a safe water supply is not available, use hot tap water or bottled mineral water to brush your teeth.

What is true for water is true for ice cubes. Americans are accustomed to ice in their drinks. We forget that contaminated water yields contaminated ice cubes. Ask for cold bottled mixes at the bar instead of "on the rocks," and wipe the mouths of your bottles or cans before opening them. When you have your morning fruit juice, be sure it is fresh and not cooled with an ice cube.

Rule 3—Be Safe: Avoid Certain Foods

Meats. All meats should be well cooked. Steak tartare or underdone meats are an invitation to tapeworm and trichina infestations.

Dairy Products. In areas where sanitation is poor or questionable, avoid milk or milk products that are not pasteurized. Mayonnaise, pastries, desserts with cream fillings, and custards are prime culture media for food poisoning unless properly refrigerated. If they are served warm, reject them. They have been out of the refrigerator too long.

Salads. Outside of northern Europe, avoid raw greens. Human waste is used as fertilizer in many parts of the world and can cause diarrhea and dysentery.

Fruits. Don't deprive yourself of the variety of fruits around the world, but skin them yourself. Fruit should be washed only in safe water.

Fish, Seafood, and Shellfish. Fresh fish and crustaceans, well cooked in hot oil, steamed, poached, or broiled, are usually safe. Shellfish, however, are carriers of hepatitis and intestinal disease and should be eaten only when deep fried or very well cooked. In Japan and Peru, raw fish is a delicacy, as is Scandinavian Gravlaks. These are usually saltwater fish. Even saltwater fish have parasites that can cause serious intestinal disorders. Perhaps you should forgo all raw fish, as you would raw meats.

Rule 4—Use Insect Repellent Liberally in the Tropics

Next to contaminated food and water, insects are the most common disease-spreading mechanism in the tropics. Malaria, the great worldwide endemic disease, which kept the populations of developing countries shivering, shaking, and anemic, was stunned by DDT. Malaria, however, is making a comeback, along with other diseases carried and spread by insects. While vaccines and medical preventives are helpful, keeping bugs away is as important. This applies to mosquitoes, which spread malaria, yellow fever, dengue, and encephalitis, and to flies, fleas, ticks, mites, lice, and other bugs that bite. Insects spread these wonderfully exotic diseases which thrill doctors. If you plan to be in out-of-the-way areas where screening is inadequate, your personal mosquito net can give you a good night's sleep and keep the bugs away. Insect repellents come in lotions, creams, and sprays. Apply them to your skin and to your clothes, too. Perfumes frequently attract insects, so beware of them. Effective products for making yourself obnoxious to insects include Cutter Inspect Repellent, 6-12, and Off. Remember, most residents of the tropics keep their skin well covered—do the same. At night, wear long sleeves and slacks, and even if you wear sandals, wear socks so as to expose as little skin as possible.

Rule 5—Pretest Travel Clothes and Shoes

Pretest your clothing before traveling to find out if it is comfortable. Nylons, polyesters, and Dacron are easy to launder but do not absorb moisture well, especially in hotter climates. Wear cotton underwear and socks of absorbent fabrics such as cotton, wool, or a blend with synthetics. Outerwear may be of Dacron and polyester. White outerwear has been found to attract insects.

Shoes should always be comfortable, and since there is nothing so comfortable as an old shoe, take several pairs that are broken in. A sore foot or a blister from new shoes may ground you for several days. Persons with blood-vessel diseases and diabetes must be especially careful about their feet, since infections occur easily and can spread rapidly. The newer cushioned running shoes make excellent walking shoes.

Rule 6—Take Care of Your Skin

Probably the biggest single risk to the skin on most trips and excursions is exposure to the sun. No one wants to come home after a long trip without the healthy tan expected of travelers. Gradual, gentle, and increasing exposure to the sun should be your guide. Start with five minutes of exposure at about 10 A.M., and add several minutes each day for several days until you are tanned. Avoid the sun when it's strongest, between 11 A.M. and 2 P.M. Wear wide-brimmed hats to shield your face, head, and neck. Be especially careful when fishing, snorkeling, and swimming; you are preoccupied and do not realize you are being burned. Sunburn can occur in surprising situations, such as on cloudy days or even in the shade when light is reflected from water or the beach. So don't worship the sun—respect it!

Protective lotions and creams are now rated for their "sun protection factor" (SPF) on a scale of 1 to 15, with 15 having the best ultraviolet ray-blocking action. Redheads and blonds are more severely affected than brunettes and must be more careful. For those who do not tan, the higher numbers are preferable, while lesser protection

may be satisfactory for those with darker skin who want a
tan.

Lotions and creams have to be reapplied regularly
every several hours, since they are washed away by per-
spiration, swimming, and simply being brushed off. Do
not neglect protecting your lips.

Rule 7—Be Careful Where You Swim

No one would deliberately swim in a sewer. Most
rivers and streams in the tropics are just that. In addition,
they harbor schistosome parasites that cause the most
prevalent parasitic disease in the world: schistosomiasis.
Infection with this parasite does not occur in the oceans.
Do not swim in tropical rivers and lakes. Oceans are for
swimming, especially far from river and sewer outlets.
Swimming pools are great if properly chlorinated.

Special Problems

Traveling with Cardiac Problems

"I have heart disease, and I can't travel," is a state-
ment that becomes less and less credible with the years.
Cardiac patients have now flown hundreds of miles, even
after an acute heart attack or open-heart surgery. Knowledge about the heart's function and its diseases has elimi-
nated many fears about heart disease. The outlook for the
heart-injured has been so improved that cardiac disability
no longer means assignment to the "old rockin' chair."

Patients with heart disease are classified according to
their ability to exert themselves without developing chest
pains, shortness of breath, irregularity of the heartbeat,
or weakness. If each heart-injured person knows his or
her capacity and keeps activity within these bounds, there
is little cause to fear travel. Just make a note of the following rules.

Diet. Many patients with heart disease or high blood pressure are on low-salt, low-fat, and low-cholesterol diets.
These are hard enough to get at home, let alone while
traveling abroad. Cruise ships can usually arrange special diets. Airlines can, too, with advance notice. The

restaurants of the world, however, are not geared to producing these special diets. In order to meet this problem, medicines that remove salt and water from the body (diuretics) may be useful for those on low-salt regimens.

The low-fat, low-cholesterol problem can be met by ordering lean cuts of meat, fish, and unbuttered vegetables. Avoid fried foods, cheese, creams, gravies, and butter. Discuss your problem with your physician and get a list of high cholesterol foods to be avoided.

Medication. The problem of cardiac drugs is somewhat different from problems with other medications. Digitalis preparations vary from one manufacturer to another. For this reason, carry your own supply, and do not rely on purchases abroad. Since most heart medications are usually taken on a regular schedule, you can estimate your needs accurately. These medications are usually stable and do not deteriorate, with the exception of nitroglycerine, which weakens with age and should be renewed every six months.

Anticoagulants. Many well-adjusted cardiac patients require continuous anticoagulant treatment for artificial heart valves, irregular heart action, or to prevent blood-clot formation in veins and arteries. Since the blood-clotting mechanism must be measured regularly to determine the proper dosage, testing laboratories must be available. I have my patients tested every two weeks; other physicians have other schedules. This treatment is given all over the world, so any large hospital is equipped to perform the prothrombin time test and regulate your medication. If your readings and dosage must be adjusted frequently, it may be better to postpone your trip until your tests are stable.

Carry a chart with you, recording the date and result of each test and the dose of medication. Generally, a lesser dose is safer than a larger one. If the dose is too high, bleeding may occur from the nose, gums, in the urine, or under the skin as black-and-blue marks. Black stools are an indication of bleeding from the stomach or the intestines. Any of these symptoms of abnormal bleeding require prompt medical attention.

Traveling with a Pacemaker. Traveling with a pacemaker is
not too different from living with one. The pacemaker
should be tested one month before a long trip, and your
cardiologist should tell you whether the batteries will
last for the duration of the trip. With current pace-
makers, the only external risks are strong magnetic or
ultrasonic radiation fields. You would not be exposed to
them unless you visited a power plant or a radar station. Carry your medical records, which show the name
of the manufacturer, type of pacemaker, model number, type of electrode, and the date of implantation.
Also have the telephone number of the cardiologist or
clinic that checks your pacemaker regularly. If necessary, your pacemaker can be checked as you travel
either by contacting a hospital in the area that does
pacemaker monitoring or by long-distance telephone—
just as you do at home.

Altitudes and the Cardiac Patient. As a general rule, cardiac
patients should be cautious about altitudes on land of
5,000 feet or more. Some may not be able to tolerate
even 5,000 feet. With increasing altitude, the oxygen in
the air is decreased. If a patient requires the same
amount of oxygen as at sea level, he or she may suffer
from shortness of breath or have chest pains at higher
altitudes. These symptoms usually subside with several days of rest and decreased activity. However, if
shortness of breath increases rapidly when resting or
with minimal exertion, or if there is an abrupt increase
in chest pains or pulse, these are danger signals requir-
ing prompt attention. Under these circumstances, get
to a lower altitude promptly or go to a medical facility
with oxygen available until you can leave.

Driving over high mountain passes requires special
attention. Some passes in the Rocky Mountains are
over 10,000 feet, posing a problem for the heart-
injured, whether as driver or passenger. Snowstorms
occur at these altitudes even during the summer. A
prolonged trip under such stressful driving conditions
can produce warning symptoms. Standard types of
portable oxygen supply can be helpful, but they may
not be sufficient. Because of this, I advise against this

kind of trip. Having stated these warnings, it is only fair to say that patients who have had heart attacks and returned to a normal life are fully capable of enjoying life in high places. You should discuss your travel plans with, and be guided by, your physician.

Traveling with Diabetes

Travelers with diabetes have special problems, too, but these are easily dealt with. It is now possible to self-test your blood sugar simply by puncturing your finger, putting a drop of blood on a special paper, and reading the result promptly, thus eliminating any doubt as to whether your diabetes is out of control.

Medication. All medications for diabetics are available abroad. Because of language difficulties, however, it is best to carry enough of your own pills. Split your supply so that if you and your luggage are temporarily parted, you will not run short.

Insulin. Insulin travels well and keeps its potency for three or more months. It need not be refrigerated, but it should not be in the luggage compartment of an airplane, where it may freeze, nor should it be kept in the trunk of an automobile in the heat of summer. Keep one month's supply, plus the necessary syringes, in your hand luggage.

Diet. Culinary adventures are as much a part of a trip as visual experiences. For all but the most brittle diabetic, exotic food is worth a try. After all, bread is bread, potatoes are potatoes, and meat is meat, here and abroad. Most desserts are similar in their carbohydrate content, so the usual food exchanges will apply. Notify the airline, tour operator, cruise ship, or resort ahead of time that you will need diabetic meals.

Jet Lag and Insulin Dosage. Whenever you fly across several time zones, meal and sleep schedules are disrupted. The timing of your insulin dose is temporarily thrown off. If you miss a meal, reduce your insulin accordingly. If you find you are spilling excessive sugar, correct by increasing the amount of insulin. It is a good idea to carry a vial of "regular" insulin to use as the supplement in such cases until you are back to a normal schedule. When you will be eating your meals regularly, and will be back on your usual dose, check your blood sugar with the finger-stick method. If you are taking tablets, an increase in your medication is usually not necessary during the transition. If you run out of insulin on the trip, be sure the insulin you buy is compatible with the syringes you carry. U100 Insulin is only available in the U.S., Canada, Australia, and New Zealand. It is not available in Great Britain or continental Europe.

Foot and Skin Care. Feet and skin require special attention, since a blister, a scratch, or a fissure can start serious infections. In warm climates, powder your feet every day with an antifungus preparation such as Desenex. Keep other damp areas of the body powdered with talcum. Only shoes that are broken in should be used on a trip. The slightest irritation should be promptly treated and sunburn carefully avoided.

Identification. Diabetics should wear an identification bracelet or necklace and should carry relevant medical information with them. The International Diabetes Federation publishes a list of branch offices throughout the world, which provide assistance in an emergency. Contact your local Diabetes Association or write James G. L. Jackson, Secretary General, International Diabetes Federation, 10 Queen Anne St., London, W1M OBD, England.

In-Flight Problems

Extra Oxygen. Patients with heart and lung disease who are short of breath while at rest will usually not tolerate the lowered oxygen pressure of long-distance flying and should consult their doctors prior to undertaking such flights. If the doctor thinks the trip can be made with supplemental oxygen, it can be supplied, but the airlines usually require a letter from the doctor certifying that the person will be able to tolerate these conditions.

Ear Problems. While many people encounter some discomfort going up and down skyscraper elevators, few experience the severe ear pain that can occur when an airliner descends and the cabin is depressurized. The eustachian tube connecting the middle ear to the back of the throat normally equalizes the pressure on both sides of the eardrum. Should this slender tube become swollen and blocked by inflammation produced by a cold or chronic sinus disease, a vacuum develops in the middle ear, and the pain becomes excruciating. For this reason some people should not fly with colds. For most, antihistamines and nasal decongestants can prevent the swelling and pain. These can be taken regularly during a flight, and a nasal spray of Afrin or Neo-synephrine about 45 minutes to an hour prior to landing is helpful. Swallowing frequently as you come down is another helpful maneuver, and flight attendants may supply hard candies or chewing gum to assist this.

Dehydration. The pressurized cabin is a dry place, and the nose, throat, and skin all tend to lose moisture. Drink fluids liberally to overcome this, and use a small amount of vaseline in each nostril at the start of a trip to lose the discomfort of nasal dryness.

Swollen Feet. This occurs frequently in healthy travelers as a result of the decreased air pressure and the immobility of the feet on a long flight. In some people it can be severe enough to cause difficulty in putting on their shoes. Move your feet frequently; walking up and down the aisle will help. A good preventive is wearing support-type hose or applying ace bandages to your ankles and legs prior to flights. These should be snug enough to produce a slight pressure on the legs, but not too tight.

Traveler's Diarrhea—"Turista"

Many travelers encounter minor episodes of diarrhea, which can be due to changes in the mineral content of the water, different foods, etc. Severe or continuing diarrhea can be painful and disabling. On occasion it can be explosive and serious. The responsible agents are usually spread by contaminated water and food. The major culprit is a toxin-producing colon bacillus, but when water is contaminated with sewage or human waste, a variety of different troublemaking organisms can also be involved.

The current recommendation is not to treat the minor incidents and not to treat the diarrhea too early, because diarrhea permits the removal of organisms and toxins. However, since pain and dehydration may be severe, after the initial expulsions, medications such as Peptobismol, Imodium, Lomotil, or paregoric can be taken every two hours or so until the diarrhea has subsided. Drinking plenty of boiled or carbonated water to which salt, bicarbonate, and syrup or sugar has been added can reduce the period of sickness and weakness while accomplishing rehydration. Should bleeding occur or high fever and pain persist, you must seek medical care.

A variety of preventives have been advocated, such as Vibramycin, Septra, or Bactrim. (Prescription required.) Pepto-Bismol is only partially successful. Vibramycin may sensitize the skin to sun, while Septra or Bactrim contain a sulfa drug and Trimethoprim, to which some may be allergic. The best prevention is not medicinal; it is caution. Observe water and food warnings carefully.

Helping Yourself and Getting Help

Exercise

We have become an exercise-conscious people in recent years. For walkers, runners, and joggers, it's a way of life just as it is for yoga and karate devotees. Regular exercise makes you feel physically at ease. It strengthens the muscles that move joints and support them. It stretches the capsules, ligaments, and tendons so as to ensure continued ease of function, free of fixation by contracted ligaments and tendons. Also, it aids the circulation to and from the limbs and various other parts of the body.

Isometric exercises are those that contract muscles but do not move the joints. These exercises tone and strengthen the muscles and are used in "muscle building." They're also excellent exercises for travelers.

How do you exercise on a transoceanic flight, on a bus, or driving a car 300 miles a day? For people who have phlebitis or who have a bad back, it is a necessity; for others, exercise can reduce the discomfort of prolonged immobile sitting.

Keeping the lower limbs active is important to prevent blood from pooling in the veins of the legs and clotting. This is especially important when varicose veins are present or if you have had phlebitis in the past. While sitting, exercise is easily accomplished by flexing and extending the ankles and pointing the toes up and down. Do this frequently. Repeat it against a resistance—e.g., by pressing the toes forward against the foot rail in front and then putting the toes under the foot rail and pulling back on the ankles. While standing, raise up on your toes, then rock back on your heels. A dozen half knee bends will loosen the knee joints and put some stress on the front thigh muscles. These can also be tightened isometrically while standing.

Save the more vigorous exercise for when you are on the ground. When traveling by bus and car you will probably be stopping every two hours. Stretch your legs, bend your knees, move your body—and use the local comfort facilities.

How to Find a Doctor Abroad

Despite your best attempts to stay healthy, it is possible that you may fall ill. It can happen anywhere, even at home. Be forearmed with the proper information. Perhaps a friend knows a physician where you are going. Take the name and address. You never know when you may need a medical friend.

Most people aren't so lucky. Two organizations have stepped into the breach with listings of properly qualified English-speaking physicians in different parts of the world.

The International Association for Medical Assistance to Travelers (IAMAT) provides a worldwide listing of English-speaking physicians and clinics accepting standard fees. In addition, IAMAT provides a well-designed chart on which your doctor can detail your clinical record and "World Immunization and Malaria Risk Charts," detailing the requirements of each country. Send your name and address to IAMAT, 736 Center St., Lewiston, NY 14092 (or phone 1-716-754-4883) for the list. There is no charge, but the organization relies on donations. If your donation is $25 or over, you will be given a set of 24 climate charts covering the whole world, including month-by-month weather predictions, notes on sanitation, and altitudes of 1,000 cities. Apply 8 weeks before departure.

Intermedic also supplies a listing of English-speaking doctors around the world. This roster was compiled for the guidance of corporations that send personnel abroad. Professional fees are standardized. Membership is $6 for an individual, $10 for a family. Write to Intermedic, 777 Third Ave., New York, NY 10017.

American consular officials and hotels in any country know both doctors and hospitals. If you cannot locate a consular official in an emergency, the American Embassy in the capital city has an official on duty 24 hours daily to respond to emergencies. In an area where you cannot find Americans to help you, find the nearest university hospital, or catch the first plane to a larger city, should your medical condition warrant such action. Wherever there's plane service, you are no more than a few hours away from a medical center.

Your Personal Medical Kit

If you wear eyeglasses, carry a copy of your prescription and an extra pair of glasses as insurance. Don't forget sunglasses or "clip-ons." If you have contact lenses, carry a spare set, or at least your prescription. Replacements are available in most large cities in the world.

Take along prescriptions for all the medications you use. The bottles should be clearly labeled. Take plastic bottles. Capsules or pills are preferable to liquids. If you have to carry liquid medicines, tape the cap with adhesive and wrap the bottle in a plastic bag to protect your clothing.

Medications required frequently for emergencies should be carried in your hand luggage so that they are readily available. Nasal decongestants should be included if you have ear trouble during flight.

Medications generally advised for a long trip include the following. (Those followed by an asterisk require a doctor's prescription.)

☐ For pain, take aspirin, acetaminophen (Tylenol and others), Darvon,* or codeine.* if you are allergic to aspirin or have peptic ulcers, use acetaminophen (Tylenol, Datril, etc.). Darvon* and codeine* are somewhat stronger and may be combined with aspirin or acetaminophen for more severe pain from injury, sunburn, burns, sprains, etc.

☐ For diarrhea, the most effective and convenient medication is Lomotil* in tablet form (diphenoxylate); Imodium* is also an effective oral preparation. Paregoric* is a liquid and, although bulky and inconvenient to carry, is effective. Codeine* is also an effective anti-diarrheal agent when ½ to 1 grain is taken. You do not need more than one of these. Pepto-Bismol is less effective but does not require a prescription.

☐ Constipation is a common complaint during travel. Even the most regular people may become constipated during a trip. Any of the standard laxatives, such as Milk of Magnesia tablets, Senokot, Ex-lax, and Colace are convenient and effective. Don't let too many days go by without a movement. Prunes, dried apricots, dates, and pears for breakfast are all helpful. Drinking adequate amounts of water is essential.

☐ For infection, antibiotics are helpful. Tetracycline* is probably the single best antibacterial compound to carry when adequate medical care is not available. It is effective in most cases of throat and ear infection and in some cases of diarrhea. The usual dosage is one capsule four times a day. You should take enough medication for one week—about 30 capsules (250mg.) for each member of your party. Tetracycline may make the skin excessively sensitive to the sun. The capsules should be kept cool and must not be used after their expiration date. Ask the pharmacist to put the expiration date on the label.

☐ For allergies and upper respiratory infections, a variety of antihistamines and nasal decongestants are available. I have found Ornade Spansules and Dimetane as good as any, but they may cause drowsiness. If this occurs, you should be very cautious about driving while taking them. Slowing of urination may also occur. Sudafed does not sedate and may be preferable. All of these may increase blood pressure, so if you have a moderately severe blood pressure problem you should take only simple antihistamines such as chlorphenira-mine. Nasal sprays such as Afrin or Neosynephrine are very helpful if used for a short period of time.

☐ "Acid stomach"—as a result of overeating and over-drinking—is easily alleviated with Gelusil, Maalox, Tums, Mylanta, or similar compounds.

☐ Motion sickness can occur on any conveyance. It is a rare adult, however, who gets motion sickness in an auto or on a commercial flight. However, if you are very sensitive to motion sickness, or if you are planning a cruise, you should have either the old reliable Dramamine or Bonine handy (available without prescription). Either of these may sedate you. You usually do not have to take the tablets unless the sea is rough. An old remedy recently brought back is powdered ginger root, now available in health food stores. It has the advantage of not causing drowsiness. Recently Transderm-scop has become popular. You simply paste the small patch behind your ear. Scopolamine, the active ingredient, is absorbed through the skin, and for 24 hours you are relieved of motion sickness. On rare occasions, an individual may react peculiarly, because scopolamine can cause disorientation and hallucinations.

☐ Sleeping pills and tranquilizers require your doctor's prescription. They may be helpful in getting over jet lag.

☐ Other supplies include:
A thermometer in a well-protected case (It is important to know if you have a fever and how high it is.)
Band-Aids in assorted sizes
Adhesive tape and paper adhesive tape
Assorted sterile bandages and gauze pads
Your own preferred skin cream and lotion

Tube of vaseline
Insect repellent
Anti-sun preparation

While we are listing the various necessary or desirable medications, remember that in most parts of the
Western world, medications are similar. You can usually
obtain them through a doctor and the local pharmacist,
just as you do at home.

What Medical Records to Take

☐ If you are a healthy person, the only records you need
are the yellow International Certificate of Vaccination. This is valuable even for domestic travel because it
tells you when you had your last tetanus injection.

☐ If you have serious allergies or adverse reactions to
medications your physician thinks are important, such
as penicillin, bee or hornet stings, or severe food reactions, you should carry a list of these in your wallet.
Potentially life threatening reactions may require you
to wear an identification bracelet or necklace. Identification bracelets and necklaces are now available in
many pharmacies at a cost of less than $5. If not availa-
ble at your pharmacy, write to Health Enterprises, Inc.,
15 Spruce St., North Attleboro, MA 02760 (1-800-
MEDIC-ID or 1-617-695-0727). Medic Alert, a non-
profit foundation, charges $15 for registration. They
will keep whatever medical information you entrust to
them on their computers. The data can be retrieved via
an emergency phone call from anywhere in the world.
They will also provide you with an identification bracelet for emergencies. Write Medic Alert, Box 1009, Tur-
lock, CA 95381 (1-800-344-3226; in California 1-209-
668-3333).

☐ If you have had any serious illness, such as heart disease, asthma, bleeding disorder, or pneumothorax, you
should carry a note from your doctor about your physical condition and what medications you are taking.

☐ If you have an artificial joint or pacemaker, or have
shrapnel from a war injury, they will be picked up by
the metal detectors at security clearance before you

board an airliner. A letter from your doctor will usually avoid an embarrassing delay.

☐ If you have had a recent electrocardiogram, ask your doctor for a photocopy. It may be of value in an emergency, whether or not you have heart disease.

Medical Insurance

Visiting the monuments and cathedrals, museums and palaces of a country is part of the tourist's itinerary. The one place no one plans to visit is the hospital. Nevertheless, illness can occur away from home. Early in your preparations, check your medical insurance to see whether it provides adequate coverage if you are traveling abroad. For example, while Blue Cross–Blue Shield will pay hospitals directly and is accepted by practically all hospitals in the United States and many in Canada, only one hospital abroad is a Blue Cross participating hospital—the American Hospital in Neuilly, a suburb of Paris. In all other foreign hospitals, you will have to pay for your care in cash or traveler's checks. Some hospitals may accept credit cards, but not many as yet.

American carriers, whether Blue Cross or commercial insurance, will honor your claims after you have paid, provided you submit valid documentation. The best documentation is the claim form of your insurance company properly completed by the hospital. Obtain these forms prior to leaving, and carry them with you. If you do not have them, get itemized detailed bills and certification of payment from the hospital. Doctor's bills should include diagnosis and a description of the services rendered as well as the charges.

Medicare does not cover services abroad. However, some Medicare supplemental insurance, those policies that pay for the Medicare deductibles, may cover hospitalization abroad. Blue Cross–Blue Shield of Greater New York's "Medicare Plus" will pay for up to 90 days in nongovernmental general hospitals, provided you are a visitor and not a resident. However, there is no uniformity within the various Blue Cross plans, so you must examine the specific benefits your policies provide.

When there is a significant "hole" in your coverage,

you may want to fill this with policies designed specifically for travelers' needs. These are short-term policies ranging from 4 days to 30 or 90 days or longer. They may cover a variety of services, such as medical expenses, baggage loss, trip cancellation, accidental injury and sickness, medical assistance, and evacuation. Medical assistance plans are usually coupled with medical evacuation. If you are sick, care can be arranged by calling a central telephone number. Doctors affiliated with the plan will decide whether you need care in a medical center and will arrange for you to be transferred if necessary. The plan pays for this, including the necessary personnel. Repatriation is also included when the plan's doctors judge it to be necessary. These plans operate in Europe, with the exception of the U.S.S.R., and in most other parts of the world.

These policies may be offered by your travel agency or your insurance broker. Or you can contact one of the many travelers' insurance companies or one of the following.

The Travelers Insurance Companies, c/o Travel Pak, One Tower Square, Hartford, CT 06115 (1-800-243-3174)

International SOS Assistance, Inc., One Neshaminy Interplex, Trevose, PA 19047 (1-800-523-8930, or 1-215-244-1500 in PA)

Assist-Card Corp. of America, 347 Fifth Ave., Suite 703, New York, NY 10016 (1-212-686-1288; toll free 1-800-221-4564)

CHAPTER 11

Dentally Speaking

by Lyonel S. Hildes, D.D.S.

No one, of course, goes off on a trip expecting to have a dental emergency. The possibility of one occurring, however, should not be overlooked in planning and preparing for an extended period away from home. Few mishaps can ruin a long-planned and eagerly anticipated trip as thoroughly as a dental emergency.

Help from a Dentist

Essential in the pre-departure planning is a thorough dental evaluation by your dentist and the elimination of any condition that could potentially become a problem.

Before You Leave

Schedule an appointment with your dentist a month or so in advance of the departure date for an extended trip, especially one abroad. Allow for sufficient time for any necessary treatment and for any post-treatment complications.

Air Force dentists recommend that their personnel do not fly for three days after dental treatment to avoid so-called "flyer's toothache." This is a sometimes painful result of the rapid change in atmospheric pressure as the plane ascends or descends. Avoid having such dental treatment immediately before a trip.

If you have a history of recurrent tooth or gum problems, make a supply of an appropriate antibiotic or analgesic part of your travel kit. Make sure that your medicaments are fresh.

Obviously, any cavities or defective restorations should be attended to. The gum tissues should be inspected and rendered any indicated treatment. Often overlooked is the possibility that a removable appliance may be fractured or lost. If a serviceable spare removable appliance is not available, an inexpensive temporary replacement can and should be obtained.

Another service that your regular dentist may be able to provide before departure is to give you a list of qualified dentists in the areas you intend to visit. On a cruise or a conducted tour, the ship's medical service or the tour guide should be able to arrange adequate emergency dental care.

While Traveling

If emergency dental care is required while traveling in the United States, the following list of potential resources, in order of reliability, may be utilized for referral.

- ☐ A relative or friend who lives in the area.
- ☐ The hotel's or resort's physician. (Ask for the name of the physician's personal dentist rather than for a random referral.)
- ☐ If you are a military retiree, military installations could provide emergency care or the medical department could suggest a competent civilian dentist.
- ☐ The local hospital probably has a dental department and could provide the names of local dentists on staff.
- ☐ A dental school in the area could suggest the name of the chief of service of the specialty involved—i.e., generalist, oral surgeon, periodontist, etc.
- ☐ The local dental society would be listed in the telephone book and could be a source of referral.
- ☐ As the last resort, a well-established pharmacist could suggest emergency treatment or provide the name of his or her personal dentist.

Sources for referral while out of the country, again in order of preference, are as follows.

☐ The family dentist of the hotel or resort physician.
☐ The tour leader.
☐ Any nearby U.S. government agency—i.e., embassy, consulate, mission, military installation, etc.
☐ An American executive of a U.S. multinational firm.
☐ A well-established and respected local pharmacist.

In situations where, for whatever reason, first aid is required prior to obtaining professional help, a small, well-stocked emergency kit can be assembled and packed for the trip. This kit should consist of medications and materials to meet any foreseeable problem. A suggested list of materials would include small quantities of the following.

MEDICATIONS
· oil of cloves
· aspirin or aspirin substitutes
· bicarbonate of soda
· Orabase with benzocaine*
· Campho Phenique
· petroleum jelly (Vaseline)
· medicated pads (Poloris)*
· Cavit (obtainable from your dentist)*
· antibiotics or analgesics if required

MATERIALS
· sterile cotton pellets*
· cotton swabs
· gauze pads*
· tea bags
· dental floss
· toothpicks
· tweezers
· paraffin (or candle wax)
· an ice bag

All of these items, with the exception of Cavit, can be obtained from a druggist. The asterisks indicate those items that are included in a prepared Emergency Dental

First-Aid Kit available from Oramedics International, 200 East Montezuma Avenue, Houghton, MI 49931.

Dental First Aid

Dental emergencies, alas, have no respect for a traveler's schedule. They may strike at the most inconvenient times—in the middle of the night, while you're bouncing along in a tour bus, or at 20,000 feet midway through a flight. Be prepared by knowing what to do in an emergency. The chart on the following pages will help.

Prevention, however, is the key word. Chances are you will not experience a dental emergency while traveling. A dental check-up and any required treatment before departure will reduce the odds considerably.

General Instructions

☐ Do *not* drink alcohol while taking medication for pain.
☐ Do *not* place aspirin directly on the gum tissue. This can cause a severe chemical burn.
☐ Do *not* eat hot or spicy foods until canker sores are healed.
☐ Do *not* place hot packs on swollen areas of face. This will make swelling worse.
☐ Do *not* attempt to repair a broken denture with over-the-counter cement or glues. The adhesive may ruin the appliance.
☐ Do *not* fly within 24 hours of an extraction. The decrease in atmospheric pressure may result in spontaneous bleeding of the partially-healed extraction site.
☐ Do *not* have a tooth extracted away from home if at all possible. Have any necessary treatment for pain and/or swelling, and control any infection with antibiotics until you can see your regular dentist.

The chart on the following pages will give you additional first-aid remedies for dental problems while traveling.

Possible dental problems and recommended self-treatment before professional help can be obtained

PROBLEM	CONDITION	FIRST AID TREATMENT
1. Aphthous Ulcer (canker sore)	pain on movement and eating	· apply Orabase with benzocaine or petroleum jelly (Vaseline) · avoid spicy food *Note:* this will resolve itself in a few days in any case.
2. Cold sores (fever blisters)	pain bleeding	· apply Campho Phenique or petroleum jelly with cotton swab as often as necessary
3. Object wedged between teeth	annoyance	· use dental floss with small knot in strand or toothpick
4. Lacerated (bitten) lip or tongue	bleeding discomfort	· apply pressure with gauze pad, napkin, handkerchief, etc. · cold compress (ice cubes in clean towel) · if bleeding persists, go to hospital emergency room

Possible dental problems and recommended self-treatment before professional help can be obtained (continued)

PROBLEM	CONDITION	FIRST AID TREATMENT
5. Inflamed gingival tissue (gum around tooth)	tender to touch bleeding	· remove debris using dental floss with small knot in strand · apply Orabase with benzocaine, *or* · rinse frequently with warm sodium bicarbonate solution (1 tablespoon in ½ glass of very warm water)
6. Periodontal abscess ("gum boil" above tooth)	painful to pressure toothache swelling	· rinse with sodium bicarbonate · apply Poloris pad · apply cold compress to face · aspirin (or equivalent) for pain
7. Periapical abscess ("abscessed tooth")	severe pain swelling elevated temperature	· clean out cavity, if any, and insert cotton pellet moistened with oil of cloves · apply Poloris pad to gum over the root of the tooth · obtain antibiotic as soon as possible

Possible dental problems and recommended self-treatment before professional help can be obtained (continued)

PROBLEM	CONDITION	FIRST AID TREATMENT
8. Fracture of tooth enamel or small filling	usually no discomfort	· none indicated
9. Large fracture of tooth or filling	irritation of tongue and/or cheek	· Cavit, *or* · cover with candle wax, chewing gum, or cotton to reduce irritation
10. Fracture of crown of tooth	moderate to severe pain on chewing sensitive to hot and/or cold	· cover with candle wax, chewing gum, or cotton · avoid hot liquids · avoid sugar · take aspirin as necessary
11. Tooth dislodged by blow (pushed out of position)	cannot bring teeth together	· gently reposition tooth with fingers · rinse frequently with sodium bicarbonate · aspirin (or equivalent) for pain · cold pack for swelling

Possible dental problems and recommended self-treatment before professional help can be obtained (continued)

PROBLEM	CONDITION	FIRST AID TREATMENT
12. Front tooth knocked out and lost	pain bleeding disfigurement	· soak tea bag in warm water, fold two times, place over socket · close teeth to hold in position for one hour · see dentist immediately
13. Front tooth knocked out and tooth root intact	pain bleeding disfigurement	· same as 12 above · retrieve tooth · hold by crown, being careful not to touch the root, and place tooth in fresh milk or wrap in wet gauze *or* · rinse tooth in warm water · rinse mouth with sodium bicarbonate solution, gently re-position tooth in the socket, and hold firmly for at least 10 minutes · after either treatment, see dentist immediately for stabilization of tooth and antibiotic coverage

Possible dental problems and recommended self-treatment before professional help can be obtained (continued)

PROBLEM	CONDITION	FIRST AID TREATMENT
14. Continued bleeding after a tooth extraction	bleeding	· same as 12 above · if bleeding does not stop, see dentist or physician immediately
15. Fractured jaw	severe pain swelling unable to close mouth properly	· place bandage, scarf, towel, etc., under jaw and tie tightly on top of head to stabilize jaw · report to hospital emergency room immediately
16. Broken denture	—	· save all pieces · wear rest of appliance, if possible, until it can be repaired
17. Tooth cap off (tooth intact)	sensitivity space may close due to adjacent teeth shifting	· fill cap with Cavit, if available, *or* · fill with petroleum jelly · re-insert cap on tooth and carefully bite into position

CHAPTER 12

Rights and Redress

Nothing is ever perfect.
Even the most carefully planned travel arrangements sometimes go awry. The hotel you booked never heard of you. The charter flight operator files for bankruptcy in the middle of your trip. You and your luggage are parted; it went on a trip around the world while you only got as far as Miami.

There's no question that these disappointments are disruptive and emotionally unsettling, but most problems can be ironed out with a little calm, or failing that, with more aggressive self-representation, i.e., speaking up firmly.

Travelers have some fundamental rights. Learning what they are provides the ammunition for on-the-spot negotiation. When that fails, there's always small claims court or heavier legal action, but no one wants a lawsuit as a postscript to a dream vacation.

Air Rights

Bumping

Denied boarding is a fancy expression for bumping. Scheduled airlines overbook flights to avoid flying half-empty planes. They do this because passengers make reservations and then don't show up.

Sometimes, however, everyone who reserved a seat arrives and the plane is overbooked. On oversold domestic flights, airlines will ask for volunteers to relinquish their seats. It's not totally a sacrifice; passengers are usually offered some kind of compensation—$50, a free pass, or perhaps a full refund of the price of their one-way ticket, plus the use of their original ticket.

When no one budges from his or her seat, airlines get tougher. Last in, first off, is usually the rule. That's why it's important to check in on time. Passengers left at the gate are not abandoned. Airlines will try to put them on their next flight or on another carrier. If they can get them to the same destination within an hour of their originally scheduled arrival, the airline has no further obligation.

If the airline can't do that, but can get the passenger to his or her destination within two hours, passengers get a 100 percent refund on a one-way ticket, up to a $200 limit, plus the use of the original ticket.

When the delay is two or more hours, the ante goes up to $400 or 200 percent of the price of the one-way ticket, plus the use of the original ticket. Airlines have the option of offering passengers cash or an equivalent pass for future flights, but if passengers insist on cash, they can get it.

On outbound international flights, the same procedure is followed, except the timing is different. Airlines suffer no penalties if they can get passengers to their destination within one hour of the original flight. There is a 100 percent penalty, up to a $200 limit on a one-way ticket, if it takes up to four hours longer. When more time elapses, passengers get 200 percent of that one-way ticket, up to a maximum of $400.

When passengers are bumped overseas by an American carrier, the airline may compensate them but they are not obligated to do so. Alternative transportation, a free pass for future travel and/or a free hotel room overnight are possible compensations that may be offered. Foreign carriers guilty of overbooking may do the same thing for

returning Americans, but, again, they are not obligated to
do so.

Flight Delays

Once upon a time, airlines were good for a free hotel
room, free meals, and free phone calls when planes were
delayed by weather, mechanical problems, acts of God,
etc. Those days are not exactly gone forever—but almost.

Today, if you are stranded at the airport, the airline is
not obliged to offer you any amenities. Each airline, however, has its own rules and regulations about what it will
do. The price of the ticket, the class, and competitive
pressures are all factors that govern their decisions.

As long as you have not been airborne, carriers don't
provide any special service. Once you are airborne and
your flight is diverted to another airport, the story
changes. Airlines have to get you to your destination on
another carrier, by bus or by train. If this occurs after
10 P.M. and no onward transportation is available, the
carrier will probably stake you to a hotel room, a long-
distance phone call, and a meal. If you're traveling on a
very low cost carrier, don't expect much.

Luggage Liability

When an airline loses, damages, or delays your bags,
what is its responsibility to you?

On a domestic flight, an airline's liability on lost
checked luggage is up to $1,250 a person. Commuter
planes are excluded unless a passenger is jointly ticketed
with an ongoing carrier. On international flights, the
carrier's liability is about $9.07 per pound, up to 70
pounds per bag.

Don't get the impression that you get all that money
without a struggle. You'll have to prove that your luggage
and its contents were actually worth that much. Sales
slips and receipts will have to support your claim. Lost
jewelry or other valuables in checked bags are disallowed.

When luggage is damaged—a handle ripped off,
zippers torn, or leather or fabric lacerated—airlines will
underwrite repair bills. If the bag is beyond repair, the
airline will probably replace it. Damages must be reported

to an airline representative before you leave the airport. The filed report will determine your future rights. Get a copy of that report and keep it.

If your bag is delayed and you are on your way to a wedding, a beach vacation, or an event that requires special clothing or equipment, you may be able to claim some expenditures for replacement of suitable attire. Renting a tuxedo, buying a bathing suit or a fresh shirt, or renting sports equipment may be justifiable expenses to rescue the real goal of your trip. Purchase only what's necessary and keep the receipts. Don't go overboard; you might have to fight the airline for your expenses.

Report missing luggage before you leave the airport. Some airlines will voluntarily supply a toilet kit or perhaps $25 to $50 for small purchases.

When bags are not lost or damaged, but contents are tampered with, you may also have a claim. A damaged or broken lock should be cause to report tampering before you leave the airport. If you find that items are missing from your luggage when you get to your hotel, call the carrier and give them your name, flight number, baggage check number, and other details. This claim is harder to prove and process, but it's still possible to do so.

Sometimes you are asked to sign a waiver absolving the carrier of any responsibility if a checked box or package is inadequately packed. If that package is damaged and may have been negligently handled, the airline may accept responsibility for it despite the waiver.

Airline Defaults

Before the recent proliferation of new airlines and the economic woes of some established ones, most airlines participated in an airline default protection plan, which obligated them to honor air tickets sold by travel agents. Ticket holders on bankrupt airlines were assured transport without any additional cost to them.

The plan ceased to be when Continental Airlines went out of business and then came back to fly again. Because of these events, you should always use your credit card when paying for airline tickets. Under the Fair Credit Billing Act, if you don't receive service or goods within 60 days of the time charges appear on your credit card bill, those charges can be abrogated if you write the credit card company explaining the circumstances.

You must write them. Passengers who already paid for unused air tickets on bankrupt airlines in cash or by check may have a long wait to get their money back, if at all. The only recourse for such passengers is to file a claim with the U.S. Bankruptcy Court.

If you're stranded by a charter airline and no transportation is offered, pay your own way back. Immediately on your return, write the charter company, its bonding company, and the bank that holds the escrow account. Explain how you paid for your ticket (check, charge card), and give the date, and the number of the charter. Act immediately!

No-Smoking Sections

If it were up to them, a growing segment of air travelers would ban smoking completely from airplanes. As it stands now, passengers are entitled to get a seat in the no-smoking section of aircraft if they get to the boarding gate within a reasonable time before departure. Lock-out rules vary—from 10 to 20 minutes before departure. Pipes and cigars are not permitted at all on commercial flights.

Complaint Department

As you read this, the Civil Aeronautics Board will be a federal regulatory agency of the past. All its good consumer works will be taken over by the Department of Transportation. If you have a complaint that warrants the attention of a government agency, write the Office of the Secretary, Department of Transportation, 400 7th St., Washington, DC 20590.

If you feel you have been wronged by an American air carrier and the condition was not resolved by talking to the flight attendant or the airline's station manager, you have another recourse. Each airline maintains a special Consumer Relations Department. It is specifically set up to handle passenger complaints. State the problem, give the flight number, the date of travel, the number of your ticket, and any other information that will help the airline adjudicate your problem fairly and satisfactorily.

U.S. Rail Problems

Lost Ticket

Losing a railroad ticket is like losing cash. There is a remote possibility that the ticket may be turned in, but before you have any claim to a refund, the loss of that ticket must be on record.

Appear in person at the Amtrak office to make that report. You also have to give them other personal information. If the ticket is turned in and Amtrak has the loss report in its computer, you may very well get a refund.

Luggage Liability

Each passenger is allowed to check up to three pieces of luggage, not to exceed 150 pounds. No bag may weigh more than 75 pounds. The railroad's liability is up to a maximum of $500. If you feel your luggage is worth more, you can purchase additional coverage up to $2,500. Extra insurance is 50 cents per $100.

Scheduled Interstate Bus Transportation

Luggage Liability

Checked luggage that's lost or damaged is insured up to a total of $250 per adult ticket by the bus company. When luggage is worth more, the company will issue additional insurance for a fee.

If your bag is indeed lost and the bus company unable to trace it in 15 days, they will file a claim that will probably take an average of 90 days from the time the company started tracing your luggage.

Bus companies are not responsible for personal items of unchecked luggage left behind on buses.

When a bus is so delayed that it causes passengers to miss connections, the company must take on some responsibility if at fault, according to regulations set by the Interstate Commerce Commission. They either have to provide alternative transportation or, if that's not possible, provide passengers with food and shelter until they can get them to their destination.

Overbooking in Hotels

Airlines aren't the only ones in the travel field guilty of overbooking. Hotels are culpable of the same practice.

Despite your confirmed reservation, there are times when hotels can't accommodate you. Guests may decide to stay on beyond their original departure date, flights may have been delayed, tour operators could have overbooked their own block of hotel rooms, or a hotel may have misjudged the number of "no shows." There's also another reason, and an unsavory one at that. Some hotels deliberately overbook and send their extra guests to hotels of lesser quality. In return, they receive a commission from the less desirable hotels.

No matter who is to blame, you are the one who is inconvenienced. Your vacation plans are disrupted, and you are justifiably aggrieved.

Having accepted your down payment, if you paid ahead, hotels have a responsibility to provide you with accommodations of equal quality.

What should you do?

First call for the manager, and be insistent. Each hotel has its own policy, but first-rate ones will try to get you a room elsewhere, pay for your first night's stay, pay your cab fare to that other hotel, and try to bring you back as soon as a room becomes available.

Hotels of lesser quality may not do that unless you insist and assert your rights. One hotel manager suggests that "walked guests" make a fuss. He claims it helps in getting cab fare. There are no laws yet dealing with the

222   TRAVEL EASY

problem, but that may be changing if the practice becomes more flagrant, according to John E. H. Sherry, President of Hotel Law at Cornell University Hotel School.

Who Is Responsible?

A group of tourists on a packaged tour of Egypt were enjoying a boat ride up the Nile when the vessel burst into flames. To escape and save themselves, the passengers jumped into the river and were rescued by Nile boatsmen.

If you believed the fine print on the back of the tour brochure, neither the tour operator nor the airline involved in packaging the trip had any responsibility to the travelers. Despite disclaimers, both the airline and the tour operator, with established reputations at stake, provided funds for emergency clothing and hotel rooms. They also refunded the cost of the tour and the air fare. Everything was done to compensate passengers for their ordeal and their inconvenience.

If you look at all the disclaimers and conditions on tour contracts, travel tickets, or other travel agreements, you get the idea that nobody takes any responsibility for anything that goes wrong on a trip. Courts in many states are now making decisions on the responsibilities of travel agents, tour operators, and even informal travel promoters.

The current practice is to shift the blame and liability. There are so many different individuals and businesses involved in putting together a tour, that it's easy to do that. Laws governing negligence, fraud, and breach of contract are being applied to travel disputes, according to Thomas A. Dickerson, a specialist in travel law.

Disclaimers are often voided by the courts, but their existence in the small print of contracts is intended to discourage law suits, Mr. Dickerson points out.

What Should You Expect?

Travelers usually don't contact tour operators or wholesalers directly. The travel agent serves as the link between them. While there are some overlapping responsibilities between the agent and the tour operator, it is the travel agent who must shoulder a great deal of that responsibility, according to Mr. Dickerson. Other lawyers may differ; you should consult your own.

Because travel agents present themselves as professional advisers and sell a particular trip, Mr. Dickerson feels that it is their job to see that clients get what they pay for. "It is up to them to check out the tour operator's reliability, financial stability, and competence to deliver what is promised," Mr. Dickerson says.

Travel agents have other responsibilities as well, Mr. Dickerson adds. They should personally check on the accuracy of reservations and the packages. Is the hotel still in business? Is the cruise still scheduled to sail, or has the health department docked it until further notice? Promised services should be verified; computers make mistakes, too. Agents should also make sure that clients have all the proper documents required for their trip—visas, health certificates, etc.

Good travel agents take their responsibilities seriously. One such agency instructs clients who run into unfulfilled promises while on tour to bring back the full names, times, places, and receipts if they had to pay extra for services due them. The agency reimburses them and battles suppliers for refunds with their own attorneys.

The Complaint Department

No one likes being taken advantage of, but litigation is costly, time consuming, and aggravating.

The first step before the last resort—that is, suing—is to deal personally with the principal or agent in a "let's work it out" manner. If this approach is unrewarding, then there are the consumer protection agencies in local, state, and federal government offices and the self-regulatory associations of business.

The previously mentioned National Tour Association, the United States Tour Operators Association, and the American Society of Travel Agents all maintain consumer relations departments to deal with consumer complaints against members. Customer relations offices are maintained by airlines, Amtrak, bus companies, steamship lines, car rental agencies, recreational vehicle associations, and others. If your efforts with these fail, you might seek further advice from various government agencies, notably the Department of Transportation and the Interstate Commerce Commission.

The Better Business Bureau is also a good complaint sounding board. Branches are located all over the country. Write to the office where the travel supplier is located. State your case clearly, with all the details. You will get advice on how to proceed with your claim. The BBB is feared by businesses, who don't want adverse opinions from them. To avoid any confrontation, they may just settle with you without any further ado.

On a local level, the chamber of commerce and the district attorney's office may deal with your problem. On the state level, the attorney general's office is an excellent place to lodge a complaint, since they know about local law as well as state law and will be able to tell you how to assert your legal rights.

When all this fails and you still feel terribly wronged, consult a lawyer. Your attorney may suggest you take your case to small claims court if the amount of money involved doesn't warrant legal fees. Small claims courts are usually "consumer friendly."

For Your Next Trip

Think about taking out insurance against unforeseen circumstances the next time you take a trip. Insurance policies will cover you against unscrupulous travel operators or failed trips.

CHAPTER 13

Countdown

Your plans are set, and travel arrangements have been worked out. Now all you have to deal with are clothing, how much money to take, what type of luggage you should use, and whatever equipment will make your trip more comfortable.

The kind of luggage you use is important, even if you're on a group tour. If Americans have gone soft on luggage, there's good reason. It's lighter. Gone are the days when porters would fight each other for the privilege of carrying your bags. Even Hong Kong airport has a dearth of porters.

Weight is your number one consideration, followed by durability and fashion. Leather bags were once the ultimate in luggage. Travelers now choose canvas, vinyl, Cordura (a nylon), and coated fabrics that are stain and water resistant.

Give consideration also to luggage with wheels. Some come with removable wheels, others with four to six wheels built into the luggage. A strap is supplied to pull the luggage along. Remove the strap when checking luggage through. It can and does get caught on conveyor belts.

A carryon piece of luggage is a must, whether you travel by plane, motorcoach, train, or even car. All the important things you need while traveling are carried in this lightweight bag—film, your camera, jewelry, toilet articles, medications, a sweater, and even a change of underwear. If your luggage is lost or delayed, you are in excellent shape with a carryon packed with high priority essentials.

What to Take

Every type of holiday has its own requirements for special equipment and clothing.

If you're planning a photo safari, you'll take your camera, film, filters, and perhaps binoculars. At a fashionable resort, you know in advance men wear jackets and women more dressy clothing. Whatever your destination or travel purpose, taking the right clothes will add to your comfort and ease.

While the rule for any trip is less clothing and more money, there are circumstances in which you might take extra things. If you travel by car and have a large trunk, you have more flexibility. You could add pairs of shoes or an extra suit or dress. From my own experience, I've found that if I don't have it, I won't miss it.

A few years ago I went on a one-week trip to Spain. My luggage was delayed. Four days into the trip I was still wearing the same clothes I started with. Every night I washed my underthings. I felt vaguely free as we drove from place to place along the Costa Del Sol. Apart from missing a change of dress, I realized I could live without my luggage.

I learned two things from that experience. If you start out with the right outfit, you can live with what you have on. Having no luggage to deal with eliminates the stress of getting in and out of hotel rooms. With nothing to pack, there's nothing to leave behind.

You have your own set of values, and your own life style, but remember don't take more than you can carry yourself!

Assess what you have in your closets, and make use of your existing wardrobe. Keep in mind your itinerary and the weather you may encounter. Experienced travelers don't usually take new clothing on trips. Travel can be rough on clothes, and it's fun to buy a new piece of clothing on a trip as a practical and attractive souvenir for yourself.

Think in terms of clothing shortcuts. Any technique you can devise to lighten your luggage is always a good idea. A bathrobe could double as a bathing suit coverup. If you're likely to run into cooler weather, consider taking thin warm underwear instead of an extra suit or sweater. Think warmth without weight. Some hotels, like the Four Seasons chain, provide guests with terrycloth bathrobes and hair dryers to use for the duration of their stay. Most hotels in Japan provide yakatas (light cotton kimonos) and sandals to guests. If you know these things in advance, you can eliminate items from your luggage. Find out what amenities hotels offer.

Coordinate colors to mix and match your wardrobe. Forget the anti-polyester bias of fashion snobs; wash and wear clothes are perfect for travel.

Comfort, too, is a priority, though there is no reason why clothing can't be both comfortable and good looking. Women should think in terms of separates. Elastic waistbands on skirts and slacks are very comfortable for motorcoach travel or on long plane rides. An overblouse is a perfect topping; it is easy dressing and less likely to wrinkle.

Cushion Your Feet

While armies move on their stomachs, tourists move on their feet. The choice of shoes is very important. Some people find that the new walking sneakers offer a great deal of stability and comfort. They are not particularly attractive to wear to fashionable restaurants, so take along other shoes, too. Women should bring along medium- to low-heeled shoes that are appropriate anywhere. Perhaps your best bet might be the kind of cushioned crepe-soled shoe that is good-looking as well as comfortable.

Basic Wardrobe for a Two-Week Trip

WOMEN	MEN
all-weather coat and head scarf	all-weather coat and hat
one skirt with jacket (or a suit)	one dress suit
pair of slacks or another skirt	one blazer or sports jacket
two or three blouses that coordinate in colors with slacks and skirt	two pairs of slacks
two dresses	three wash and wear dress shirts (avoid shirts requiring cuff links)
one knit dress, suitable for evenings	a few ties
a sweater	two knit sports shirts
one pair of walking shoes	sweater
one pair of dress shoes	five pairs of socks
one pair of crepe-soled shoes or sneakers	three pairs of shoes— walking, dress, cushioned sole or sneakers
four pairs of hose	four sets of underwear
three changes of underwear	
one nightdress—fast drying	pair of pajamas—fast drying
one lightweight robe and slippers	lightweight bathrobe slippers
flat evening purse (large enough to hold travel documents; nice enough for evening activities)	half a dozen handkerchiefs
wear a shoulder-strap bag (strap can be worn across body, leaving hands free)	

This is a basic clothing guide. Of course, you will add your toiletries and such items as bathing suits for travel to a resort and other clothing suitable for the kind of vacation you plan.

Tip

A handy, pocket weather and clothing guide called Weather Travelpack has just been introduced. It provides a quick reference to what clothing to pack for 50 U.S. cities for every month of the year. There are also guides to

Europe and Latin American cities. Bookstores carry them for about $4.95. If not available, write Weather Trends International, Ltd., 565 Fifth Ave., New York, NY 10017.

Helpful Aids You Might Consider Taking

☐ Pocket calculator (comes in handy in foreign countries when you want to figure cost of purchases or weights and measures)
☐ Travel alarm clock
☐ Pocket knife with corkscrew and bottle opener (put in checked luggage)
☐ Money belt or a Safe Sac (holds money, worn under clothing like a pendant)
☐ Folding cup (handy on long bus rides; perhaps someone will pass along a drink to you)
☐ Immersion heater for a fast cup of coffee in your hotel room, packets of instant coffee and soups, tea bags, etc.
☐ Electric shaver
☐ Moist towelettes and packets of tissues
☐ Magnifying glass to read fine print
☐ Hair dryer, if needed, and perhaps a curling iron
☐ Small pocket radio, if you want to hear morning news or music

If you are going overseas and want to take small electrical equipment, most foreign countries have electrical current at 220 to 240 volts. If you don't want your electrical appliances to blow, you'll need a voltage converter and a set of proper plugs. Wall outlets in foreign countries take five different-sized pronged plugs. The country's tourist offices can tell you the kind of plugs you might need. Bathrooms in modern hotels in Europe, Latin America, and Asia are equipped to take your standard 110-120 volt electric shaver without incident.

Packing

Everybody has a system for packing. I personally put my clothing on wire hangers and pack them so they can be taken out of the suitcase and hung up directly. I do this because I have an aversion to hotel hangers, which come in parts and require the dexterity of a microsurgeon to reattach. It's my personal pique.

I find the wire hanger system works well. Just remember to put paper or masking tape around the wire edge to protect your clothes from being impaled on it. Plastic bags from the cleaners placed in between your clothes will keep them from wrinkling; air trapped in them does the trick.

Take along plastic tape to tape bottle tops closed, and whenever you can, switch the contents of glass bottles to plastic ones. You want to keep your luggage light.

Make a list of the items you put in your bags, and keep that list somewhere else. If your luggage is lost, you'll be able to tell insurance people what was in the bags. Never pack valuables in checked luggage!

Many people swear by garment bags. I find them too bulky. If you try to hang them up on an airplane, it's hard work. The closets are too small to accommodate all the garment bags people bring on board.

Things to Remember

Side Pockets. Each section of your suitcase has a use. Side pockets are invaluable for holding a sewing kit, shoe polish, safety pins, cellophane tape, a tape measure, and a rubber stopper for a leaky hotel basin.

Bottom of Bag. Put heavier things on the bottom, lighter things on top. The reason? Your clothes are less likely to crease that way. Remember, last in is first out. Pack nightclothes last.

Corners and Sides of Bag. Use the corners of the bag for rolled-up underwear and film in plastic bags. Use the sides for shoes, packed heel to toe in plastic bags. Stuff shoes with socks and breakable items like alarm clocks.

Packing Jackets. Always button jackets before packing, and zip up dresses. Leave belts on if you can, otherwise leave them open and let them hug the sides of the luggage.

Itinerary. A copy of your itinerary taped inside the luggage can be helpful if your luggage is lost. You should also make sure your name and address are taped inside.

Pocket Dictionary. If you're going overseas, remember to
  pack a foreign-language dictionary. It can come in very
  handy.
For Rainy Weather. A folding umbrella is always a good item
  to carry, and it's not too heavy.

Money Matters

How much money to take on a trip and whether it should
be in cash, traveler's checks, or a credit card, are questions
worthy of considerable thought. (See the chapter on
Homework for estimating amounts.)

A credit card, backed up with cash and travelers'
checks, could be your best bet. With a credit card you don't
have to worry about how much money to carry; hotels,
restaurants, shops, and department stores generally accept
cards for payment. Mastercard, Diner's, Visa, American
Express, and Carte Blanche are well known here and
abroad.

There may be rare instances where credit cards are
not acceptable; in such cases, travelers' checks or cash will
do nicely.

For overseas travel your trip will cost about $100 a
day per person, if not more, for moderate to luxury living.
That is after you pay for transportation costs. Hotels and
meals are your most costly expenses. If you go economy
class and stay at less expensive hotels and cut corners on
food, you may be able to trim your costs to about half that
figure.

For travelers on packaged tours, where everything is
prepaid—hotels, meals and tips—$25 to $30 a day is reasonable for pocket money. And you may have money left
over. Do not include shopping expenses in this figure.

The safest way to carry money is in travelers' checks,
now offered free by a number of banking institutions and
also issued free with membership in some clubs. When
not free, they cost about one percent of the total amount
purchased.

Barclay's Bank, Thomas Cook, American Express,
Visa, and Mastercard checks are widely accepted in for-

eign countries. When cashing them, expect to pay a small exchange fee, especially overseas. Banks, including airport banks, probably will give you the best rate.

The best reason for buying travelers' checks rather than carrying cash is safety. If checks are lost or stolen, you can get replacement funds quickly.

When you get travelers' checks, buy them in denominations of $10, $20, and $50. If you were to buy checks in $100 denominations, you might have trouble cashing them, especially for small purchases, and overseas you might have an excess of foreign currency. When you change foreign currency back into American dollars, you could lose money in the transaction.

Cash, too, should be carried. Take along a supply of one dollar bills—about 20—to take care of small purchases when you don't want to break a travelers' check or a $10 bill.

For overseas travel, buy enough foreign currency for your immediate needs on arrival—tips, cabs, a bottle of soda water—about $30 worth. You can do this at the airport before you leave or buy some from a foreign exchange specialist in your own city. Changing a lot of money when you've just come off a long flight can be a mistake, especially if you don't fully understand the country's currency. Change your money the next day, when your mind is refreshed and you are more alert. If you're due to arrive in a foreign country over the weekend, when banks are closed, buy more money before you leave, or get more at the airport when you arrive. You can always get money at your hotel, even though you might lose a little in this transaction. Just don't exchange too much.

Last-Minute Details

Before you close the books on your planning stage and take off, discuss trip cancellation insurance, baggage insurance, health insurance, and any other kind of insurance, with your travel agent. Also make provisions for mail to be held, your plants watered, your newspapers stopped. It might also be a good idea to get timers to turn lights on and off in your home automatically to thwart would-be intruders. If you live in an apartment, this may not be necessary, but tell neighbors you will be away.

Before you leave the house, check off the following items to take with you, and *have an alternative plan* should you forget to take essentials—like medications.

- ☐ Tickets
- ☐ Valid passport (if needed)
- ☐ Travelers' checks
- ☐ Credit card
- ☐ Emergency cash
- ☐ Important phone numbers and addresses
- ☐ All your medications and their generic names
- ☐ Extra glasses and/or a prescription for them
- ☐ Emergency medical kit
- ☐ Confirmed reservations in writing if an independent traveler
- ☐ List of gifts with clothing sizes
- ☐ A folding umbrella
- ☐ Film, camera, pocket radio, if you want one, and your pocket calculator
- ☐ Personal identification
- ☐ International Driver's permit, if needed
- ☐ Extra luggage keys

HAVE A WONDERFUL TRIP.

APPENDIX A

State and National Tourist and Travel Offices

NOTE: all 800 numbers are toll-free phone calls.

United States

Alabama
Bureau of Publicity and Information   205-252-2262
532 S. Perry St., Montgomery, AL 36104   800-252-2262

Alaska
Division of Tourism   907-465-2010
Pouch E. 445, Juneau, AK 99811

Arizona
Office of Tourism   602-255-3618
3507 North Central Ave., Phoenix, AZ 85012

Arkansas
Department of Parks and   in AR: 800-482-8999
Tourism   outside AR: 800-643-8383
1 Capitol Mall, Little Rock, AR 72201

California
Department of Economic and Business Affairs   916-322-1396
Office of Tourism
1030 13th St., Suite 200
Sacramento, CA 95814

Colorado
Division of Commerce and Development   303-779-1067
Office of Tourism
5500 South Syracuse Circle, Suite 267
Englewood, CO 80111

Connecticut
Department of Economic Development   203-566-3948
Tourism Division
210 Washington St., Hartford, CT 06106

Delaware
State Travel Service   in DE: 800-282-8667
99 Kings Highway, P.O. Box 1401   outside DE: 800-441-8846
Dover, DE 19903

District of Columbia
Washington Area Convention and Visitors Assn.   202-789-7000
1575 I St., Suite 250
Washington, DC 20005

Florida
Department of Commerce   904-487-1462
Division of Tourism
126 Van Buren St., Tallahassee, FL 32301

Georgia
Tourist Division   404-656-3590
Dept. of Industry and Trade
P.O. Box 1776, Atlanta, GA 30301

Hawaii
Visitors Bureau   808-923-1811
2270 Kalakaua Ave., Honolulu, HI 96815
Offices also in New York, Chicago, Los Angeles,
San Francisco, and Vancouver, B.C.

Idaho
Division of Economic and Community Affairs   208-334-2470
Visitor Information   800-635-7820
Room 108, State Capitol Building, Boise, ID 83720

Illinois
Tourist Information Center   312-793-2094
100 W. Randolph St.   in IL: 800-252-8987
State of Illinois Bldg.   nearby states: 800-637-8560
Chicago, IL 60601

Indiana
Tourism, Development Division   317-232-8860
1 North Capitol Ave., Suite 700   in IN: 800-622-4464
Indianapolis, IN 46204/2243

Iowa
Visitor and Tourism Division   515-281-3210
600 East Court Ave., Suite A
Des Moines, IA 50309

Kansas
Travel and Tourism Division   913-296-2009
503 Kansas Ave., Topeka, KS 66603

Kentucky
Travel and Development   800-225-8747
Department of Tourism
Capitol Plaza Tower, Frankfort, KY 40601

Louisiana
Office of Tourism   800-231-4730
P.O. Box 44291   504-925-3860
Baton Rouge, LA 70804

Maine
Publicity Bureau   207-289-2423
97 Winthrop St.
Hallowell, ME 04347

Maryland
Office of Tourist Development   301-269-2686
45 Calvert St.
Annapolis, MD 21401

Massachusetts
Division of Tourism   617-727-3201
Department of Commerce and Development
100 Cambridge St.
Boston, MA 02202

Michigan
Travel Bureau   517-373-1195
Dept. of Commerce   800-248-5700
P.O. Box 30226   in MI: 800-292-2520
Lansing, MI 48909

Minnesota
Office of Tourism   612-296-5029
240 Bremer Building   800-328-1461
419 North Robert St.   in MN: 800-652-9747
St. Paul, MN 55101

Mississippi
Dept. of Economic Development   601-359-3414
Division of Tourism   800-647-2290
P.O. Box 849
Jackson, MS 39205

Missouri
Division of Tourism   314-751-4133
308 East High St., P.O. Box 1055
Jefferson City, MO 65102

Montana
Travel Promotion Bureau   in MT: 406-444-2654
Dept. of Highways   800-548-3390
1424 Ninth Ave., Helena, MT 59620

Nebraska
Division of Travel and Tourism   402-471-3796
P.O. Box 94666   800-228-4307
301 Centennial Mall South
Lincoln, NE 68509

Nevada
Nevada Commission on Tourism   702-885-4322
Capitol Complex, Suite 207
Carson City, NV 89710

New Hampshire
Office of Vacation Travel   603-271-2343
P.O. Box 856, Concord, NH 03301

New Jersey
Division of Travel and Tourism   609-292-2470
P.O. Box CN 826, Trenton, NJ 08625

New Mexico
Economic Development and Tourism Department   505-827-6230
Travel Division   800-545-2040
Bataan Memorial Building, Room 130
Santa Fe, NM 87503

New York
Division of Tourism   518-474-4116
State Dept. of Commerce   in nearby states: 800-225-5697
1 Commerce Plaza
Albany, NY 12245

New York City
New York Convention and Visitors Bureau   212-397-8222
2 Columbus Circle
New York, NY 10019

North Carolina
Travel and Tourism Division   919-733-4171
430 North Salisbury St.   in NC: 800-334-1051
Raleigh, NC 27611   800-438-4404

North Dakota
Tourism Promotion Division   701-224-2525
Liberty Memorial Building   in ND: 800-472-2100
State Capitol Grounds   800-437-2077
Bismarck, ND 58505

Ohio
Office of Travel and Tourism   800-282-5393
P.O. Box 1001, Columbus, OH 43216

Oklahoma
Tourism Promotion Division   405-521-2409
500 Will Rogers Building
Oklahoma City, OK 73105

Oregon
Economic Development
Tourism Division
595 Cottage St., Northeast
Salem, OR 97310

800-547-7842
in OR: 800-233-3306

Pennsylvania
Department of Commerce
Bureau of Travel Development
416 Forum Building, Harrisburg, PA 17120

800-233-7366

Rhode Island
Department of Economic Development
Tourism
7 Jackson Walkway, Providence, RI 02903

401-277-2601
in nearby states: 800-556-2484

South Carolina
Department of Parks, Recreation and Tourism
Division of Tourism
1205 Pendleton St., Suite 110
Columbia, SC 29201

803-758-8570

South Dakota
Division of Tourism
P.O. Box 1000, Pierre, SD 57501

in SD: 800-952-2217
800-843-1930

Tennessee
Department of Tourist Development
P.O. Box 23170, Nashville, TN 37202

615-741-2158

Texas
Travel and Information Division
Department of Highways and
Public Transportation
P.O. Box 5064, Austin, TX 78763

512-475-2028

Utah
Travel Council
Council Hall, Capitol Hill
Salt Lake City, UT 84114

801-533-5681

Vermont
Travel Division
134 State St., Montpelier, VT 05602

802-828-3236

Virginia
Division of Tourism
202 North Ninth St., Suite 500
Richmond, VA 23219

804-786-2051

Washington
Commerce and Economic Development
Tourism Division
General Administration Bldg., Room G3
Olympia, WA 98504

in WA: 800-562-4570
800-541-9274

West Virginia
Travel Development   304-348-2286
Building 6, Room 564, State Capitol   800-624-9110
Charleston, WV 25305

Wisconsin
Department of Development   608-266-2161
Division of Tourism
123 West Washington Ave., Madison, WI 53707

Wyoming
Travel Commission   307-777-7777
I-25 at College, Cheyenne, WY 82002   800-443-2784

Canada and Mexico

Canada
Tourism Canada
New York: 1251 Avenue of Americas   212-757-4917
                New York, NY 10020
Chicago: 310 South Michigan Ave.   312-427-1666
                Chicago, IL 60604
Los Angeles: 510 West 6th St.   213-622-4292
                Los Angeles, CA 90014

Mexico
Mexican National Tourist Council
New York: 405 Park Ave.   212-755-7212
                New York, NY 10022
Los Angeles: 10100 Santa Monica Blvd.   213-203-8151
                Los Angeles, CA 90069

The Caribbean and Nearby Islands

Caribbean Tourist Association   212-682-0435
20 East 46th St., New York, NY 10017

Aruba
Aruba Tourist Board   212-246-3030
1270 Avenue of Americas
New York, NY 10020

The Bahamas
Bahama Tourist Office   212-757-1611
10 Columbus Circle, Suite 1660   800-327-0787
New York, NY 10019

Barbados
Barbados Board of Tourism   212-986-6516
New York: 800 2nd Ave.
             New York, NY 10017
Los Angeles: 3440 Wilshire Blvd., Suite 1215   213-380-2198
             Los Angeles, CA 90010   800-221-9831

Bermuda
Bermuda Department of Tourism   212-397-7700
630 Fifth Ave.   in NY: 800-223-6107
New York, NY 10111   outside NY: 800-223-6106

Cayman Islands
Cayman Islands Dept. of Tourism   212-682-5582
420 Lexington Ave., New York, NY 10017

Curacao
Curacao Tourist Board   212-751-8266
400 Madison Ave., Suite 311, New York, NY 10017

Haiti
Haiti Tourist Bureau   212-757-3517
1270 Avenue of Americas, Suite 508
New York, NY 10020
Miami: 150 Southeast Second Ave.   305-371-9420
        Republic Bank Building, Suite 1013
        Miami, FL 33131

Jamaica
Jamaica Tourist Board
New York: 2 Dag Hammarskjold Plaza   212-688-7650
             New York, NY 10017
Chicago: 36 South Wabash Ave., Suite 1210   312-346-1546
             Chicago, IL 60603
Los Angeles: 3440 Wilshire Blvd., Suite 1207   213-384-1123
             Los Angeles, CA 90010

Puerto Rico
Puerto Rico Tourism Co.   212-541-6630
1290 Avenue of Americas, New York, NY 10104
Chicago: 11 East Adams St.   312-922-9701
             Chicago, IL 60603
Los Angeles: 3575 West Cahuenga Blvd.   213-874-5991
             Los Angeles, CA 90068
Offices also in Orlando, FL, and Toronto, Canada.

United States Virgin Islands
Division of Tourism, U.S. Virgin Islands   212-582-4520
1270 Avenue of Americas, New York, NY 10020
Chicago: 343 South Dearborn St., Suite 915   312-461-0180
             Chicago, IL 60604
Los Angeles: 3450 Wilshire Blvd.   213-739-6138
             Los Angeles, CA 90010

Central and South America (Selected)

Argentina
Consulate General, Argentina   212-397-1400
12 West 56th St.
New York, NY 10019

Brazil
Brazilian Tourist Authority   212-286-9600
60 East 42nd St., Suite 1336
New York, NY 10023

Chile
Consulate General, Chile   212-980-3366
866 United Nations Plaza
New York, NY 10017

Colombia
Colombian Government Tourist Office   212-688-0151
140 East 57th St.
New York, NY 10022

Costa Rica
Costa Rica Tourist Office
New York: 630 Fifth Ave.   212-245-6370
          New York, NY 10111
Miami: 200 Southeast 1st St., Suite 400   800-327-7033
          Miami, FL 33131

Ecuador
Consulate General, Ecuador   212-683-7555
18 E. 41st St., Room 1800
New York, NY 10017

Peru
Peru National Tourist Office   212-949-4020
489 Fifth Ave., Room 3001
New York, NY 10017

Venezuela
Venezuelan Government Tourist and   212-355-1101
Information Center
7 E. 51st St., New York, NY 10022

Europe

Austria
Austrian National Tourist Office
New York: 500 Fifth Ave.   212-944-6880
             New York, NY 10110
Chicago: 500 N. Michigan Ave., Suite 544   312-644-5556
             Chicago, IL 60611
Los Angeles: 3440 Wilshire Blvd., Suite 906   213-380-3309
             Los Angeles, CA 90010

Belgium
Belgian National Tourist Office   212-758-8130
745 Fifth Ave., New York, NY 10151

Cyprus
Cyprus Tourist Organization   212-686-6016
13 East 40th St., New York, NY 10016

Czechoslovakia
Cedok Czechoslovakian Travel Bureau   212-689-9720
10 East 4th St., New York, NY 10016

Denmark
Danish Tourist Board   212-949-2333
655 Third Ave., New York, NY 10017

Finland
Finnish Tourist Board   202-949-2333
655 Third Ave., New York, NY 10017

France
French Government Tourist Office
New York: 610 Fifth Ave.   212-757-1125
               New York, NY 10020
Chicago: 645 N. Michigan Ave.   312-337-6301
               Chicago, IL 60611
Los Angeles: 9401 Wilshire Blvd.   213-271-2665
               Los Angeles, CA 90212

German Democratic Republic (East Germany)
Embassy of German Democratic Republic   202-232-3134
1717 Massachusetts Ave., N.W.
Washington, DC 20036

Federal Republic of Germany (West Germany)
German National Tourist Office   212-308-3300
New York: 747 Third Ave.
               New York, NY 10017
Los Angeles: 444 South Flower St.   213-688-7332
               Los Angeles, CA 90071

Greece
Greek National Tourist Organization
New York: 645 Fifth Ave.   212-421-5777
               New York, NY 10022
Chicago: 168 N. Michigan Ave.   312-782-1084
               Chicago, IL 60601
Los Angeles: 611 West 6th St., Suite 1198   213-626-6696
               Los Angeles, CA 90017

Hungary
Hungarian Travel Bureau IBUSZ   212-582-7412
630 Fifth Ave., Suite 520
New York, NY 10111

Iceland
Iceland Tourist Board   212-949-2333
655 Third Ave., New York, NY 10017

Ireland
Irish Tourist Board   212-869-5500
New York: 590 Fifth Ave.
               New York, NY 10036
Chicago: 230 N. Michigan Ave.   312-726-9356
               Chicago, IL 60601
San Francisco: 625 Market St., Suite 502   415-957-0985
               San Francisco, CA 94105

Italy
Italian Government Travel Office
New York: 630 Fifth Ave.   212-245-4822
               New York, NY 10111
Chicago: 500 N. Michigan Ave.   312-644-0990
               Chicago, IL 60611
San Francisco: 360 Post St.   415-392-6206
               San Francisco, CA 94108

Luxembourg
Luxembourg National Tourist Office   212-370-9850
801 Second Ave., New York, NY 10017

Malta
Consulate of Malta   212-725-2345
249 East 35th St., New York, NY 10016

Monaco
Monaco Government Tourist Bureau   212-759-5227
845 Third Ave., New York, NY 10022

Netherlands
Netherlands National Tourist Office
New York: mailing address only: 212-223-8141
               576 Fifth Ave.
               New York, NY 10036
               437 Madison Ave.
               New York, NY 10022
San Francisco: 605 Market St.   415-543-6772
               San Francisco, CA 94105

Norway
Norwegian National Tourist Office   212-949-2333
655 Third Ave., New York, NY 10017

Poland
Polish National Tourist Office   212-391-0844
500 Fifth Ave., New York, NY 10110

Portugal
Portuguese National Tourist Office   212-354-4403
548 Fifth Ave., New York, NY 10036

Romania
Romanian National Tourist Office 212-697-6971
573 Third Ave., New York, NY 10016

Spain
Spanish National Tourist Office
New York: 665 Fifth Ave.   212-759-8822
               New York, NY 10022
Chicago: 845 N. Michigan Ave.   312-944-0215
               Chicago, IL 60611
San Francisco: 1 Hallidie Plaza   415-346-8100
               San Francisco, CA 94102
Office also in Houston, TX.

Sweden
Swedish Tourist Board 212-949-2333
655 Third Ave.
New York, NY 10017

Switzerland
Swiss National Tourist Office
New York: 608 Fifth Ave.   212-757-5944
               New York, NY 10020
San Francisco: 250 Stockton St.   415-362-2260
               San Francisco, CA 94108

Turkey
Turkish Tourism and Information Office
New York: 821 United Nations Plaza   212-687-2194
               New York, NY 10017

United Kingdom
British Tourist Authority
New York: 40 West 57th St.   212-581-4700
               New York, NY 10019
Chicago: John Hancock Center, Suite 3320   312-787-0490
               875 N. Michigan Ave.
               Chicago, IL 60611
Dallas: Plaza of the Americas, Suite 750   214-748-2279
               North Tower LB 346
               Dallas, TX 75201
Los Angeles: 612 South Flower St.   213-623-8196
               Los Angeles, CA 90017

U.S.S.R.
Intourist 212-757-4127
630 Fifth Ave.
New York, NY 10111

Yugoslavia
Yugoslav State Tourist Office 212-757-2801
630 Fifth Ave.
New York, NY 10111

Africa and the Middle East (Selected)

Egypt
Egyptian Government Tourist Office
New York: 630 Fifth Ave.   212-246-6960
                   New York, NY 10111
San Francisco: 323 Geary St., Suite 608   415-781-7676
                   San Francisco, CA 94102

Israel
Israel Government Tourist Office
New York: Empire State Building   212-560-0650
                   350 Fifth Ave.
                   New York, NY 10118
Chicago: 5 S. Wabash Ave.   312-782-4306
                   Chicago, IL 60603
Los Angeles: 6380 Wilshire Blvd.   213-658-7462
                   Los Angeles, CA 90048

Kenya
Kenya Tourist Office
New York: 424 Madison Ave.   212-486-1300
                   New York, NY 10017
Beverly Hills: 9100 Wilshire Blvd.   213-274-6634
                   Doheny Plaza, Suite 111
                   Beverly Hills, CA 90212

Morocco
Moroccan National Tourist Office
New York: 20 East 46th St., Suite 503   212-557-2520
                   New York, NY 10017

South Africa
South African Tourism Board
New York: 747 Third Ave.   212-838-8841
                   New York, NY 10017
Chicago: 307 N. Michigan Ave.   312-726-0517
                   Chicago, IL 60601
Beverly Hills: 9465 Wilshire Blvd., Suite 721   213-275-4111
                   Beverly Hills, CA 90212

South Pacific

Australia
Australian Tourist Commission
New York: 489 Fifth Ave.   212-489-7550
                   New York, NY 10017
Los Angeles: 3550 Wilshire Blvd., Suite 1740   213-380-6060
                   Los Angeles, CA 90010

New Zealand

New Zealand Travel Commission

New York:	630 Fifth Ave.	212-586-0060
	New York, NY 10111	
Los Angeles:	Tishman Building, Suite 1530	213-477-8241
	10960 Wilshire Blvd.	
	Los Angeles, CA 90024	
San Francisco:	Alcoa Building, Suite 970	415-788-7430
	Maritime Plaza	
	San Francisco, CA 94111	

Tahiti

Tahiti Tourist Development Board
B.P. 65
Papeete, Tahiti
French Polynesia

U.S. Representative, California   213-475-2010

Asia

China

China National Tourist Office   212-867-0271
60 East 42nd St., Suite 465, New York, NY 10165

Hong Kong

Hong Kong Tourist Association

New York:	548 Fifth Ave.	212-869-5008
	New York, NY 10036	
San Francisco:	421 Powell St., Suite 200	415-781-4582
	San Francisco, CA 94102	
Chicago:	333 N. Michigan Ave., Suite 2422	312-782-3872
	Chicago, IL 60601	

India

Government of India Tourist Office

New York:	30 Rockefeller Plaza	212-586-4901
	New York, NY 10112	
Chicago:	230 N. Michigan Ave.	312-236-6899
	Chicago, IL 60601	
Los Angeles:	3550 Wilshire Blvd.	213-380-8855
	Los Angeles, CA 90010	

Indonesia

Indonesian Tourist Promotion Center

New York:	Consulate General	212-879-0600
	5 East 68th St.	
	New York, NY 10021	
San Francisco:	Consulate	415-892-8966
	351 California St., Room 700	
	San Francisco, CA 94104	

Japan
Japan National Tourist Office
New York: 630 Fifth Ave.   212-757-5640
               New York, NY 10111
Chicago: 333 North Michigan Ave.   312-332-3975
               Chicago, IL 60601
San Francisco: 360 Post Rd., Suite 401   415-989-7140
               San Francisco, CA 94108

Macao
Macao Tourist Information Bureau
New York: 608 Fifth Ave., Suite 309   212-581-7465
               New York, NY 10020
Los Angeles: 3133 Lake Hollywood Drive   213-851-3400
               Los Angeles, CA 90068
Offices also in Honolulu, Toronto, and Vancouver.

Nepal
Nepal Consulate General   212-370-4188
820 Second Ave., Suite 1200, New York, NY 10017

Singapore
Singapore Tourist Promotion Board   212-687-0385
342 Madison Ave., New York, NY 10173

Sri Lanka
Ceylon (Sri Lanka) Tourist Board   212-935-0369
609 Fifth Ave., Suite 714, New York, NY 10017

Korea
Korea National Tourism Corporation
New York: 460 Park Ave., Suite 400   212-688-7543
               New York, NY 10022
Los Angeles: 510 West 6th St., Suite 323   213-623-1226
               Los Angeles, CA 90014
Chicago: 230 N. Michigan Ave., Suite 1500   312-346-6660
               Chicago, IL 60601

Taiwan
Taiwan Visitors Association
New York: Suite 8855, 1 World Trade Center   212-466-0691
               New York, NY 10048
San Francisco: 166 Geary St., Suite 1605   415-989-8677
               San Francisco, CA 94108   989-8694
Los Angeles: 3325 Wilshire Blvd., Suite 515   213-739-8898
               Los Angeles, CA 90010   739-8899

Thailand
Tourism Authority of Thailand
New York: Room 2449, 5 World Trade Center   212-432-0433
               New York, NY 10048
Los Angeles: 3440 Wilshire Blvd., Suite 1101   213-382-2353
               Los Angeles, CA 90010

APPENDIX B

Reading List

Hotels and Lodgings

Directories

Directory of Hotel and Motel Systems. New York: American Hotel and Motel Association. Updated annually. Lists hotels, motels, chains. Can be purchased ($24.50) from the association, 888 Seventh Ave., New York, NY 10019.

Hotel and Motel Redbook. Walnut Creek, Calif.: Pactel Publishing Company. Updated annually. Includes maps, list of hotels and motels, rates, car rental information. Available in most libraries. Cost: about $40.

Regional Guides

American Automobile Association Guides. Guides for 26 regions are available with membership in the AAA. Contact your local club for information.

Mobil Travel Guides. Chicago: Rand McNally. Updated annually. Guides with hotels and ratings available for seven regions. About $7.95 each.

Bed and Breakfast

American Bed and Breakfast Association, *A Treasury of Bed and Breakfast* and *Bed and Breakfast Hostline*. Both are available from the association, P.O. Box 23294, Washington, DC. The *Treasury*, published in 1984, describes 2,700 homes and lists reservations systems. Available by mail order for $12.95 plus $3 postage. *Hostline*, updated semiannually, lists hosts in 1,500 cities. Available by mail for $5.95, postage included.

Gieseking, Hal. *Frommer Guide to Bed and Breakfast, North America.* New York: E.P. Dutton, 1984. Offers descriptions and details features of 480 homes and 99 reservation agencies in 50 states and Canada.

249

Lanier, Pamela, *The Complete Guide to Bed & Breakfast, Inns and Guesthouses.* Santa Fe: John Muir Publications, 1984. Lists over 2,000 lodgings in the U.S. and Canada.

Rundback, Betty, and Kramer, Nancy, *Bed and Breakfast, U.S.A.* New York: E.P. Dutton, 1984. Offers descriptions and details features of 480 homes and 99 reservation agencies in 50 states and Canada.

Small Hotels and Inns

Crossette, Barbara, *America's Wonderful Little Hotels and Inns.* New York: Congdon and Weed, 1984. Covers more than 600 distinctive smaller hotels and inns in U.S., Canada, and Puerto Rico.

Regional Country Inns, by variety of authors in The Compleat Traveler series. New York: Burt Franklin, Publisher, 1984-85.

Budget Accommodations

Carlson, Raymond, *National Directory of Budget Motels.* New York: Pilot Books, 1985. Available for $3.50 by mail order from Pilot Books, 103 Cooper St., Babylon, NY 11702. Lists low-cost chain motels.

Spas

Babcock, Judy, and Kennedy, Judy, *The Spa Book.* New York: Crown, 1983. Tour of spas in North America, including Mexico.

Wilkens, Emily, *More Secrets from the Super Spas.* New York: Dembner/Norton, 1983. Detailed profile on super spas in America and abroad.

Attractions

Shemanski, Frances, *A Guide to Fairs and Festivals in the United States.* Westport, Conn.: Greenwood Press, 1984. Features descriptions and calendar of major events in 50 states and territories.

Van Meer, Mary and Pasquarelli, and Michael Anthony, *Free Attractions, USA.* Santa Fe: John Muir Publications, 1984. Where to enjoy free events in U.S.

Transportation

Travel by Ship

Blum, Ethel, *The Total Traveler by Ship.* Miami: Travel Publications, Inc., 1985. An excellent hand-holder for first-time or experienced voyagers.

DeLand, Antoinette, *Fielding's Worldwide Cruises*. New York: Fielding Travel Books/William Morrow and Co. Updated annually. Describes ports, lists cruise lines, and describes ships and specialty cruises.

Rail Travel

Fistell, Ira, *America by Train*. New York: Burt Franklin, Publisher, 1984–85. Describes regions and attractions along train routes.

Saltzman, Kathryn and Marvin L., *Eurail Guide—How to Travel Europe and All the World by Train*. Malibu, Calif.: Eurail Guide Annual. Updated Annually. What to see on train routes overseas.

Other Topics

Retirement Spots

Dickinson, Peter A., *Travel and Retirement Edens Abroad*. New York: E.P. Dutton, 1983. Nuts and bolts of retirement overseas plus descriptive text detailing more popular places.

Dickinson, Peter A., *Sunbelt Retirement*. New York: E. P. Dutton, 1980. A state-by-state guide to retiring in the South and West of the United States.

Handicapped Travel

Weiss, Louise, *Access to the World*. New York: Facts On File, 1983. Handbook for handicapped travelers, from slightly disabled to wheelchair tourists.

Learning Vacations

Eisenberg, Gerson G., *Learning Vacations*. Princeton: Peterson's Guides, 1982.

Senior Money Savers

Palmer, Paige. *The Senior Citizen's Guide to Budget Travel in Europe*. Babylon, N.Y.: Pilot Books, 1985. $3.50—postage included. Mail order only, 103 Cooper St., Babylon, NY 11702. The same author has written *The Senior Citizen's Guide to Budget Travel in the U.S.* 1985. $3.95 from Pilot Books.

Weintz, Caroline and Walter. *The Discount Guide for Travelers Over 55*. New York: E.P. Dutton, 1983.

Free literature is available from the following government agencies.

From U.S. Customs, P.O. Box 7118, Washington, D.C. 20044
> *Know Before You Go*—customs hints
> *GSP & The Traveler*—duty-free imports from developing nations
> *Tourist Trademark Information*—list of popular prohibited items

From the Bureau of Consular Affairs, Department of State, Washington, D.C. 20520
> *Travel Tips for Senior Citizens*—helpful hints
> *Your Trip Abroad*—how to get a passport and other tips on overseas travel

From U.S. Department of Agriculture, Washington, D.C. 20250
> *Travelers' Tips on Bringing Food, Plant and Animal Products into the United States*—spells out what you can and can't bring in

General Travel Books

Fielding, Arthur Frommer, Fisher Annotated Travel Guides, Fodor, and *Stephen Birnbaum Travel Guides* are among a number of distinguished publications with multiple titles. They cover individual countries, cities, and even states. Some are geared to low-budget travel, others to all tourists. Visit your bookstore and ask for help for specific destinations or contact specialized mail order travel book resources, many of which publish catalogues. These include Forsyth Travel Library, P.O. Box 2975, Shawnee Mission, KA 66201; The Complete Traveller Bookstore, 199 Madison Ave., New York, NY 10016; Traveller's Bookstore, 22 W. 52nd St., New York, NY 10019, and Book Passage, 57 Post St., San Francisco, CA 94104.

APPENDIX C

Maps of Key Tourist Sites

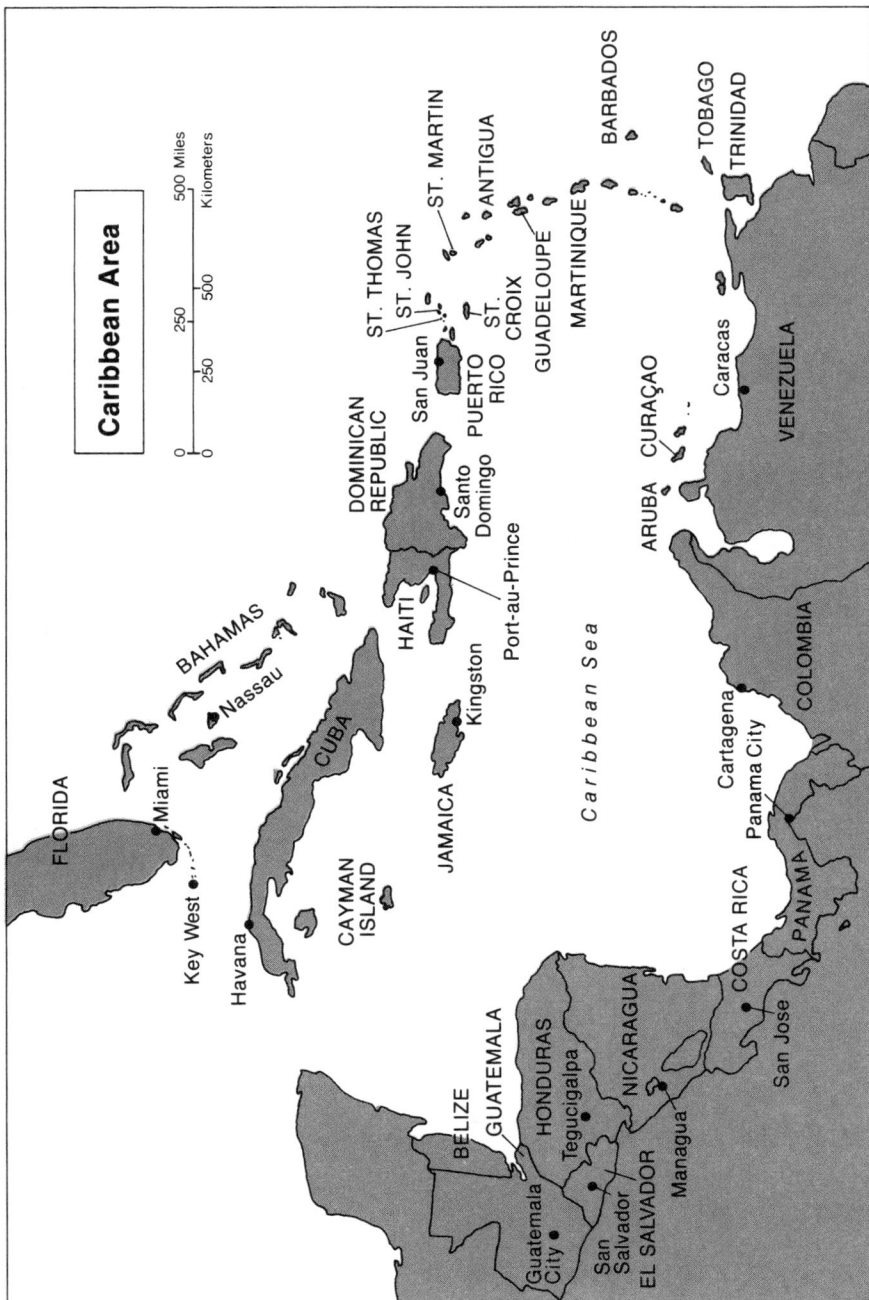

Caribbean Area

500 Miles
Kilometers

FLORIDA

Miami

Key West

Havana

CUBA

BAHAMAS

Nassau

CAYMAN ISLAND

JAMAICA

Kingston

HAITI

Port-au-Prince

DOMINICAN REPUBLIC

Santo Domingo

San Juan

PUERTO RICO

ST. THOMAS

ST. JOHN

ST. CROIX

ST. MARTIN

ANTIGUA

GUADELOUPE

MARTINIQUE

BARBADOS

TOBAGO

TRINIDAD

Caribbean Sea

ARUBA

CURAÇAO

Caracas

VENEZUELA

COLOMBIA

Cartagena

Panama City

PANAMA

COSTA RICA

San Jose

NICARAGUA

Managua

HONDURAS

Tegucigalpa

EL SALVADOR

San Salvador

GUATEMALA

Guatemala City

BELIZE

255

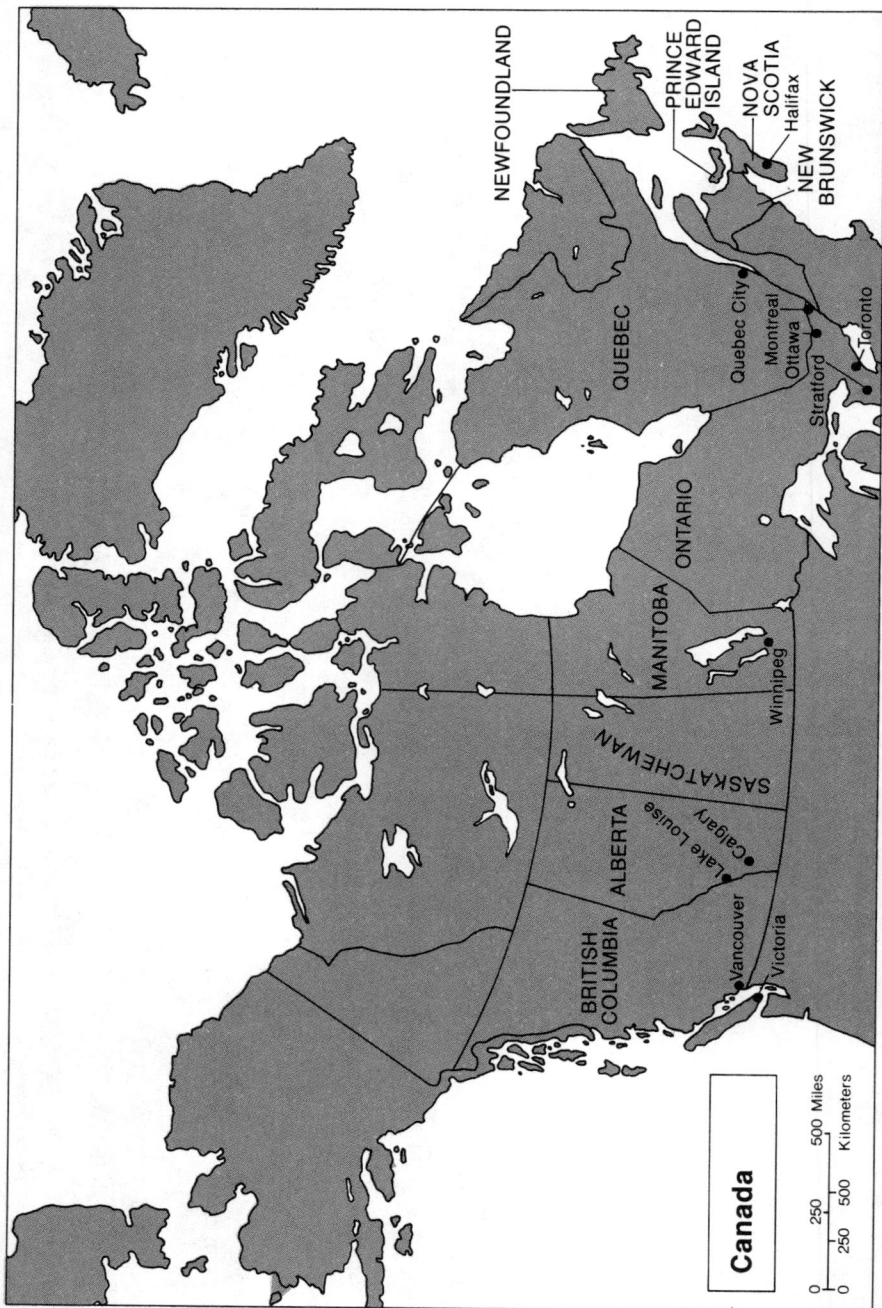

Canada

NEWFOUNDLAND

PRINCE EDWARD ISLAND

NOVA SCOTIA
Halifax

NEW BRUNSWICK

QUEBEC

Quebec City
Montreal
Ottawa
Stratford
Toronto

ONTARIO

MANITOBA

SASKATCHEWAN

Winnipeg

ALBERTA

Lake Louise
Calgary

BRITISH COLUMBIA

Vancouver
Victoria

0   250   500 Miles
0 250 500 Kilometers

256

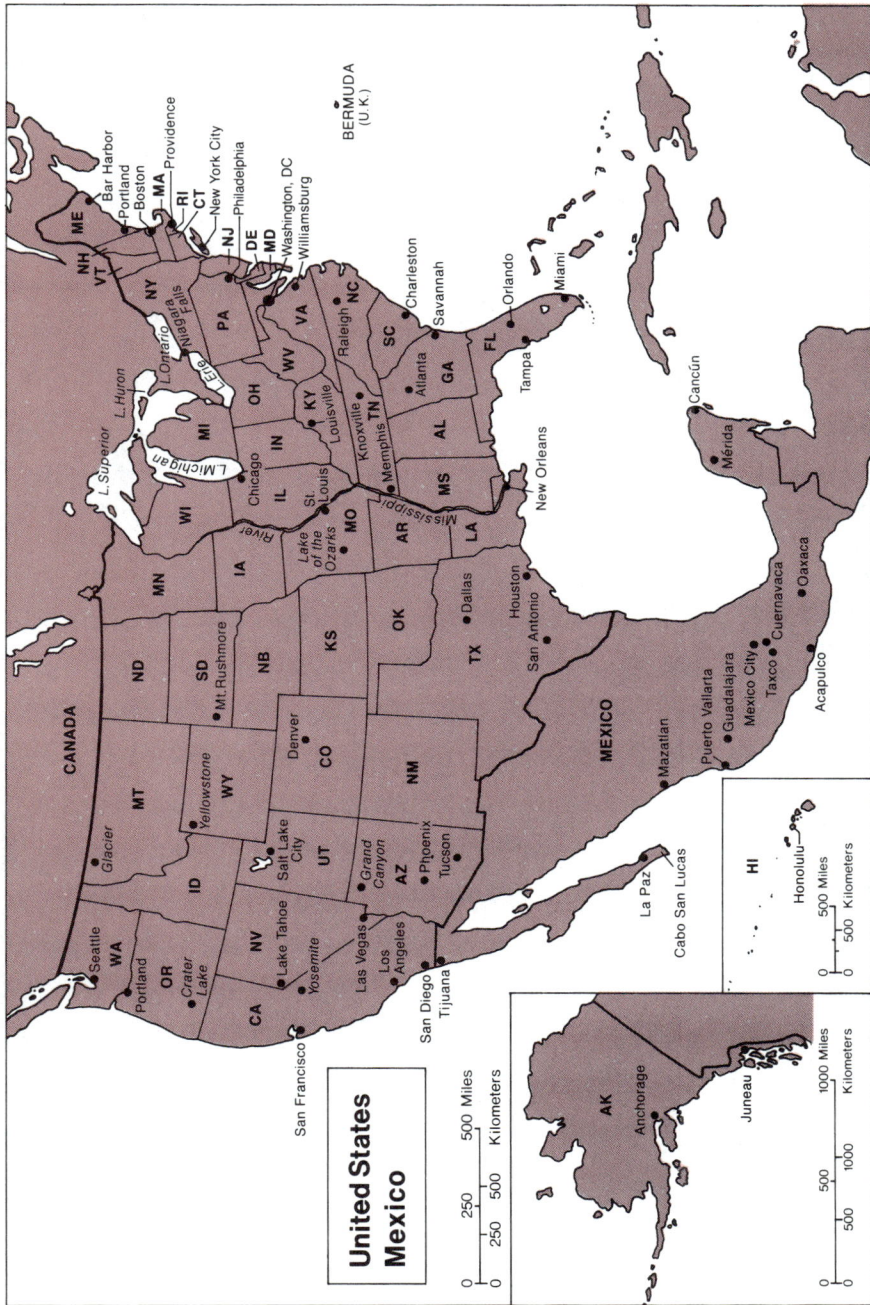

United States
Mexico

CANADA

States and Abbreviations:
ME, NH, VT, MA, RI, CT, NY, NJ, DE, MD, PA, WV, VA, NC, SC, GA, FL, OH, KY, TN, AL, MS, MI, IN, IL, WI, MN, IA, MO, AR, LA, ND, SD, NB, KS, OK, TX, MT, WY, CO, NM, ID, UT, AZ, NV, WA, OR, CA, AK, HI

Cities and Landmarks:
Bar Harbor, Portland, Boston, Providence, New York City, Philadelphia, Washington, DC, Williamsburg, Niagara Falls, Charleston, Savannah, Raleigh, Orlando, Miami, Atlanta, Cancún, Mérida, Tampa, Louisville, Knoxville, Memphis, Chicago, St. Louis, New Orleans, Lake of the Ozarks, Dallas, Houston, San Antonio, Mt. Rushmore, Denver, Yellowstone, Mazatlán, Puerto Vallarta, Guadalajara, Mexico City, Taxco, Cuernavaca, Oaxaca, Acapulco, Salt Lake City, Grand Canyon, Phoenix, Tucson, Seattle, Glacier, Portland, Crater Lake, Lake Tahoe, Yosemite, Las Vegas, Los Angeles, San Diego, Tijuana, San Francisco, La Paz, Cabo San Lucas, Honolulu, Anchorage, Juneau

Water features:
L. Superior, L. Huron, L. Michigan, L. Ontario, L. Erie, Mississippi River

BERMUDA (U.K.)

MEXICO

HI

AK

Scale bars:
500 Miles / Kilometers
250 / 250 Miles / Kilometers
500 / 500 Miles / Kilometers
1000 Miles / Kilometers
500 / 1000 Kilometers

257

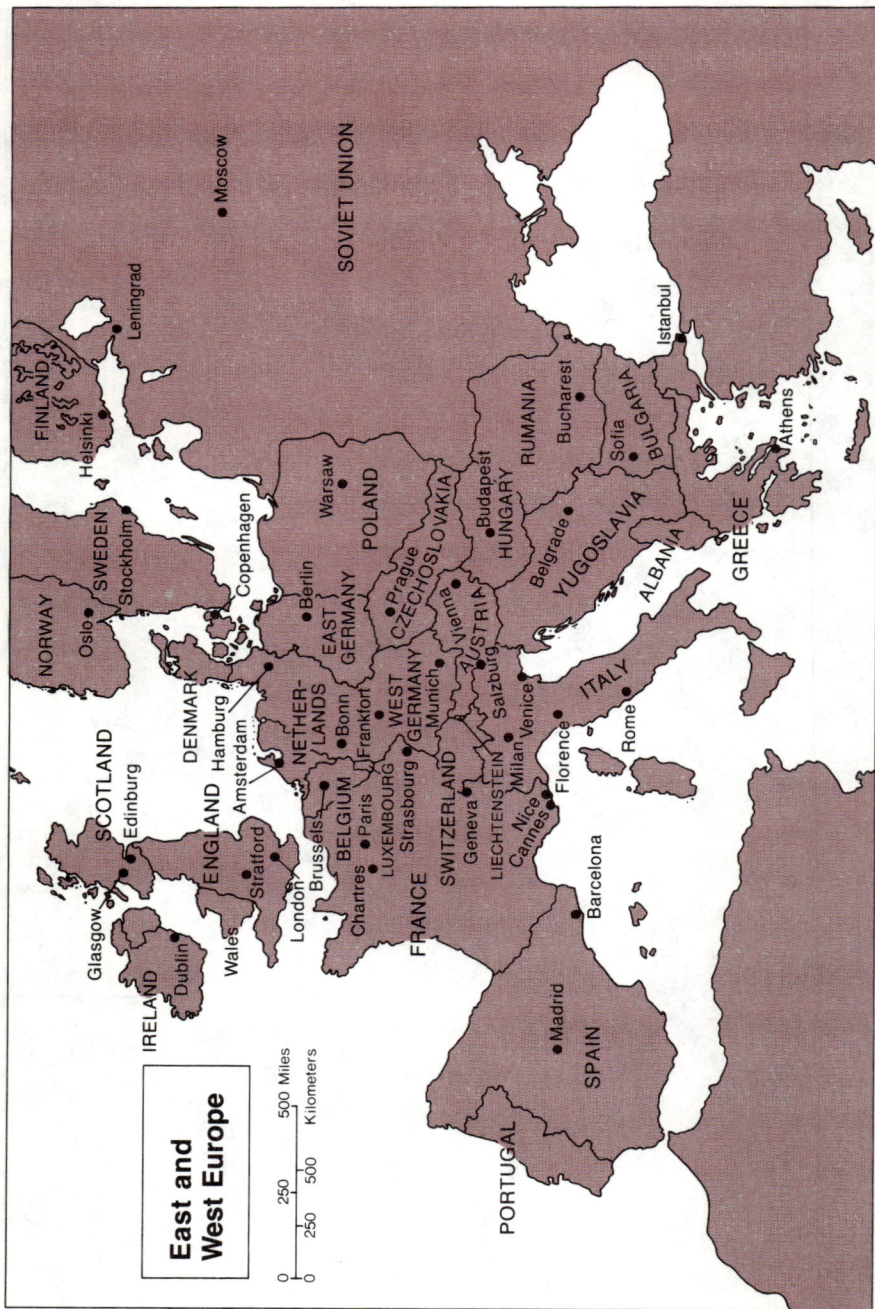

East and
West Europe

500 Miles
Kilometers

250   500

250   500

0

SOVIET UNION

• Moscow

Leningrad

FINLAND

Helsinki

SWEDEN

Stockholm

Oslo

NORWAY

Copenhagen

DENMARK

Warsaw

POLAND

Berlin

EAST GERMANY

Prague

CZECHOSLOVAKIA

Budapest

HUNGARY

Vienna

AUSTRIA

Salzburg

Bucharest

RUMANIA

Sofia

BULGARIA

YUGOSLAVIA

Belgrade

ALBANIA

Istanbul

Athens

GREECE

NETHER-
LANDS

Amsterdam

Hamburg

Bonn

Frankfort

WEST
GERMANY

Munich

SWITZERLAND

Geneva

LIECHTENSTEIN

Nice

Cannes

Milan

Venice

Florence

ITALY

Rome

SCOTLAND

Edinburg

Glasgow

ENGLAND

Strafford

London

Wales

BELGIUM

Brussels

LUXEMBOURG

Strasbourg

Paris

Chartres

FRANCE

IRELAND

Dublin

Barcelona

SPAIN

Madrid

PORTUGAL

258

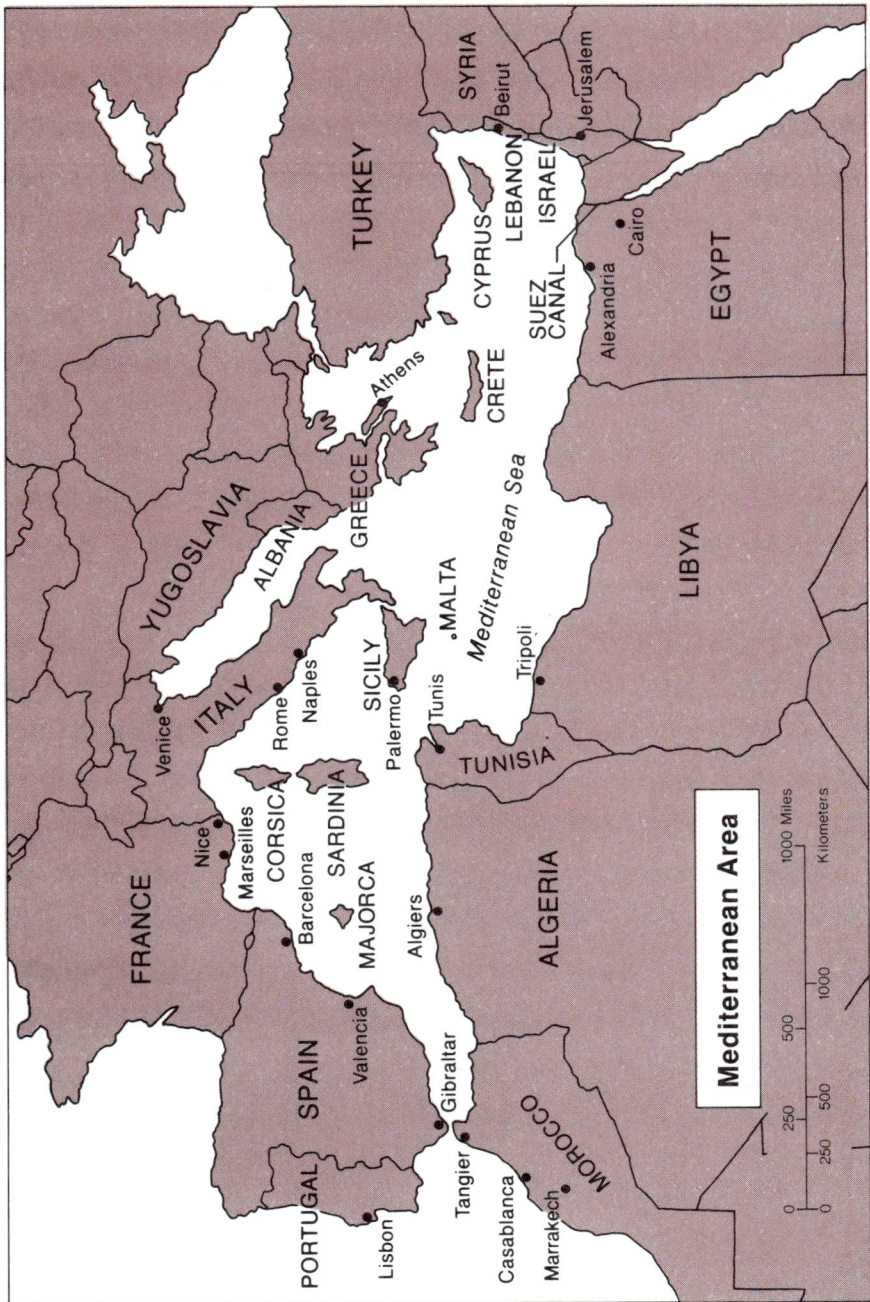

Mediterranean Area

SYRIA
Beirut
Jerusalem
TURKEY
LEBANON
ISRAEL
CYPRUS
Cairo
SUEZ CANAL
EGYPT
CRETE
Alexandria
Athens
GREECE
Mediterranean Sea
YUGOSLAVIA
ALBANIA
MALTA
LIBYA
ITALY
Rome
Naples
SICILY
Tripoli
Venice
Palermo
Tunis
Nice
Marseilles
CORSICA
SARDINIA
TUNISIA
FRANCE
Barcelona
MAJORCA
Algiers
ALGERIA
Valencia
SPAIN
Gibraltar
MOROCCO
PORTUGAL
Tangier
Casablanca
Lisbon
Marrakech

1000 Miles
Kilometers
1000
500
500
250
250
0
0

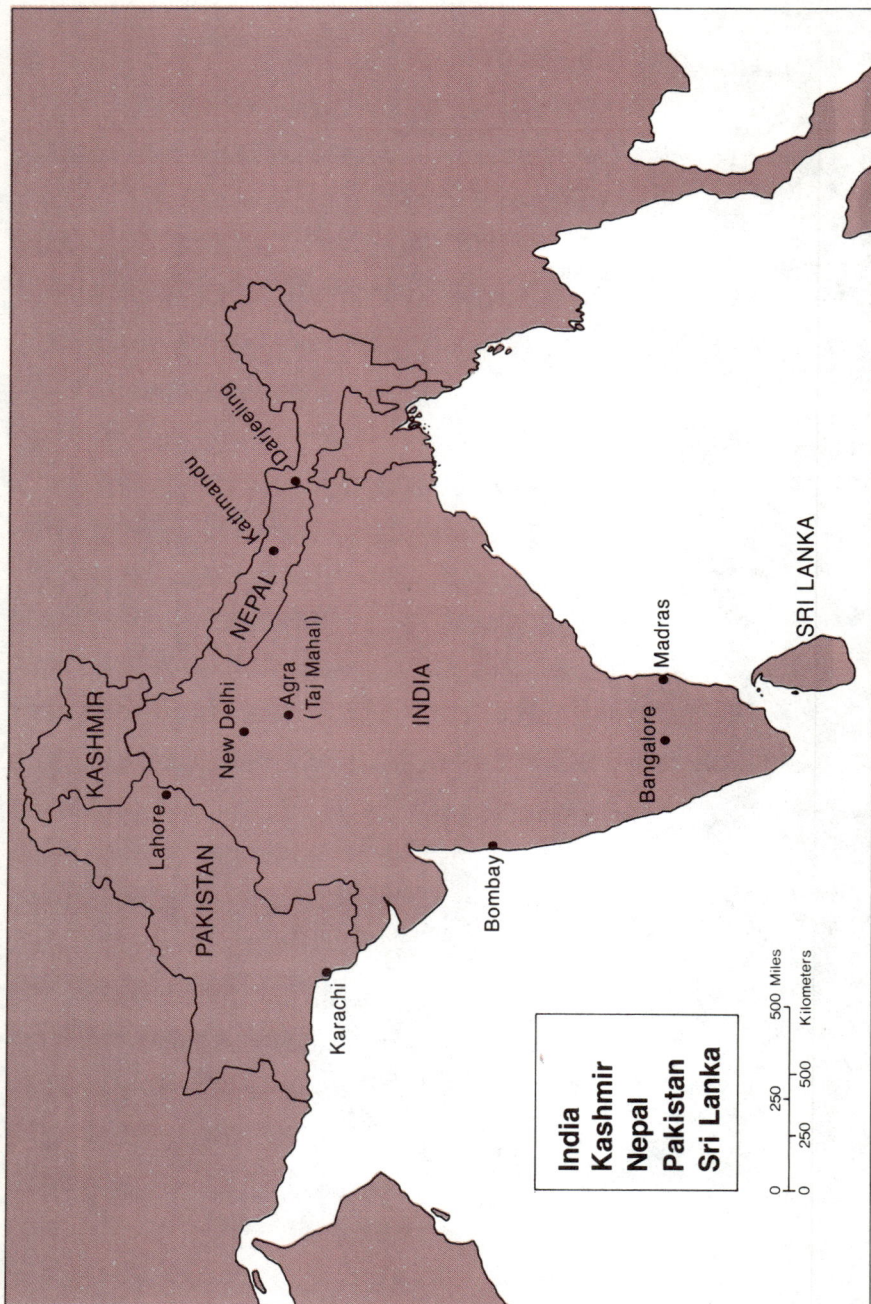

India
Kashmir
Nepal
Pakistan
Sri Lanka

KASHMIR

PAKISTAN

Lahore

Karachi

New Delhi

Agra
(Taj Mahal)

NEPAL

Kathmandu

Darjeeling

INDIA

Bombay

Bangalore

Madras

SRI LANKA

0   250   500 Miles

0   250   500 Kilometers

260

Africa

| 0 | 500 | 1000 Miles |
| 0 | 500 | 1000 | Kilometers |

MOROCCO
Tangier
Casablanca
Rabat
Marrakech
Algiers
Tunis
TUNISIA
Tripoli
ALGERIA
LIBYA
EGYPT
Cairo
Luxor
MAURITANIA
MALI
Tombouctou
NIGER
CHAD
SUDAN
Khartoum
SENEGAL
GUINEA
SIERRA LEONE
Monrovia
LIBERIA
IVORY COAST
Abidjan
GHANA
Accra
NIGERIA
Lagos
CAMEROON
Addis Ababa
ETHIOPIA
SOMALIA
UGANDA
KENYA
Nairobi
ZAIRE
Kilimanjaro
Mombasa
TANZANIA
Dar es Salaam
ANGOLA
ZAMBIA
MOZAMBIQUE
Victoria Falls
ZIMBABWE
MADAGASCAR
NAMIBIA
BOTSWANA
Pretoria
Johannesburg
SOUTH AFRICA
Cape Town

Far East
Australia
New Zealand

Cartagena

Caracas

VENEZUELA

GUYANA

SURINAME

FRENCH GUIANA

•Bogotá

COLOMBIA

Galápagos

ECUADOR Quito

Guayaquil

Belém

PERU

BRAZIL

Lima

Machu
Picchu

Lake
Titicaca

•La Paz

•Brasilia

BOLIVIA

Rio de Janeiro

PARAGUAY

Iguassu
Falls

Asuncion•

Sao Paulo

CHILE

ARGENTINA

Santiago•

Buenos Aires

Mar del Plata•

URUGUAY

Montevideo

South America

0	500	1000 Miles
0	500	1000	Kilometers

Index

Pepto-Bismol, 198, 201
Peru, 165
Pneumococcus immunization, 185
P & O Cruises, 141
Poland, 4, 101, 165, 181
Polio, 186, 189
Polish Ocean Lines, 145
Polaris, 208
Portugal, 52–53, 101, 167
Prepackaged tours, 22
Princess Cruises, 105, 137, 138
Promotional airfares, 84
Prudential Lines, 145
P.T. International, 43
Puerto Rico, 136
Puerto Vallarta, 137, 138

Quality Inns International, 98

Ramada Inns, 98
Recreational Vehicle Association, 68
Recreational Vehicle Dealers
    Association of North America,
    68
Recreational vehicles, 66–69
Red Sea cruises, 143
Republic Airlines, 89
Resorts, 38–39, 40
Respiratory infections, medications
    for, 201–202
Rest, need for adequate, 187–88
Rhine River cruises, 141
Rio de Janeiro, 21
River cruises, 140–43
Rodeway Inns, 98
Romania, 4, 165, 181
Roommate, finding, 15–16
Royal Caribbean, 137
Royal Cruise Line, 137
Royal Hawaiian Airlines, 89
Royal Viking, 137, 138

Sabin vaccine, 186
Saga International Holidays, 50, 52,
    126
Saguenay Fjord, 139
St. Lawrence River, 139
St. Martin, 136
Salk vaccine, 186
Salt and Pepper Tours, Inc., 142
San Jose de Purua, 4

Saratoga Springs, N.Y., 39
Savannah, 140
Scandinavian countries, 99
Scopolamine, 202
Scottish Inns, 98
Scottsdale, Arizona, 39
Security checks, for airplane travel,
    78–79
Senior Air Fares, 88–89
Senior citizen groups, 14–15
Senior Seasons, 101–102
Senokot, 201
September Day Club, 89, 96, 98
Septra, 198
Shakespeare festival, 102
Shell Motor Club, 60
Shenandoah National Park, 45
Sheraton Hotels and Inns, 98
Sherry, John E. H., 221
Shoes, 191, 227
Shopping
    airport shops, 167–68
    flea markets, 166–67
    getting bargains in, 106–108
    hours of operation, 166
    and overseas travel, 164–70
    sending packages home, 168–70
Shore excursions, 150
Single, traveling as, 9–16, 114
Sitmar, 137, 138
Skin, care for, 191–92
Sleeping pills, 202
Smoking/no-smoking sections
    on airplanes, 219
    on tours, 130
Society Expeditions, 131–32, 143
South Africa, 132
Southwest Airlines, 85
Soviet Union, 181
Spain, 52, 101, 165, 167
Spa vacations, 3–4
Special equipment, choice of, for
    travel, 226–29
Special-interest tours, 125
Specialty Travel Index, 125
Sports vacations, 5
Spur of the Moment Cruises, 104
Stand-Bys, Ltd., 97
Star system of rating hotels,
    motels, and resorts, 37
State tourist offices, 18,
    Appendix A
Stay-put Tours, 113
Stella Solaris, 143

About the Author

In her years of travel to more than 90 countries for pleasure and as a travel writer, **Rosalind Massow** has nearly
fulfilled a childhood dream of "dipping my toes in every
major ocean and river in the world." She is a former
on-staff reporter and feature writer for Hearst newspapers and women's editor of *Parade* magazine. She has been
a travel editor and writer for several other magazines and
newspapers and is the author of *Now It's Your Turn to Travel*
(1976), the first book published for the older traveler. A
member of the Society of American Travel Writers and
other professional associations, she is the recipient of
three Front Page awards for excellence in journalism.

Norton M. Luger, M.D., is a clinical associate professor of
medicine at Cornell University Medical School and a practicing physician. He is a medical consultant to the Society
of American Travel Writers and a weekly medical colum-
nist for *The Star* newspaper.

Lyonel S. Hildes, D.D.S., is an associate clinical professor in the New York University College of Dentistry
and a practicing dentist in White Plains, New York.

Other AARP Books

ALONE—NOT LONELY: Independent Living for Women Over Fifty
by Jane Seskin
673-24814-3 $6.95

THE ESSENTIAL GUIDE TO WILLS, ESTATES, TRUSTS, AND DEATH TAXES
by Alex J. Soled
673-24809-7 $12.95

KEEPING OUT OF CRIME'S WAY, The Practical Guide for People Over 50
by J. E. Persico with George Sunderland
673-24801-1 $6.95

LIFE AFTER WORK
by Allan Fromme, Ph.D.
673-24821-6 $6.95

THE OVER EASY FOOT CARE BOOK
by Timothy P. Shea, D.P.M., and Joan K. Smith
673-24807-0 $6.95

PLANNING YOUR RETIREMENT HOUSING
by Michael Sumichrast, Ronald G. Shafer, and Marika Sumichrast
673-24810-0 $8.95

POLICY WISE: The Practical Guide to Insurance Decisions for Older Consumers
by Nancy H. Chasen
673-24806-2 $5.95

SURVIVAL HANDBOOK FOR WIDOWS (and for relatives and friends who want to understand)
by Ruth J. Loewinsohn
673-24820-8 $5.95

WHAT TO DO WITH WHAT YOU'VE GOT: The Practical Guide to Money Management in Retirement
by Peter Weaver and Annette Buchanan
673-24805-4 $7.95

For complete information write AARP Books, 1900 East Lake Avenue, Glenview, IL 60025, or contact your local bookstore.

Prices subject to change.

Scott, Foresman and the American Association of Retired Persons have joined together to create . . . AARP BOOKS

These comprehensive guides, written by experts, will help you manage your money, choose where to live, plan your estate, save on insurance, and help those you care about to live a better life.

What to Do with What You've Got: The Practical Guide to Money Management in Retirement
A wealth of information on how to protect and increase your assets. Turn investments into money producers. Figure your net worth. Cut your expenses (without cutting back). Highly recommended. **$7.95**

Planning Your Retirement Housing
Should you own or rent? Move or stay put? Buy land? A condo? Helps you weigh the options and decide what's best for you. Secure financing. Save on energy and repairs. Discover tax breaks. **$8.95**

The Essential Guide to Wills, Estates, Trusts, and Death Taxes
This easy-to-follow guide lets you organize your affairs legally and economically. Find out how to write a will. Reduce your estate's tax liability. When to consider a trust fund. An excellent resource. **$12.95**

Policy Wise: The Practical Guide to Insurance Decisions for Older Consumers
$5.95

AARP INFORMATION BOOKS
YOU CAN COUNT ON

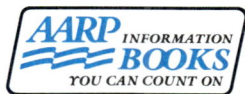

Join AARP today and enjoy valuable benefits!

Join the American Association of Retired Persons, the national organization which helps people like you, age 50 and over, realize their full potential in so many ways! The rewards you'll reap with AARP will be many times greater than your low membership dues. And your membership also includes your spouse!

Your AARP benefits...

- Modern Maturity magazine
- Legislative work benefiting mature persons
- Nonprofit Pharmacy Service
- Quality Group Health Insurance
- Specially priced Motoring Plan
- Community Volunteer Activities
- Hotel & Car Rental Discounts
- Travel Service
- Tax-Aide Program to help with your taxes

☐ one year/$5
☐ three years/$12.50 (saves $2.50)
☐ ten years/$35 (saves $15)
☐ Check or money order enclosed, payable to AARP. DO NOT SEND CASH.
☐ Please bill me.

Name (please print)

Address   Apt.

City

State   Zip

Date of Birth _____mo/_____ day/_____ year

L9AB

55% of dues is designated for Association publications. Dues outside continental U.S.: $7 one year, $18 three years. Please allow 3 to 6 weeks for receipt of membership kit.

It's Your Choice: The Practical Guide to Planning a Funeral $4.95

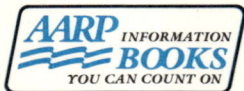

The Over Easy Foot Care Book
Your guide to healthy and happy feet! How to select shoes that fit. The right way to treat corns. Exercises and over-the-counter medications that effectively relieve foot pain. Plus much more! $6.95

ORDER INFORMATION
Complete the following information and return it **along with your name and address** (be sure to include ZIP code) to the address below. All orders must be prepaid.

AARP Books
400 South Edward Street
Mount Prospect, IL 60056

AARP INFORMATION *BOOKS*
YOU CAN COUNT ON

Check method of payment:
☐ Check   (make payable to AARP Books)
☐ Money Order
☐ Visa   ☐ MasterCard

Card Number   Expiration Date

Name of book(s)   Price:

subtotal:

add $1.45 shipping per order: $1.45

total:

AARP Books are also available in your local bookstore, distributed by Farrar, Straus and Giroux.